DATE DUE

BEYOND

THE

BORDER

Published in the United States by Cleis Press Inc., P.O. Box 8933, Pittsburgh, Pennsylvania 15221, and P.O. Box 14684, San Francisco, California 94114.

Printed in the United States.
Cover design: Ellen Toomey
Typesetting: CaliCo Graphics
Logo art: Juana Alicia

First Edition.
10 9 8 7 6 5 4 3 2 1
ISBN: 0-939416-42-5 cloth
ISBN: 0-939416-43-3 paper

Grateful acknowledgment is made to the following for permission to reprint previously published material: "The Immigrant" appeared in *Diana's Second Almanac* edited by T. Ahern. Providence, RI: Diana's Bymonthly Press, 1980. Reprinted with permission of T. Ahern. "Up Among the Eagles" appeared in *Open Door*. San Francisco: North Point Press, 1988. Copyright 1988, 1978, 1976 by Luisa Valenzuela. "Mercedes Benz 220 SL" also appears in *The Youngest Doll* by Rosario Ferré. University of Nebraska Press, 1991. "The Judge's Wife" by Isabel Allende originally appeared in *Granta Magazine*.

Acknowledgments

Our special thanks go to Deanna Heikkinen, who typed the manuscript so quickly and efficiently. Without her assistance this work would not have been possible.

BEYOND

THE

BORDER

**A NEW AGE IN
LATIN AMERICAN
WOMEN'S FICTION**

EDITED BY
NORA ERRO-PERALTA
CARIDAD SILVA-NUÑEZ

Cleis Press

Translators

Bertie Acker
Nick Castor
Marguerite Feitlowitz
Rosario Ferré
Lucía Fox
Eloah F. Giacomelli
Anne Hohenstein
Ian Martin
Nora Erro-Peralta
Margaret Sayers-Peden
Brenda Segall
Caridad Silva-Núñez
Cynthia Steele
Lisa Wyant

Contents

Beyond the Border:
A Critical Introduction 7

Isabel Allende 23
The Judge's Wife 24
Bibliography 30

Lydia Cabrera 34
The Prize of Freedom 35
Bibliography 37

Aída Cartagena Portalatín 45
**A Passion for
Donna Summer** 46
Bibliography 48

Lygia Fagundes Telles 50
The Hunt 51
Bibliography 53

Rosario Ferré 59
Mercedes Benz 220 SL 60
Bibliography 68

Lucía Fox 72
The Wedding 73
Bibliography 77

Elena Garro 79
Perfecto Luna 80
Bibliography 87

Angélica Gorodischer 95
**Under the Yubayas
in Bloom** 96
Bibliography 111

Sylvia Lago 113
Homelife 114
Bibliography 124

Elena Poniatowska 125
**Slide in, My Dark One,
Between the Crosstie
and the Whistle** 126
Bibliography 143

Armonía Somers 149
The Immigrant 150
Bibliography 165

Gloria Stolk 168
**Crickets and
Butterflies** 169
Bibliography 176

Luisa Valenzuela 178
Up Among the Eagles 179
Bibliography 184

Rima Vallbona 190
**The Secret World of
Grandmamma Anacleta** 191
Bibliography 196

The Short Story,
Feminism and Latin
American Women Writers:
A Bibliography 203

BEYOND THE BORDER:
A CRITICAL INTRODUCTION

The evolving tradition of Latin American women writers can be dated as far back as Isabel de Guevara who, in 1556, wrote a letter of complaint to the Spanish Queen Doña Juana about the mistreatment that she had received upon her arrival in the New World. From that early voice on, Latin American women writers have pressed for justice, and for the defense of the weakest elements of society: women, children, Indians, blacks, and the lower classes.

Women writers were isolated from one another during the period of colonization and up to the twentieth century. The first and most prominent Latin American woman writer was Sor Juana Inés de la Cruz (Juana Ramírez de Asbaje, 1651-1695). Her life and work reflect the unfortunate situation of Latin American women at the time, who were offered two choices, indeed two forms of prison: marriage or the convent. Faced with such limited options, Sor Juana, an intelligent woman from a well-to-do family, chose the convent as the only means to fulfill her hunger for knowledge. Nevertheless, she still was not free to continue her studies, for church authorities soon demanded that she abandon her intellectual activities as researcher and writer altogether. Although she defended her right to intellectual freedom, eventually she gave up her studies and died at an early age, the victim of an epidemic, but also of society.[1] She left behind an accomplished body of literature: poetry, drama, and essays. In most of her work, she denounced the unfair rules imposed by men upon women and, in so doing, became the forerunner of Latin American feminism. Her best known work, *Respuesta a Sor Filotea de la Cruz* (Reply to Sor Philotea of the Cross, 1691), a clever essay on women's rights addressed to Sor Filotea de la Cruz, the pseudonym used by the Bishop of Puebla, is considered a masterpiece by critics.[2] Her literary works were recognized as the best of the period and gained her the name "The Tenth Muse" of the New World.

Two centuries later Gertrudis Gómez de Avellaneda (1814-1873), a Spanish/Cuban, voiced her defense of Indians and blacks.[3] Born in Cuba in 1814, she lived in Spain from the age of twenty-four until her death. She wrote poems, plays, and novels, among which was a famous anti-slavery novel, *Sab* (1841), in which she pointed out similarities between the lives of slaves and women, both victims of society. Although her writing was praised for its excellence, she was severely criticized and censured by her society for her defiance of social convention.

Following this tradition of literary brilliance combined with personal rebellion against patriarchy, a Peruvian, Clorinda Matto de Turner (1852-1909), initiated the "novela indigenista" (indigenist novel) with her work

Aves sin nido (*Birds Without a Nest*, 1889). Although her work gained national recognition and led writers into a new form of narrative, she herself was excommunicated and exiled by religious and political authorities for her anticlerical, liberal stand.[4] Another illustrious Peruvian woman of the nineteenth century, and a friend of Matto de Turner, was Mercedes Cabello de Carbonara, who wrote a famous novel, *Blanca Sol* (1888), denouncing colonialism. Both women participated actively in a *tertulia*, a regular meeting of intellectuals—in the Spanish tradition—at which ideas were discussed over a wide range of subjects.

Two other women, both Argentine, shared the literary stage during this period: Juana Manuela Gorriti (1819-1892) and Juana Paula Manso (1819-1875). Gorriti made a pioneer contribution to indigenous literature with her novels *El tesoro de los incas* (The Treasure of the Incas, n.d.) and *El pozo del Yocci* (The Well of Yocci, 1869), and gave us a vivid historical portrait of her times in the serial story *La hija del Mashorquero* (The Daughter of the Mashorquero). Manso collaborated with Argentine president Domingo Faustino Sarmiento in the field of education, where she dared to break with traditional structures in teaching methodology. Her political novel *Los misterios del Plata* (The Mysteries of the River Plate, 1846), published during the dictatorship of Juan Manuel Rosas, captured the feeling of the time with an artistic mastery equalled only by José Mármol's *Amalia* (1851), a classic of the romantic movement. Both Gorriti and Manso faced reprisals and ferocious criticism for their ideas on liberation and educational reform.

The first half of the twentieth century brought important women writers to the narrative scene.[5] Although they were not recognized as genuine innovators by standard histories of Latin American literature, and were praised only condescendingly by male critics of their time, these writers broke new ground in the areas of fictional theme, language, and literary techniques, and pointed Latin American fiction towards a new direction. With their personal achievements, many of them also challenged society's assumptions about women. Such was the case of the Argentine Victoria Ocampo (1890-1979), who not only wrote her *Testimonios* (Testimonies, 1935-1977), but also ten volumes of essays on a variety of subjects and an *Autobiografía* (Autobiography, 1979) which was published posthumously. In these works she spoke candidly and openly about herself in the first person, criticizing the restrictions that society imposed on women, even wealthy, beautiful women, as she was. Her life and work reflected an enduring commitment to self-development and to literature. As a young woman she wrote to her friend Delfina Bunge in 1908:

> Can you see me burying myself with domestic cares? Because, needless to say, someone will have to take charge of the house.

Can you see me leading that colorless life? That would be a true suicide of the intellect, of "the self." Never, never in my life will I be able to resign myself to abdicating my personality. And I understand that one must make this sacrifice for love. But not me, I can't.[6]

Earlier, in 1907, she had written to her friend: "I've made up my mind to have only one great love: Art!"[7]

Ocampo was also a translator, a critic, the founder of the prestigious literary review *Sur* (South, 1931), and of the publishing house of the same name which promoted the works of many writers, among them *La última niebla* (*The House of Mist*, 1935) by María Luisa Bombal. Ocampo's travels, her encounters with famous artists from numerous countries, and her analytical insights into the human psyche constitute a fascinating source of aesthetic pleasure for the reader of her *Testimonios* and *Autobiografía*. In 1977 Victoria Ocampo became the first woman elected to the Argentine Academy of Letters. She dedicated this honor to all women whose efforts have never been recognized by history. Ocampo's life story is a profound testimony to the fact that society's canons can be changed through personal achievement.

Teresa de la Parra, born in Venezuela in 1890 to a wealthy family, had a short life marked by illness. Parra wrote two novels: *Ifigenia, diario de una señorita que escribió porque se fastidiaba* (Iphigenia: Diary of a Young Lady Who Wrote Because She Was Bored, 1924) and *Memorias de Mamá Blanca* (*Mama Blanca's Memoirs*, 1929). *Ifigenia* is a novel of 494 pages, translated into French by the prestigious poet Francis de Miomandre. While it achieved immediate recognition and success in Paris, it was severely criticized in Venezuela as an evil influence on women readers. The novel's protagonist, María Eugenia Alonso, writes to a friend in Europe and later keeps a diary about her decision, based on social and economic pressures, to marry a man whom she does not love, and about the subsequent changes she observes in her personality. Her writing becomes a search for self-knowledge, during which she eventually accepts her weaknesses and inability to rebel. The process of self-inquiry is presented to the reader through a first person narrator. However, Parra manages to avoid the intimate confessional tone usually associated with female writers by using different points of view and by maintaining a lucid narrative distance from her material. Her real purpose is to expose Latin American society's mistreatment of women. Yet her protagonist's inner journey represents a skillful exploration of analytical psychology by means of literature. This novel was widely read and, in spite of bitter criticism by Parra's own society, gained her immediate recognition abroad.

The House of Mist, by the Chilean María Luisa Bombal (1910-1980), was another work of fiction that, when it appeared in 1935, was considered avant-garde because it dared to present the repressed sexual desires of an unhappily married woman who fantasizes an affair with a stranger. The nameless protagonist is unable to realize meaning in her life, becoming alienated from a husband who pays her no attention and a society which does not acknowledge her needs. She lives in a mental fog which prevents her from articulating her needs and integrating them into her life. Bombal's extensive use of poetic devices allows her to present the woman's sensuality in a frank but metaphoric manner which brought to the novel the success of seven editions and publication in eight languages.[8] Bombal's novel was one of the first in Latin American literature to discuss the issue of women's sexuality; her efforts bore fruit during the second half of the century, when this issue was treated by many women writers with great success.

An important literary figure of the early part of the century is the Cuban Lydia Cabrera (1900-). She became famous after the publication of her *Cuentos negros* (Black Tales, 1940) in Paris. These short stories drew upon African popular culture in Cuba and the tradition of Latin American *criollista* literature, attempting to preserve the Afro-Cuban legends for history and to capture their world through innovative language. Cabrera also wrote numerous fables and collections of short stories. Her work represents one of the early successful female forays into the field of the short story, a genre which reached its peak later in the century in the fiction of the well-known Argentine writer, Jorge Luis Borges (1899-1986), whose work brought to Latin American literature international acclaim. The publication of *Antología de la literatura fantástica* (Anthology of Fantastic Literature, 1940) by Jorge Luis Borges, Bioy Casares, and Silvina Ocampo, inaugurated a period of increased creativity, renewal, and intellectual achievement in Latin American literature, especially fiction, which has not yet diminished. The 1950s and 1960s were marked by high productivity of authors and publishers. For the first time in the history of Latin American fiction, many authors were—and still are—translated and their works successfully marketed abroad, reaching best seller status in New York, Paris, Madrid, Barcelona, and other major cultural centers. With writers such as Carlos Fuentes, Mario Vargas Llosa, Jorge Luis Borges, Guillermo Cabrera Infante, Gabriel García Márquez (Nobel Prize 1968), Manuel Puig, and many others, the short story again became a popular literary form.[9]

However, the international success of Latin American fiction—known in literary circles as the Boom—really meant the success of primarily male writers. Women have been largely ignored by Hispanic critics, historians and anthologists. In response to this situation, and as early as 1950, the Mexican writer Rosario Castellanos (1925-1974) began to call attention to works written by women, particularly in her essays: *Sobre cultura femenina* (On Feminine Culture, 1950), *Juicios sumarios* (Summary Arguments, 1966), *Mujer que sabe latín* (Woman Who Knows Latin, 1973) and *El uso de la palabra* (The Use of Language, 1974). She published many articles and short stories which strongly protested the victimization of women in Latin American societies and demanded change. Following in her footsteps, the Mexican writer Elena Poniatowska denounced the difficulties which women writers faced. The academics Rose Minc and Beth Miller compiled many studies of female literature. Lucía Fox Lockert, Gabriela Mora, Celia Correas de Zapata, Juana Arancibia and Lygia Johnson broke new ground in research about Latin American women writers.

The journals *Letras femeninas*, *FEM*, and *Hispamérica* became effective forums in which to publish—and promote—the work of women writers. The United Nations declared 1975 to be International Women's Year, setting in motion a number of congresses devoted to the study of the works of women writers, among them Latin American women writers. The First Interamerican Congress of Women Writers took place at Carnegie-Mellon University, in Pittsburgh, Pennsylvania, in 1975; the second such congress, at San Jose State University, California, in 1976; the third, at the University of Ottawa, Canada, 1978; and the fourth, at the Universidad Nacional Autónoma de México in Mexico City in 1981. The efforts of North American female academics helped Latin American women intellectuals overcome their traditional isolation.

It is important to mention the names of a few women whose dynamism and generosity have made possible a continuous dialogue between North and South America: Juana Alcira Arancibia, Celia Correas de Zapata, Margo Glantz, Martha Martínez, Beth Miller, Yvette Miller, Victoria Pueyrredón, Elba Torres de Peralta, Victoria Urbano, Rima Vallbona and Alaide Foppa (tragically missing in Guatemala since 1980). These women continue the tradition of their intellectual sisters who, since the beginning of the century, have been working on their own to promote the arts in general and the works of women in particular. Victoria Ocampo, of the Plate Region, was a pioneer in this and founder of the Argentine Women's Union, as well as of *Sur*. In the Caribbean, the collective work of a group of women led by Elena Mederos resulted in a major cultural contribution through the Liceum of Habana, Cuba. In Puerto Rico, Nilita Vientós Gastón founded and published *Asomante*, later *Sin Nombre*, a literary journal which has served as a distinguished cultural forum for Spanish American intellectuals.

By the 1960s, there was a noticeable increase in the number and quality of short stories written by women, due to a variety of circumstances (whose study falls beyond the scope of this book), such as: the economic prosperity of the 1960s; the support given by UNESCO to Latin American cultural activities; the establishment of more, and more accessible, publishing companies which, in turn, produced a significant increase in the number of readers; the international feminist movement, and a greater involvement of women in the work force.

Over the last two decades, Latin American women writers produced a considerable body of literature, particularly fiction. Many writers have shown tremendous creative ability in experimenting with new forms of narrative which go beyond the boundaries of traditional genres. Such is the case of Luisa Valenzuela, *El gato eficaz* (Cat-O-Nine-Deaths, 1972); Rosario Ferré, *Papeles de Pandora* (Pandora's Papers, 1976); and Elena Poniatowska, *Hasta no verte Jesús mío* (Until I See You Again, 1969). Others have successfully cultivated several literary genres: Elena Garro, Marta Lynch, Julieta Campos, Hilda Perera, Griselda Gambaro, Beatriz, Guido, Lucia Fox, Aída Cartagena Portalatín, among others.

Although it is now an indisputable fact that there is a rich and valuable body of fiction by Latin American women, female writers still face a traditional obstacle: the network which guarantees writers a place in literary history remains reluctant to register works by women and, in so doing, condemns to obscurity the experiences, contributions and existence of half of humanity. When we look at distinguished contemporary anthologies in Spanish, many of which are used as reference books or as textbooks at the university level, we notice that they ignore fiction by Latin American women.[10] Most works by female writers are published in national, limited editions which are poorly distributed. Frequently, anthologies and histories of Latin American literature repeat the names of a few women considered as rare classic phenomena, and always associate them with the same short story. A typical example is that of María Luisa Bombal and her story "The Tree." Some researchers, mostly women, are beginning to reverse this pattern. In the last nine years, three short story anthologies have been published in Spanish: (1) *Detrás de la reja* (Behind Bars, 1983) by Celia Correas de Zapata and Lygia Johnson, (2) *Mujeres en espejo* (Women in the Mirror, 1983) by Sara Sefchovich, and (3) *Puerta abierta: la nueva escritora latinoamericana* (Open Door: the New Latin American Woman Writer, 1986) by Caridad Silva-Núñez and Nora Erro-Orthmann.

When we compare the number of available English translations of male Latin American writers, especially those associated with the Boom, and the excellent response these received from English readers, with the limited availability of works by major Latin American women writers, it becomes evident that there is a need to translate, study and promote women's fiction in English. There are only two English anthologies devoted entirely to short stories written by Latin American women writers: *Other Fires* edited by Alberto Manguel, 1986 and *Short Stories by Latin American Women: The Magic and the Real* by Celia Correas de Zapata, 1990. There is also a recent, and excellent, effort by Marian Arkin and Barbara Shollar entitled *Longman Anthology of World Literature by Women 1875-1975*. This volume devotes a whole section to Latin American women writers with an introduction by Margarite Fernández Olmos.[11]

There is certainly a need to go beyond current boundaries in terms of both geography and gender. We conceived this anthology with the hope of transcending the traditional boundaries which confine women's writings to an asphyxiatingly small space. This volume intends to go beyond the cultural and linguistic frontiers which limit human exchange between the United States and Latin America.

The process of selection was difficult because Latin American women writers have produced an abundance of short stories, most of high caliber. Our choices were guided primarily by a deep concern for literary quality. We also gave priority to short stories that have not appeared in English before. We refused to confine our selections to only those few themes often used to classify women's writings, and instead stressed a wide diversity of themes and styles. Additionally, this collection represents as many Latin American countries as possible, given the availability of material and projected length of this volume.

The bibliography lists the numerous studies that have appeared in the field of female narrative and women's studies, and it also reveals the output of the writers included in this anthology as well as criticism about them.[12] We hope that this material can be used by both students and critics of literature while waiting for a most-needed history of Latin American literature by women.

We planned *Beyond the Border* with two goals in mind: (1) to introduce the general reader to a new literary experience, and (2) to offer critics and students readings of sufficient complexity as to stimulate their intellect. We trust that this book will also be useful in the following disciplines: Latin American studies, interdisciplinary studies, sociology, women's studies and comparative literature.

The critical readings of dozens of contemporary Latin American short stories made us realize that it is impossible to classify them into literary schools or movements in the traditional sense, due to their enormous individuality and their vast diversity of themes and techniques. However, we noticed that—taking into account themes, narrative structures and linguistic codes—we could detect three areas of concern and general commonality. These areas do not refer to chronological periods of literary evolution in the traditional sense. On the contrary, all of them coexist chronologically, and authors moved through them according to their own personal artistic development. Each area enriches the technical, thematic, and linguistic complexities of the next, and at the same time is nourished by it. Some of the stories we present can be identified as belonging to one of these areas of development; others exhibit a comprehensive sum of all three of them.

, The first area of literary development highlights certain predominant themes: the unhappy marriage, women's passivity, sexual repression, unfulfilled love, loneliness, mother's duties, lack of self-expression, dependency, evasion. There is a need to articulate women's issues from an emotional point of view. Authors use traditional literary techniques, first-person narration, and the female protagonist. The narrative tone is frequently confessional and dramatic.[13]

A second area of creative development is characterized by open and militant language and a pronounced feminist approach which denounces unfairness and demands social changes. From this new point of view, some of the same issues presented in the first area are reintroduced and new themes appear: the urgent need for women's active involvement in society, the metaphysical quest, politics, social problems, sexual needs and the struggle for personal development. Literary techniques are more elaborate: use of multiple narrative voices, parody and humor. Language becomes direct and creative.[14]

A third commonplace of development not only compounds many of the same themes but also transforms them into more complex issues which lend themselves to multiple interpretations and interdisciplinary analysis. Stories from this stage often draw from different literary genres and fields: poetry, drama, history, journalism, oral literature, fable. Almost all of them use demystification as means to subvert institutions and traditional male mythology. This stage of development projects a deep metaphysical quest directed towards an almost constant inquiry into human relationships and into the spiritual and subconcious aspects of universal/female knowledge. The solidarity of women with other marginal elements of society is also apparent, as well as political commitment and the exploration of violence. The use of complex technical structures and linguistic codes is almost always present in these stories. It becomes very important to break away from traditional rhetoric and to use language on all possible levels of symbolic meaning through both the self-reflexive mode and intertextuality. These texts seek the reader's active participation, stress multiple narrators, humor, synthesis of opposition, ambiguity, female eroticism, innovative use of time and narrative space, and extremely individualistic characters.[15]

"The Judge's Wife" offers at least two possible readings. It may be read as entertainment: the unfolding, intriguing story of a man trying to avoid his predicted fate; or it may be read on the feminist level: the weak, disadvantaged position in which a patriarchal society places women, and the personal power of a woman to challenge and change this position. These readings are not mutually exclusive, but rather complement one another.

The omniscient narrator displays a light sense of irony and uses metaphorical analogies to demythicize male values while amusing the reader. The central plot is deceptively simple and presents the traditional marriage of a tough, older judge and his young, fragile wife. The wife exerts a positive influence on her husband, gradually converting him into a kinder human being. As a subplot the narrator tells the story of a born outcast who manages to survive and win the respect of his fellow men through the use of violence.

The destinies of these three characters are surprisingly connected in a deadly game in which the locus of power moves from one character to another; finally, the reader is offered a deeply humane reconception of power when the ostensibly weakest character, the wife, proves to be the strongest. Her use of power rejects the traditional hierarchical concept, instead evincing a new understanding of personal freedom.

This story explores human relations at the primitive level of sexual attraction as well as on a more sophisticated level, conveying both psychological and social dimensions. The interaction of the central characters gradually emphasizes the history of women dependent upon male rules, and the difficulties they undergo in order to defend themselves and become the creators of their own fate.

"The Prize of Freedom" creates a world of legend and fable in which the unfolding clues of a moral lesson keep alive the narrative suspense. A rich imagination, combined with a healthy sense of humor, gives new insight into the meaning of freedom and teaches the importance of preserving one's own liberty against encroachment from the outside world. Freedom is a personal treasure not to be trusted to anyone's care, even that of a friend. The story can also be interpreted at a socio-political level.

"A Passion for Donna Summer" presents the theme of racial discrimination in an innovative literary form. The structure is organized as a spontaneous monologue/stream of consciousness through which Colita/Dawn, the female protagonist, denounces discrimination of blacks in the Dominican Republic, New York City, and South Africa, while reviewing her own life. She is a poor black woman who realizes her own situation as victim of society but finds herself incapable of overcoming the world of hostility around her. The constant use of the present tense, plus a rich exuberant language full of free association and ironic humor, gives movement to the mental action. The references to Donna Summer's music add a sensual, nostalgic lament to Dawn's monologue and set the narrative space and tone of the story.

"The Hunt" shares some thematic characteristics with "Perfecto Luna." It underlines the paradox implicit in using a standard concept of time when dealing with perceptions of life and death, limit and the infinite. In this story the vehicle of thematic expression is an art object:

a tapestry hung in an antique store. The carefully detailed, yet dynamic description of a still scene represented in an old tapestry, in contrast with scenes—also carefully portrayed—in which a man contemplates the tapestry, convey movement to the plastic action and the literary plot, creating an impression of art within art and reality within fiction. The increasing identification of the man with the scene portrayed in the tapestry transforms him into the plastic protagonist and evokes in him visions of an illusive experience which may have taken place in the past (perhaps in another life) and in which he was either the hunter or the hunted. The variety of techniques used to evoke time, and the elusive connection between the scene in the tapestry and the scene in which the man is contemplating it, require the active participation of the reader and invite him/her to reflect on the mystery and the nature of time, art, and life itself.

"Mercedes Benz 220 SL" is marked by a sensual hallucinating language. This story deals with many of the social problems experienced today in Puerto Rico, particularly the indifference of the rich towards the poor, and the very few options offered to women by society. One of the central characters of "Mercedes Benz 220 SL" is a rich white woman who is a prisoner of the very circumstances which, on the one hand, assure her physical survival, but on the other bring about her spiritual death: an unhappy marriage, asphyxiating social rules, and her own ignorance. Ironically, she collaborates in her own oppression. The story exhibits a provocative avant garde literary structure by fracturing time at different levels of narration and by using multiple narrative voices and a complex montage which demands the reader's constant involvement.

"The Wedding" presents one of the most difficult subjects of patriarchal pathology: incest. The story is told from the point of view of a third person narrator, Fernanda, a friend of another character, Elsa, who is the victim of her father's desire. Through subtle description and short, interrupted dialogue, the narrator reveals the tragedy of a young girl and her mother, both of whom try to regain their freedom in desperate ways: one through marriage, the other through suicide. The father maintains his social standing and reputation by declaring his daughter ungrateful and his wife crazy. The story adopts a low-key poetic tone which, in contrast with the hidden violence that moves the plot, invites the reader to take a severely critical stand, and avoids a traditional sentimental response in which the reader often feels compassion for the aggressor's sickness.

"Perfecto Luna" depicts the elusive nature of the boundary between life and death through a narrator/protagonist who believes himself alive, although the ending of the story suggests that he has been dead from the beginning. In a highly mysterious, although realistic narrative space, the ambiguity of existence prevails beyond physical death. The "naiveté" and simplicity of the protagonist illustrate the idea that metaphysical anguish is apparent at all levels of human experience.

"Under the Yubayas in Bloom" presents an imaginary, hierarchical male society, its power structures and its functioning, at a metaphorical level by mixing parables, reality and legend. This fiction explores the intellectual and sexual relationships of male prisoners. Women appear only in the parables that the "Ancient Master," leader of a group of prisoners, uses in his discourses. Women have no identity of their own; they acquire it only through the interpretative versions of men. The story achieves a provocative intellectual dimension by questioning fundamental concepts of society such as the value placed on male culture/ education, and the idea of God, both pillars of a hierarchical system which supports the power of some individuals over others. Male spiritual and sexual needs are explored, and the use of sex as a ritual of power is denounced as an act which eliminates true emotional intimacy. The fact that the narrator/protagonist describes and interprets the world around him, while admitting that he understands neither that world nor the parables of the Ancient Master, allows the reader to interpret the text on several levels. The structure of this story centers around a main plot, presented by a narrator/protagonist and interpreted through five parables told by the Ancient Master, and is amplified by occasional dialogues of the prisoners. This kind of structure allows maximum flexibility to the theme. The language is rich in symbolic meaning and labyrinthine descriptions which offer great intellectual pleasure to the reader. Parody and irony play a fundamental role, adding a healthy, creative humor to the depth of thought presented in this story.

"Homelife" brings up the dilemma of an average bourgeois housewife whose ambitions for a happy family life conflict with the political reality of her country, which demands a militant commitment from everyone —a conflict which eventually destroys her homelife. The dilemma is graphically illustrated by interpolating certain narrative fragments which the protagonist introduces through her monologue/letter to her husband, now a political prisoner. The frequent fragmentation of the main level of narration visually expresses the breakdown of the protagonist's world: her husband imprisoned, her son killed by the regime, and her daughter in hiding underground after enduring jail and torture. This story questions the detached political attitude of the traditional housewife, yet it maintains profound respect for and understanding of all its characters.

"Slide in, My Dark One, Between the Crosstie and the Whistle" is a nostalgic exploration of the love which Pancho, a railroad man, feels for his engine. It is also a metaphorical lament of a worker who loses his intimate relationship with his job to a highly technological society which alienates him from his identity. The story is quite effective in its long, detailed descriptions of healthy sexual encounters between Pancho and his mistress Teresa and suggested comparison with Pancho's erotic feelings for his engine. The careful psychological descriptions of Pancho and Teresa lead the reader into a fascinating world of sensual spontaneity. The plot gradually reveals the history of a railroad company and the struggle of its workers for their rights. In so doing, it offers a critical reflection on management's disregard for human needs. The narrator uses ambiguity to provide a mysterious ending in which feelings of love and solidarity prevail over profit and power.

"The Immigrant" challenges the traditional meaning of the mother's role and opens it to new possibilities. The protagonist is a mature, strong, sensible woman who sustains a healthy, honest relationship with her son while, at the same time, playing the role of mother/lover, model/ teacher to satisfy a young woman's needs and her own. The plot explores the sexual and emotional intimacy between two women and stresses the importance of sharing a transcendental experience with another human being. The literary structure is based on a complex montage technique, the use of alternative narrative voices, and the use of the epistolary style. The story requires active participation from the reader in order to edit the narrative material and to expand the text to several levels of possible interpretation. Proclaiming the individual's right to intellectual and personal freedom, the story defies dogmas and traditional myths to assert the primacy of human dignity.

"Crickets and Butterflies," although traditional in structure, deals with a theme only infrequently discussed: the abuse and commercial use of children in society. The story achieves a poetic harmony in balancing scenes of extreme cruelty with others in which human generosity keeps alive the hope for a better future.

Like many innovative feminist short stories of our time, "Up Among the Eagles" offers at least two possible readings. One, at the anecdotal level, describes the adventures of a foreign female amongst the strange inhabitants of a remote city in the mountains. Another possible reading offers a philosophical dissertation about the concept of time, as defined and practiced in Western culture, and an attempt to subvert it.

The central plot presents the reflections and daily chores of the protagonist in a world totally foreign to her identity, one in which she accidentally finds herself and which she is afraid to leave. The story explores the myths, rituals, and beliefs of these weird people who constantly manipulate time from the "heights" of the "mind" in order to deny old age and death. By analogy the reader discovers ironic similarities with patriarchal efforts to manipulate time through reason. The approach of the protagonist, to the contrary, accepts old age and death as the natural passing of a time which is energy and essence. She offers a feminist avant garde vision which opposes one of the fundamental principles of patriarchal society, i.e., the chronological or linear concept of time and its resultant dichotomies: man/woman, logic/intuition, life/ death, heaven/earth.

The protagonist concludes that this kind of interpretation of the universe lacks authenticity because it fragments the whole. Past, present, and future form an integral whole which constantly recreates itself; so she rejects the Cartesian division of mind and body and decides that to be is an eternal becoming, while "to be afraid of dying is to be already dead." This story seeks active involvement from the reader, who must decode the metaphorical clues of the narrative in order to understand the hidden demythifying message.

The use of humor and irony make "The Secret World of Grandmamma Anacleta" a marvelous piece of entertainment. The plot is full of surprises and double meaning as it creates an intriguing, capricious character: Grandmamma Anacleta, who seems to represent all the faults traditionally associated with old grandmothers and yet emerges as a unique personality fully capable of shaping her own destiny. The story questions the myth of old age, the dependency of women and the elusive meaning of power. It also challenges modern media to pay attention to real marvels of human achievement rather than to "brutality and pornography." Precisely because of its unusual theme, this story is extremely refreshing.

These selections make a significant contribution to the establishment of an authentic female identity through the process of deconstruction/re-construction at various levels: language, learning how to re-read, and subversion of traditional patriarchal mythology.

It is our hope that this volume will be a source of information on contemporary fiction by women writers and a discovery of important similarities and variations between Latin American women authors and their counterparts elsewhere in the world.

Finally, we invite all our readers—students, researchers, writers, teachers and those who read solely to take pleasure from literature—to enjoy the excitement of aesthetic re/creation.

NOTES

1. For differing views of Sor Juana's final decision to abandon her studies and devote herself entirely to religion, see: Octavio Paz, *Sor Juana Inés de la Cruz: o las trampas de la fé* Mexico: Fondo de Cultura Económica, 1982; Dorothy Schons, "Some Obscure Points in the Life of Sor Juana Inés de la Cruz" *Modern Philology* 24 (1926): 141-62, and "Nuevos datos para la biografía de Sor Juana" *Contemporáneos* 9 (1929): 161-76.

2. We have translated titles of essays, short stories and novels into English but have not italicized them unless they have been published in English.

3. Critics have debated the true nationality of Gómez de Avellaneda. Both Spain and Cuba claim her as their own.

4. Some important writers of the indigenist narrative movement are: Jorge Icaza,

Alcides Arguedas, Ciro Alegría, José María Arguedas, Gregorio López y Fuentes and Rosario Castellanos.

5. For a fairly complete list of twentieth century women fiction writers, see: Sara Sefchovich, *Mujeres en espejo* Vol. I. Mexico: Folios, 1983. 25-43.

6. Doris Meyer, *Victoria Ocampo. Against the Wind and the Tide*. New York: George Braziller, 1979. 36.

7. Doris Meyer, *Victoria Ocampo. Against the Wind and the Tide*. New York: George Braziller, 1979. 35.

8. Marta Brunet (1901-1967), also a Chilean writer, published *Montaña adentro* (Deep in the Mountain, 1923), a novel that presents among others the theme of seduction in an open, shameless tone.

9. Many of the narrative works of these writers have been successfully transcribed into films: Manuel Puig, *The Kiss of the Spider Woman*; Gabriel García Márquez, *Eréndira*; Carlos Fuentes, *Old Gringo*; Mario Vargas Llosa, *The City and the Dogs*; Julio Cortázar, *Blow Up*.

10. Two recent attempts to improve this situation are: Raquel Chang-Rodríguez and Malva Filer, *Voces de hispanoamérica. Antología literaria*. Boston: Heinle and Heinle, 1989, and a collection of critical essays by Patricia Elena González and Eliana Ortega, *La sartén por el mango*. Río Piedras, Puerto Rico: Huracán, 1984.

11. For available English translations of works by authors included in this anthology, see our bibliography. There are also English translations of a few other Latin American women writers: an anthology of Rosario Castellanos' writings in *A Rosario Castellanos Reader* by Maureen Ahern; one of Marta Traba's novels, *Mothers and Shadows* by Jo Labanyi; Sor Juana Inés de la Cruz's essays in *A Woman of Genius: The Intellectual Autobiography of Sor Juana Inés de la Cruz* by Margaret Sayers Peden; and short stories by María Luisa Bombal in *New Islands and Other Stories* by Richard and Lucía Cunningham. In the last decade a variety of studies on Latin American women writers has appeared in English. They encompass different genres and approaches. Two biographical studies: Carlos Solé, *Latin American Writers,* and Diane Marting, *Women Writers of Spanish America*. Translations and interviews by Evelyn Picón Garfield in *Women's Fiction from Latin America* and *Women's Voices from Latin America*. Three anthologies which include all literary genres: Barney J. Luby and Wayne H. Finke, *Anthology of Contemporary Latin American Literature, 1960-1984*; Doris Meyer and Margarite Fernández Olmos, *Contemporary Women Authors of Latin America*; and Alicia Partnoy, *You Can't Drown the Fire: Latin American Women Writing in Exile*. Two critical studies: *Plotting Women* by Jean Franco and *Reflections-Refractions: Reading Luisa Valenzuela* by Sharon Magnarelli. There is only a handful of Latin American women's writing translated prior to 1980. These references are included in our bibliography.

12. Some of the short stories, novels and essays have been reprinted several times. In order to avoid repetition we have listed the first edition as well as the edition that was available to us.

13. Two short stories not included in this anthology, "El último verano" ("The Last Summer") by Amparo Dávila and "La hija del filósofo" ("The Philosopher's Daughter") by Elena Poniatowska, illustrate many of these characteristics.

14. The short story "Homelife" exhibits many of these characteristics. "Mercedes Benz 220 SL" and "A Passion for Donna Summer" deal with political and social problems. "Perfecto Luna" and "The Hunt" reflect an existential problem, and both

make use of complex literary and stylistic techniques. All these stories are included in this anthology.

15. "The Immigrant," "Under the Yubayas in Bloom," and "The Judge's Wife" are the most representative stories in this area.

ISABEL ALLENDE
Chile

I sabel Allende was born in Lima, Peru in 1942, but she considers Chile her native country since she lived there from childhood until President Salvador Allende, her uncle, was overthrown by a coup d'état. She now lives in California with her husband. Isabel Allende has written many plays and short stories, but above all she has been a journalist since the age of seventeen; she is also a theatrical director and a director of *Mampato*, an important children's magazine. Her first novel, *La casa de los espíritus* (*The House of the Spirits,* 1982), became an instant best-seller in Spain, France, Germany, Japan, and the United States. This novel alone makes her the most widely read Latin American woman writer of all times.

Allende has been a strong supporter of democracy and human rights in Chile. She also has shown great solidarity with the global cause of women's rights. Allende believes that Latin American women writers still suffer gender descrimination: "If we compare the decade of the 1950s with that of the 80s, undoubtedly there is a noticeable difference in Latin America; nevertheless, I think we still have a long way to go. Our women writers have had to struggle and are still struggling against the prejudices of editors, who think that masculine literature is better or sells better, and the critics who keep a strategic silence about women's literary works."[1]

NOTES

1. Michael Moody, "Una conversación con Isabel Allende." *Chasqui* 16, 2-3 (1987): 53. Translated by Nora Erro-Peralta and Caridad Silva-Núñez.

THE JUDGE'S WIFE

Nicolas Vidal always knew he would lose his head over a woman. So it was foretold on the day of his birth, and later confirmed by the Turkish woman in the corner store the one time he allowed her to read his fortune in the coffee grounds. Little did he imagine, though, that it would be on account of Casilda, Judge Hidalgo's wife. It was on her wedding day that Vidal first glimpsed her. He was not impressed, preferring his women dark-haired and brazen. This ethereal slip of a girl in her wedding gown, eyes filled with wonder, and fingers obviously unskilled in the art of rousing a man to pleasure, seemed to him almost ugly. Mindful of his destiny, he had always been wary of any emotional contact with women, hardening his heart and restricting himself to the briefest of encounters whenever the demands of manhood needed satisfying.

Casilda, however, appeared so insubstantial, so distant, that he cast aside all precaution and, when the fateful moment arrived, forgot the prediction that usually weighed in all his decisions. From the roof of the bank, where he was crouching with two of his men, Nicolas Vidal peered down at this young lady from the capital. She had a dozen equally pale and dainty relatives with her, who spent the whole of the ceremony fanning themselves with an air of utter bewilderment, then departed straight away, never to return. Along with everyone else in the town, Vidal was convinced the young bride would not withstand the climate, and that within a few months the old women would be dressing her up again, this time for her funeral.

Even if she did survive the heat, and the dust that filtered in through every pore to lodge itself in the soul, she would be bound to succumb to the fussy habits of her confirmed bachelor of a husband. Judge Hidalgo was twice her age, and had slept alone for so many years he didn't have the slightest notion of how to go about pleasing a woman. The severity and stubbornness with which he executed the law, even at the expense of justice, made him feared throughout the province. He refused to apply any common sense in the exercise of his profession, and was equally harsh in his condemnation of the theft of a chicken and of a premeditated murder. He dressed formally in black, and despite the all-pervasive dust in this god-forsaken town, his boots always shone with beeswax.

A man such as the Judge was never meant to be a husband, and yet not only did the gloomy wedding-day prophecies remain unfulfilled, Casilda emerged happy and smiling from three pregnancies in rapid succession. Every Sunday at noon she would go to mass with her husband, cool and collected beneath her Spanish mantilla, seemingly untouched by the pitiless summer, as wan and frail-looking as on the day of her arrival: a perfect example of delicacy and refinement. Her loudest words were a soft-spoken greeting; her most expressive gesture was a graceful nod of the head. She was such an airy, diaphanous creature that a moment's carelessness might mean she disappeared altogether.

So slight an impression did she make that the changes noticeable in the Judge were all the more remarkable. Though outwardly he remained the same—he still dressed as black as a crow and was as stiff-necked and brusque as ever—his judgments in court altered dramatically. To general amazement, he found the youngster who robbed the Turkish shopkeeper innocent, on grounds that she had been selling the boy short for years, and the money he had taken could therefore be seen as compensation. The Judge also refused to punish an adulterous wife, arguing that since her husband himself kept a mistress, he did not have the moral authority to demand fidelity. Word in the town had it that the Judge was transformed the minute he crossed the threshold at home: that he flung off his gloomy apparel, rollicked with his children, chuckled as he sat Casilda on his lap. Though no one ever succeeded in confirming these rumors, his wife got the credit for his new-found kindness, and her reputation grew accordingly.

None of this was of the slightest interest to Nicolas Vidal, who as a wanted man was sure there would be no mercy shown him the day he was brought in chains before the Judge. He paid no heed to the talk about Doña Casilda, and the rare occasions he glimpsed her from afar only confirmed his first impression of her as a lifeless ghost.

Born thirty years earlier in a windowless room in the town's only brothel, Vidal was the son of Juana the Forlorn and an unknown father. The world had no place for him. His mother knew it, and so tried to wrench him from her womb with sprigs of parsley, candle butts, douches of ashes and other violent purgatives, but the child clung to life. Once, years later, Juana was looking at her mysterious son and realized that, while all her infallible methods of aborting may have failed to dislodge him, they had nevertheless tempered his soul to the hardness of iron. As soon as he came into the world, he was lifted in the air by the midwife who examined him by the light of an oil lamp. She saw he had four nipples.

"Poor creature: he'll lose his head over a woman," she predicted, drawing on her wealth of experience.

Her words rested on the boy like a deformity. Perhaps a woman's love would have made his existence less wretched. To atone for all her attempts to kill him before his birth, his mother chose him a beautiful first name, and an imposing family name picked at random. But the lofty name of Nicolas Vidal was no protection against the fateful cast of his destiny. His face was scarred from knife fights before he reached his teens, so it came as no surprise to decent folk that he ended up a bandit. By the age of twenty, he had become the leader of a band of desperados. The habit of violence toughened his sinews, but the solitude he imposed on himself for fear of falling prey to a woman lent his face a sad expression. As soon as they saw him, everyone in the town knew from his eyes, clouded by tears he would never allow to fall, that he was the son of Juana the Forlorn. Whenever there was an outcry after a crime had been committed in the region, the police set out with dogs to track him down, but after scouring the hills they invariably returned empty-handed. In all honesty they preferred it that way, because they could never have fought him. His gang gained such a fearsome reputation that the surrounding villages and estates paid to keep them away. This money would have been plenty for his men, but Nicolas Vidal kept them constantly on horseback in a whirlwind of death and destruction so they would not lose their taste for battle. Nobody dared take them on. More than once, Judge Hidalgo had asked the government to send troops to reinforce the police, but after several useless forays the soldiers returned to their barracks and Nicolas Vidal's gang to their exploits. On one occasion only did Vidal come close to falling into the hands of justice, and then he was saved by his hardened heart.

Weary of seeing the laws flouted, Judge Hidalgo resolved to forget his scruples and set a trap for the outlaw. He realized that to defend justice he was committing an injustice, but he chose the lesser of two evils. The only bait he could find was Juana the Forlorn, as she was Vidal's sole known relative. He had her dragged from the brothel where by now, since no clients were willing to pay for her exhausted charms, she scrubbed floors and cleaned out the lavatories. He put her in a specially made cage which was set up in the middle of the Plaza de Armas, with only a jug of water to meet her needs.

"As soon as the water's finished, she'll start to squawk. Then her son will come running, and I'll be waiting for him with the soldiers," Judge Hidalgo said.

News of this torture, unheard of since the days of slavery, reached Nicolas Vidal's ears shortly before his mother drank the last of the water. His men watched as he received the report in silence, without so much as a flicker of emotion on his blank, lone wolf's face, or a pause in the sharpening of his dagger blade on a leather strap. Though for many years he had had no contact with Juana, and retained few happy childhood memories, this was a question of honor. No man can accept such an insult, his gang reasoned as they got guns and horses ready to rush into the ambush and, if need be, lay down their lives. Their chief showed no sign of being in a hurry. As the hours went by, tension mounted in the camp. The perspiring, impatient men stared at each other, not daring to speak. Fretful, they caressed the butts of their revolvers and their horses' manes, or busied themselves coiling their lassos. Night fell, but Nicolas Vidal was the only one in camp who slept. At dawn, opinions were divided. Some of the men reckoned he was even more heartless than they had ever imagined, while others maintained their leader was planning a spectacular ruse to free his mother. The one thing that never crossed any of their minds was that his courage might have failed him, for he had always proved he had more than enough to spare. By noon, they could bear the suspense no longer, and went to ask him what he planned to do.

"I'm not going to fall into his trap like an idiot," he said.

"What about your mother?"

"We'll see who's got more balls, the Judge or me," Nicolas Vidal coolly replied.

By the third day, Juana the Forlorn's cries for water had ceased. She lay curled on the cage floor, with wildly staring eyes and swollen lips, moaning softly whenever she regained consciousness, and the rest of the time dreaming she was in Hell. Four armed guards stood watch to make sure nobody brought her water. Her groans penetrated the entire town, filtering through closed shutters and being carried by the wind through the cracks in doors. They got stuck in corners, where dogs worried at them, and passed them on in their howls to the newly born, so that whoever heard them was driven to distraction. The Judge couldn't prevent a steady stream of people filing through the square to show their sympathy for the old woman, and was powerless to stop the prostitutes going on a sympathy strike just as the miners' fortnight holiday was beginning. That Saturday, the streets were thronged with lusty workmen desperate to unload their savings, who now found nothing in town apart from the spectacle of the cage and this universal wailing carried mouth to mouth from the river to the coast road. The priest headed a group of Catholic ladies to plead with Judge Hidalgo for Christian mercy and to beg him to spare the poor old innocent woman such a frightful death, but the man of the law bolted his door and refused to listen to them. It was then that they decided to turn to Doña Casilda.

The Judge's wife received them in her shady living room. She listened to their pleas looking, as she always did, bashfully down at the floor. Her husband had not been home for three days, having locked himself in his office to wait for Nicolas Vidal to fall into his trap. Without so much as looking out of the window, she was aware of what was going on, for Juana's long-drawn-out agony had forced its way even into the vast rooms of her residence. Doña Castilda waited until her visitors had left, dressed her children in their Sunday best, tied a black ribbon around their arms as a token of mourning, then strode out with them in the direction of the square. She carried a food hamper and a bottle of fresh water for Juana the Forlorn. When the guards spotted her turning the corner, they realized what she was up to, but they had strict orders, and barred her way with their rifles. When, watched now by a small crowd, she persisted, they grabbed her by the arms. Her children began to cry.

Judge Hidalgo sat in his office overlooking the square. He was the only person in the town who had not stuffed wax in his ears, because his mind was intent on the ambush and he was straining to catch the sound of horses' hoofs, which would be the signal for action. For three long days and nights he put up with Juana's groans and the insults of the townspeople gathered outside the courtroom, but when he heard his own children start to wail he knew he had reached the bounds of his endurance. Vanquished, he walked out of the office with his three days' beard, his eyes bloodshot from keeping watch, and the weight of a thousand years on his back. He crossed the street, turned into the square and came face to face with his wife. They gazed at each other sadly. In seven years, this was the first time she had gone against him, and she had chosen to do so in front of the whole town. Easing the hamper and the bottle from Casilda's grasp, Judge Hidalgo himself opened the cage to release the prisoner.

"Didn't I tell you he wouldn't have the balls?" laughed Nicolas Vidal when the news reached him.

His laughter turned sour the next day, when he heard that Juana the Forlorn had hanged herself from the chandelier in the brothel where she had spent her life, overwhelmed by the shame of her son leaving her to fester in a cage in the middle of the Plaza de Armas.

"That Judge's hour has come," said Vidal.

He planned to take the judge by surprise, put him to a horrible death, then dump him in the accursed cage for all to see. The Turkish shopkeeper sent him word that the Hidalgo family had left the same night for a seaside resort to rid themselves of the bitter taste of defeat.

The Judge learned he was being pursued when he stopped to rest at a wayside inn. There was little protection for him there until an army patrol could arrive, but he had a few hours' start, and his motorcar could outrun the gang's horses. He calculated he could make it to the next town and summon help there. He ordered his wife and children into the car, put his foot down on the accelerator and sped off along the road. He ought to have arrived with time to spare, but it had been ordained that Nicolas Vidal was that day to meet the woman who would lead him to his doom.

Overburdened by the sleepless nights, the townspeople's hostility, the blow to his pride and the stress of this race to save his family, Judge Hidalgo's heart gave a massive jolt, then split like a pomegranate. The car ran out of control, turned several somersaults and finally came to a halt in the ditch. It took Doña Casilda some minutes to work out what had happened. Her husband's advancing years had often led her to think about what it would be like to be left a widow, yet she had never imagined he would leave her at the mercy of her enemies. She wasted little time dwelling on her situation, knowing she must act at once to get her children to safety. When she gazed around her, she almost burst into tears. There was no sign of life in the vast plain baked by a scorching sun, only barren cliffs beneath an unbound sky bleached colorless by the fierce light. A second look revealed the dark shadow of a passage or cave on a distant slope, so she ran towards it with two children in her arms and the third clutching her skirts.

One by one she carried her children up the cliff. The cave was a natural one, typical of many in the region. She peered inside to be certain it wasn't the den of some wild animal, sat her children against its back wall, then, dry-eyed, kissed them goodbye.

"The troops will come to find you a few hours from now. Until then, don't for any reason whatsoever come out of here, even if you hear me screaming—do you understand?"

Their mother gave them one final glance as the terrified children clung to each other, then clambered back down to the road. She reached the car, closed her husband's eyes, smoothed back her hair and settled down to wait. She had no idea how many men were in Nicolas Vidal's gang, but prayed there were a lot of them so it would take them all the more time to have their way with her. She gathered strength pondering on how long it would take her to die if she determined to do it as slowly as possible. She willed herself to be desirable, luscious, to create more work for them and thus gain time for her children.

Casilda did not have long to wait. She soon saw a cloud of dust on the horizon and heard the gallop of horses' hoofs. She clenched her teeth. Then, to her astonishment, she saw there was only one rider, who stopped a few yards from her, gun at the ready. By the scar on his face she recognized Nicolas Vidal, who had set out all alone in pursuit of Judge Hidalgo, as this was a private matter between the two men. The Judge's wife understood she was going to have to endure something far worse than a slow death.

A single glance at her husband was enough to convince Vidal that the Judge was safely out of his reach in the peaceful sleep of death. But there was his wife, a shimmering presence in the plain's glare. He leaped from his horse and strode over to her. She did not flinch or lower her gaze, and to his amazement he realized that for the first time in his life another person was facing him without fear. For several seconds that stretched to eternity, they sized each other up, trying to gauge the other's strength, and their own powers of resistance. It gradually dawned on both of them that each one was up against a formidable opponent. He lowered his gun. She smiled.

Casilda won each moment of the ensuing hours. To all the wiles of seduction known since the beginning of time she added new ones born of necessity to bring this man to the heights of rapture. Not only did she work on his body like an artist, stimulating his every fiber to pleasure, but she brought all the delicacy of her spirit into play on her side. Both knew their lives were at stake, and this added a new and terrifying dimension to their meeting. Nicolas Vidal had fled from love since birth, and knew nothing of intimacy, tenderness, secret laughter, the riot of the senses, the joy of shared passion. Each minute brought the detachment of troops and the noose that much nearer, but he gladly accepted this in return for her prodigious gifts. Casilda was a passive, demure, timid woman who had been married to an austere old man in front of whom she had never even dared appear naked. Not once during that unforgettable afternoon did she forget that her aim was to win time for her children, and yet at some point, marveling at her own possibilities, she gave herself completely, and felt something akin to gratitude towards him. That was why, when she heard the soldiers in the distance, she begged him to flee to the hills. Instead Nicolas Vidal chose to fold her in a last embrace, thus fulfilling the prophecy that had sealed his fate from the start.

Translated by Nick Castor

Bibliography: Isabel Allende

Fiction

Allende, Isabel. *La casa de los espíritus*. Barcelona: Plaza & Janés, 1982.

————. *De amor y de sombra*. Barcelona: Plaza & Janés, 1984.

————. *The House of the Spirits*. Trans. Magda Bogin. New York: Knopf, 1985.

————. *Eva Luna*. Barcelona: Plaza & Janes, 1987.

————. *Of Love and Shadows*. Trans. Margaret Sayers Peden. New York: Bantam Books, 1987.

————. "Rosa the Beautiful." [Selections from the novel *The House of the Spirits*.] Trans. Magda Bogin. *Women's Fiction from Latin America: Selections from Twelve Contemporary Authors*. Ed. Evelyn Picón Garfield. Detroit: Wayne State University Press, 1988. 317-37.

————. "The Spirits Were Willing." Trans. Jo Anne Engelbert. *Lives on the Line: The Testimony of Contemporary Latin American Authors*. Ed. Doris Meyer. Berkeley: University of California Press, 1988. 235-42.

————. "Los libros tienen sus propios espíritus." *Los libros tienen sus propios espíritus*. Ed. Marcelo Coddou. Xalapa: Universidad Veracruzana, 1986. 15-20.

————. *Eva Luna*. Trans. Margaret Sayers Peden. New York: Bantam Books, 1989.

————. *Cuentos de Eva Luna*. Buenos Aires: Editorial Sudamericana, 1990.

Essays

Allende, Isabel. "La magia de las palabras." *Revista Iberoamericana* 51.132-33 (1985): 447-52.

Criticism on the Works of Isabel Allende

Agosín, Marjorie. "Isabel Allende: *La casa de los espíritus*." *Revista Interamericana de Bibliografía/Inter-American Review of Bibliography* 35.4 (1985): 448-58.

Agosín, Marjorie and Cola Franzen. "Entrevista a Isabel Allende/Interview with Isabel Allende." *Imagine: International Chicano Poetry Journal* 1.2 (1984): 42-56.

Aguirre, María Elena. "Isabel y sus espíritus." *Carola* 9 April 1984: 23.

Alegría, Fernando. *Nueva historia de la novela hispanoamericana*. Hanover, NH: Ediciones del Norte, 1986. 395-97.

Badra, Nadia F. "Una historia de amor desvela a Isabel." *Gente* 29 April 1984: 3-4.

Campos, Jorge. "*La casa de los espíritus*, de Isabel Allende." *Insula: Revista de Letras y Ciencias Humanas* Feb.-Mar. 1983: 19.

Campos, René. "*La casa de los espíritus* : mirada, espacio, discurso de la otra historia." *Los libros tienen sus propios espíritus*. Ed. Marcelo Coddou. Xalapa: Universidad Veracruzana, 1986. 21-28.

Coddou, Marcelo. "Dimensión del femenino en Isabel Allende." *Los libros tienen sus propios espíritus*. Ed. Marcelo Coddou. Xalapa: Universidad Veracruzana, 1986. 29-53.

————. Introducción. "*La casa de los espíritus*: de la historia a la Historia." *Los libros tienen sus propios espíritus*. Ed. Marcelo Coddou. Xalapa: Universidad Veracruzana, 1986. 71-78.

————. "Las ficciones de Isabel Allende." *Literatura Chilena: Creación y Crítica* Jan.-Mar. 1987: 11-12.

————. ed. *Los libros tienen sus propios espíritus*. Xalapa: Universidad Veracruzana, 1986.

————. "Para leer a Isabel Allende: su vida en su obra." *Araucaria de Chile* 38 (1987): 125-36.

Eberenz, Rolf. "La imaginación como libertad: *La casa de los espíritus* de Isabel Allende." *Iberoamericana* [Frankfurt] 8.22-23 (1984): 102-8.

Engelbert, Jo Anne and Linda Gould Levine. "The World is Full of Stories: An Interview with Isabel Allende." *Review* 34 (1985): 18-20.

Fischer, Amalia E. "De sus espíritus a los míos, Isabel." *FEM* 11.53 (1987): 38-40.

Foster, Douglas. "Isabel Allende Unveiled." *Mother Jones* Dec. 1980: 42-46.

Freixas, Ramón. "*La casa de los espíritus*." *Quimera* 28 Feb. 1983: 69.

García Pinto, Magdalena, ed. *Historias íntimas: conversaciones con 10 escritoras latinoamericanas*. Hanover, NH: Ediciones del Norte, 1988. 1-26.

Gazarian Gautier, Marie-Lise. "Isabel Allende." *Interviews with Latin American Writers*. Elmwood Park, Ill.: Dalkey Archive Press, 1989. 5-24.

Glickman, Nora. "Los personajes femeninos en *La casa de los espíritus*." *Los libros tienen sus propios espíritus*. Ed. Marcelo Coddou. Xalapa: Universidad Veracruzana, 1986. 54-60.

Gordon, Ambrose. "Isabel Allende on *Love and Shadows*." *Contemporary Literature* 28.4 (1987): 530-42.

Herlinghaus, Hermann. "Una novela chilena-latinoamericana sobre *La casa de los espíritus* de Isabel Allende." *Lateinamerika* 21.1 (1985): 143-50.

Hernán-Gómez, Beatriz. "Las violencias circulares: notas a *La casa de los espíritus*." *Studi di letteratura ibero-americana offertia Giuseppe Bellini* Rome: Bulzoni, 1984. 333-48.

Jara, René. "Narrativa chilena post-golpe: en las huellas de la esperanza." *Araucaria de Chile* 39 (1987): 109-17.

———. *El revés de la arpilla: perfíl literario de Chile*. Madrid: Ediciones Hiperión, S.L., 1988. 232-36.

Levine, Linda Gould. "A Passage to Androgyny: Isabel Allende's *La casa de los espíritus*." Ed. Carol Maier and Noel Valis. *In the Feminine Mode: Essays on Hispanic Women Writers*. Lewisburg, Pa.: Bucknell University Press, 1990.

Magnarelli, Sharon. "*The House of the Spirits*." *Latin American Literary Review* 14.28 (1986): 101-4.

Marcos, Juan Manuel. "*La casa de los espíritus*." *Revista Iberoamericana* 51.130-31 (1985): 401-6.

———. "Isabel viendo llover en Barataria." *Revista de Estudios Hispánicos* 19.2 (1985): 129-37.

Marcos, Juan Manuel, and Teresa Mendez-Faith. "Multiplicidad, dialéctica y reconciliación del discurso en *La casa de los espíritus*." *Los libros tienen sus propios espíritus*. Ed. Marcelo Coddou. Xalapa: Universidad Veracruzana, 1986. 61- 70.

Medwick, C. "The Amazing Isabel Allende." *Vogue* March 1985: 506.

Moody, Michael. "Entrevista con Isabel Allende." *Discurso Literario: Revista de Temas Hispánicos* 4.1 (1986): 41-53. Rpt. in *Hispania* 69.1 (1986): 149-51.

———. "Isabel Allende and the Testimonial Novel." *Confluencia: Revista Hispanica de Cultura y Literatura* 2.1 (1986): 39-43.

———. "Una conversación con Isabel Allende." *Chasqui: Revista de Literatura Latinoamericana* 16.2-3 (1987): 51-59.

Mora, Gabriela. "Las novelas de Isabel Allende y el papel de la mujer como ciudadana." *Ideologies and Literatures: A Journal of Hispanic and Luso-Brazilian Studies* 2.1 (1987): 53-61.

———. "Ruptura y perseverancia de estereotipos en *La casa de los espíritus*." *Los libros tienen sus propios espíritus*. Ed. Marcelo Coddou. Xalapa: Universidad Veracruzana, 1986. 71- 78.

Rodríguez, Mario. *"La casa de los espíritus."* *Atenea* 448 (1983): 270-73.

―――. "García Márquez/Isabel Allende: relación textual." *Los libros tienen sus propios espíritus*. Ed. Marcelo Coddou. Xalapa: Universidad Veracruzana, 1986. 79-82.

Rojas, Mario A. *"La casa de los espíritus*, de Isabel Allende: Un caleidoscopio de espejos desordenados." *Revista Iberoamericana* 51.132-133 (1985): 917-25. Rpt. in *Los libros tienen sus propios espíritus*. Ed. Marcelo Coddou. Xalapa: Universidad Veracruzana, 1986. 83-90.

―――. *"La casa de los espíritus* de Isabel Allende: una aproximación sociolingüística." *Revista de Crítica Literaria Latinoamericana* 11.21-22 (1985): 205-13. Rpt. in *Los libros tienen sus propios espíritus*. Ed. Marcelo Coddou. Xalapa: Universidad Veracruzana, 1986. 91-99.

Romero, Graciela. "Isabel Allende: diez años de soledad." *Mundo* 12 Nov. 1983: 28-29.

Rubilar, Luis and Virginia Vidal. "Crónica e historia de medio siglo en una novela chilena." *Araucaria de Chile* 23 (1983): 187-93.

Shapiro, H. "Salvador's Niece Builds a House of the Spirits from the Ashes of Exile." *People Weekly* 10 June 1985: 145-46.

Smith, Amanda. "Publishers Weekly Interviews: Isabel Allende." *Publishers Weekly* 17 May, 1985: 119-20.

Zamudio, Alfredo. "Isabel Allende: a vivir con alegría." *Hoy* 385 Dec. 1984: 31-33.

LYDIA CABRERA
Cuba

Lydia Cabrera was born in Habana, Cuba, in 1900. Her artistic interests took her to Paris in the 1920s, where she immersed herself in vanguardism, particularly surrealism. She became acquainted with significant artists of that time, among them Teresa de la Parra, with whom she lived for several years. Although Cabrera has traveled extensively and has lived in exile from Cuba since 1960, her work has always focused on her native country.

She published her first book, *Cuentos negros* (Black Tales), in France in 1936. This collection of twenty-one stories, mostly of Yoruba origin, gained her considerable recognition in Europe and was published in its original Spanish in Habana in 1940.

Influenced by the great pioneer work of her brother-in-law, Fernando Ortiz, on black Cuban heritage, Lydia Cabrera distinguished herself by her devotion to the study of Afro-Caribbean (especially Afro-Cuban) culture. She published exceptional research about Bantú, Ewe, and Yoruba religion, traditions, and language, which also served as foundation for her creative literary work.

Chronologically, Lydia Cabrera belongs to the women's generation of the first quarter of the twentieth century. Yet because of its innovative literary quality her work continues to be published to the present time.

THE PRIZE OF FREEDOM

Back when animals used to talk, were good friends with each other and got along with man, the Dog was already a slave.

In that age of never rushing, of elastic hours, the Cat, the Dog, and the Mouse were inseparable, Cuba's best pals. They usually got together in the backyard of a large house along the plaza, in whose stained-glass windows, still not so long ago, reflections from the sea went to die. There, at the foot of a laurel—murdered eventually, along with its birds, by the new age—they chatted away the early evening.

Once the Mouse, who was big in the book business (he was a scholar), and the Cat were singing the praises of liberty and discussing at length the rights of all the sons of the earth, including those of the air and water. The Dog realized that he was a slave and it made him sad. The next day he went to see Olofi:

"Bada dide odiddena!"*

and he asked him for a license to be free.

The old man, the oldest of the heavens, was a bit at a loss. Narrowing his crafty eyes which saw everything in advance, and scratching behind his ear, he had serious doubts about whether he should accommodate the Dog. But at last, after shrugging his shoulders and shooting black spit out from behind his eye-tooth—which is what he always did when he made a decision—he put his signature on a sheet of parchment and, with everything in order, gave the Dog the longed-for liberty license. That same night, the Dog, feeling very pleased with himself, showed it to his friends.

"Listen, pal, put it away in a safe place, and guard it like gold," advised the Cat when he said good-bye. And the Dog, thinking that in no other place could it be safer—not having pockets—tucked it away in his rear-end. But the precious document, shut up in there, stung terribly. It caused a disturbing condition that got worse with time. He was forced to walk in a grotesque way, his back paws immodestly spread apart, and didn't dare make even the slightest gesture to express any feeling with his tail. Then all of a sudden he'd feel an overwhelming need to itch, which gave rise to a violent urge to run, to rub himself desperately against the ground without measuring the consequences of such an act; when, to his shame, these outbursts took place in public, they made absolutely everyone laugh. It was torture. Constant worry over losing the document occupied his thoughts day in and day out. The fear of some careless slip that might smudge the text made the Dog abstain from eating; and at last, not knowing which to choose, freedom or martyrdom, the Dog pulled out the document and gave it to his friend the Cat for safekeeping.

* Get up, old man, get up!

The Cat thought that exposing a liberty license to the elements, and to risky roof-top living, was a big responsibility. So he took it to the house of his friend the Mouse, whose roof was at least over his head. The Mouse had gone to buy cheese at a bodega. The Mousewife came to the door, and having given her full instructions, the Cat entrusted her with the license. But the Mousewife was having labor pains. She grabbed the license, ripped it up, and made her nest.

Meanwhile the Dog had quarrelled bitterly with his owner.

The Dog had said, "Give me another bone!"

The Master had replied, "I don't feel like it."

The Dog stood up to the man. The man was about to lift the whip.

"I need to eat much more because I am free!"

The man said, "You were born a slave. You will eat as much as I think! You are my slave!"

"No Señor, my Master, I am not your slave"—and his tail wildly confirmed the fact. "I have my liberty license."

"If that's so, show it to me immediately!"

The Dog went out to the backyard and called on the Cat.

"Hurry, my friend. My liberty license!"

The Cat called on the Mouse.

"My friend the Mouse, hurry! Your wife has our friend's liberty license."

The Mouse ran back with a heavy heart, and whispered into the Cat's ear. The Cat put his paws on his head, and for the first time let out a "Hissss!" and jumped, claws bared, on the Mouse; and this was the first time that the Dog jumped on the Cat and sank his fangs into the nape of his neck.

With eyes of green fire, the Cat defended himself, claws on all four paws bared; it made for a cycle of howling, whacking, biting and blood. The Mouse, since he was small, slipped away into his hole.

The Cat, bristling and battered, clambered up on the laurel; from one branch he reached the roof, and from the eaves he hissed, challenging the Dog, his back arched like a bow.

But the Dog went to lick the hand of his owner, throwing himself at his feet without further explanation.

Translated by Lisa Wyant

Bibliography: Lydia Cabrera

Fiction

Cabrera, Lydia. *Contes nègres de Cuba*. Trans. Francis de Miomandre. Paris: Gallimard, 1936.

———. "Cuentos negros de Cuba." *Estudios Afrocubanos* 2 (1938): 58-71.

———. *Cuentos negros de Cuba*. La Habana: Imprenta La Verónica, 1940. Rpt. in Madrid: Ramos, 1972.

———. "Un buen hijo." *Cuentos cubanos contemporáneos*. Ed. José Antonio Portuondo. Mexico City: Editorial Leyenda S.A., 1947. 91-104.

———. "Eggüe o Vichichi finda." *Revista Bimestre Cubana* [La Habana] 60 (1947): 42-120.

———. "La jicotea endemoniada." *Orígenes*. La Habana 7.24 (1948): 3-9.

———. *Por qué . . . cuentos negros de Cuba*. La Habana: Colección del Chicherekú, Ediciones C.R., 1948. Rpt. in Madrid: Ramos, 1972.

———. "La virtud del árbol Dagame." *Antología del cuento en Cuba*. Ed. Salvador Bueno. La Habana: Ediciones del Cincuentenario, 1953. 141-45.

———. *Pourquoi; nouveaux contes negres de Cuba*. Trans. Francis de Miomandre. Paris: Gallimard, 1954.

———. "Cundió brujería mala." *Selección de cuentos cubanos*. La Habana: Editorial Nacional de Cuba, 1962. 29-37.

———. "El dueño de Ewe (Oluwa-Ewe)." *Memoire de l'Institut Français de l'Afrique Noire* Paris 37 (1963): 169-180.

———. "Turtle's Horse." *From the Green Antilles*. Ed. Barbara Howes. New York: MacMillan, 1966. 275-76.

———. "Walo-Wila." *From the Green Antilles*. Ed. Barbara Howes. New York: MacMillan, 1966. 277-79. Rpt. in *Longman Anthology of World Literature by Women 1875-1975*. Eds. Marian Arkin and Barbara Shollar. New York: Longman, 1989. 376-77.

———. "Y así fue . . ." *El Tiempo*. New York, "Página Literaria," 18 Jan. 1970.

———. *Ayapá: cuentos de jicotea*. Zaragoza: Ediciones Universal, 1971. Miami: Ediciones Universal, 1971.

———. "Babalú Ayé-San Lázaro. Mitos y leyendas. (Ilustraciones de Hernán García): Guanaroca. La Tatagua. La cabeza de Patricio. San Félix, número 13. El diablo y la mujer." *La enciclopedia de Cuba*. vol. 6. San Juan-Madrid: Editorial Playor, 1974. 263-303.

———. "El baile de las Cucarachas y las Gallinas." *La enciclopedia de Cuba*. vol. 6. San Juan-Madrid: Editorial Playor, 1974. 394.

———. "Boloya." *La enciclopedia de Cuba*. vol. 6. San Juan-Madrid: Editorial Playor, 1974. 384.

———. "Cholé la holgazana y su buena vecina Daraya." *La enciclopedia de Cuba*. vol. 6. San Juan-Madrid: Editorial Playor, 1974. 388.

———. "Como a Jicotea la coronaron Rey." *La enciclopedia de Cuba*. vol. 6. San Juan-Madrid: Editorial Playor, 1974. 386.

———. "El granito de arena." *La enciclopedia de Cuba*. vol. 6. San Juan-Madrid: Editorial Playor, 1974. 383.

———. "Historia de Elewá Echeún y de lo que le aconteció con su hermano envidioso y Ekué Kekeré, la Jutía." *La enciclopedia de Cuba*. vol. 6. San Juan-Madrid: Editorial Playor, 1974. 391.

———. "Oyé Ogbó. Refranes y ejemplos. Como enseñaban a sus hijos los viejos lucumíes y taitas criollos. Refranes criollos. Refranes Abakuá. Refranes Lucumí (Yoruba)." *La enciclopedia de Cuba*. vol. 6 San Juan-Madrid: Editorial Playor, 1974. 349-82.

———. *Francisco y Francisca. Chascarrillos de negros viejos*. Miami: Peninsular Printing Inc., 1976.

———. "Francisco y Francisca." *Caribe* 2 (1977). Rpt. in *Repertorio latinoamericano* 5.40 (1979): 29.

———. "El sabio desconfía de su misma sombra." *Cuentos fantásticos hispanoamericanos*. Ed. Mignon Dominguez. Buenos Aires: Editorial Crea, 1980. 183-211.

———. "Tres cuentos (El insomnio de un marinero; Romualdo Nalganes; ¡Se va por el río!)" *Escandalar* 3.2 (1980): 60-63.

———. "Apopoito Miamá." *El cuento cubano: Panorámica y Antología*. Ed. Pedro Izquierdo Tejido. San José, Costa Rica: Litografía e Imprenta LIL, S.A., 1983. 158-63.

———. *Cuentos para adultos niños y retrasados mentales*. Miami: Ultra Graphics, 1983.

———. "The Hill Called Mambiala." Trans. Elizabeth Millet. *Contemporary Women Authors of Latin America: New Translations*. Eds. Doris Meyer and Margarite Fernández Olmos. New York: Brooklyn College Press, 1983. 147-57.

———. "Obbara Lies but Doesn't Lie." Trans. Suzanne Jill Levine and Mary Caldwell. *Contemporary Women Authors of Latin America: New Translations*. Ed. Doris Meyer and Margarite Fernández Olmos. New York: Brooklyn College Press, 1983. 147-57.

———. "Se dice que no hay hijo feo para su madre." *El cuento cubano: Panorámica y Antología*. Ed. Pedro Izquierdo Tejido. San José, Costa Rica: Litografía e Imprenta LIL, S.A., 1983. 149-55.

———. "La tierra le presta al hombre y éste tarde o temprano, le paga lo que le debe." *El cuento cubano: Panorámica y Antología*. Ed. Pedro Izquierdo Tejido. San José, Costa Rica: Litografía e Imprenta LIL, S.A., 1983. 156-57.

———. C'est arrivé." *Cuba: Nouvelles et contes d'aujourd'hui*. Paris: L'Harmattan, 1985. 35-37.

———. "Deux Contes Populaires." *Cuba: Nouvelles et contes d'aujourd'hui*. Paris: L'Harmattan, 1985. 35-37.

———. "How the Monkey Lost the Fruits of His Labor." Trans. Mary Caldwell and Suzanne Jill Levine. *Other Fires: Short Fiction by Latin American Women*. Ed. Alberto Manguel. Toronto: Lester & Orpen Dennys, 1986. 200-205.

————. "La tesorera del diablo." *Puerta abierta: la nueva escritora latinoamericana*. Ed. Caridad L. Silva-Velázquez and Nora Erro-Orthmann. Mexico City: Joaquín Mortiz, 1986. 37-57.

————. "The Mire of Almendares." Trans. Evelyn Picón Garfield. *Women's Fiction from Latin America: Selections from Twelve Contemporary Authors*. Ed. Evelyn Picón Garfield. Detroit: Wayne State University Press, 1988. 19-22.

————. "Tatabisako." Trans. Evelyn Picón Garfield. *Women's Fiction from Latin America: Selections from Twelve Contemporary Authors*. Ed. Evelyn Picón Garfield. Detroit: Wayne State University Press, 1988. 23-27.

Essays

Cabrera, Lydia. "La Ceiba y la sociedad secreta Abakuá." *Orígenes* [La Habana] 7.25 (1950): 16-47.

————. *El monte*. La Habana: Colección de Chicherekú, Ediciones C.R., 1954. Rpt. in Miami: Editorial Universal, 1975.

————. "El sincretismo religioso de Cuba. Santos, Orisha, Ngangas, Lucumís, y Congos." *Orígenes* [La Habana] 36 (1954): 8-20.

————. *Refranes de negros viejos*. La Habana: Ediciones C.R., 1955; Miami: Colección del Chicherekú en el exilio, Ediciones C.R., 1970.

————. *Anagó, vocabulario lucumí* (El Yoruba que se habla en Cuba), Prologue Roger Bastide, La Habana: Colección del Chicherekú, Ediciones C.R., 1957. Rpt. in Miami: Colección del Chicherekú, Ediciones C.R., 1970.

————. *La sociedad secreta Abakuá, narrada por viejos adeptos*. La Habana: Colección del Chicherekú, Ediciones C.R., 1958; Miami: Colección de Chicherekú, Ediciones C.R., 1970.

————. "El Indísime Bebe la Mokuba que lo consagra Abakuá." *Lunes de Revolución* [La Habana] 2 30 Mar. 1959. 5-6.

————. "Iemanjá en Cuba." *Iemanjá e Suas Lendas*. Ed. Zora A. Seljan. Río de Janeiro: Gráfica Record, 1967. 49-58.

————. "Ritual y símbolos de la iniciación en la sociedad secreta Abakuá." *Journal de la Societé des Americanistes* Paris 58 (1969): 139-71.

————. *Otán Iyebiyé, las piedras preciosas*. Miami: Colección del Chicherekú en el exilio, Ediciones C.R., 1970. Rpt. in Miami: Ediciones Universal, 1970.

————. *La laguna sagrada de San Joaquín*. (Photographer Josefina Tarafa), Madrid: Ediciones Erre, 1973.

————. *Yemayá y Ochún*. Kariocha, Iyalorichas y Olorichas, notas de la contraportada by Pierre Verger, Madrid: Colección del Chicherekú en el exilio, Ediciones C.R., 1974. Rpt. in New York: Ediciones C.R., 1980.

————. "Notas sobre Africa, la negritud y la actual poesía Yoruba." *Revista de la Universidad Complutense* Madrid 24.95 (1975): 9-58.

————. *Anaforuana: ritual y símbolos de la iniciación en la sociedad secreta Abakuá*. Madrid: Ediciones C.R., 1975. Rpt. in Miami: Ediciones Universal, 1976.

————. *Itinerarios del insomnio: Trinidad de Cuba*. Miami: C.R., Peninsular Printing Inc., 1977.

————. *La Regla Kimbisa del Santo Cristo del Buen Viaje*. Miami: Peninsular Printing, Inc., 1977. Rpt. in 1986.

————. *Reglas de congo: Palo monte mayombé*. Miami: Peninsular Print, 1979.

————. "Damas." *Journal of Caribbean Studies* 1.1 (1980): 1-2.

————. *Koeko Iyawó, aprende novicia: pequeño tratado de regla lucumí*. (Pequeño tratado de Regla Lucumbí). Miami: Ultra Graphics, 1980.

————. "Más diablo que el diablo." *Vuelta* 5.60 (1981): 7-9.

————. *La medicina popular de Cuba*. Miami: Ultra Graphics, 1984.

————. *El monte*. Trans. Morton Marks. New York: n.p., 1984.

————. *El monte. Piante e Magia: Religioni, medicina, e folklore delle culture afrocubane*. Trans. Laura González. Milano: Rizzoli Editore, 1984.

————. *Vocabulario Congo: (el Bantú que se habla en Cuba)*. Miami: C.R., 1984.

————. *Supersticiones y buenos consejos*. Miami: Universal, 1987.

————. *Los animales en el folklore y la magia de Cuba*. Miami: Editorial Universal, 1988.

————. *La lengua sagrada de los Nañigos*. Miami: Ediciones C.R., 1988.

Criticism on the Works of Lydia Cabrera

Acosta Saignes, Miguel. "*El monte* de Lydia Cabrera." *Revista Bimestre Cubana* [La Habana] 71 (1956): 286-87.

Anhalt, Nedda G. de. "Lydia Cabrera, la Sikuanekua." *Vuelta* [Mexico] Apr. 1987: 35.

Arocha, José Antonio. "Vislumbración de Lydia Cabrera." *Alacrán azul* 1.1 (1970): 6-7.

Ben-Ur, Lorraine Elena. "Diálogo con Lydia Cabrera." *Caribe* 2.2 (1977): 131-37.

Carpentier, Alejo. "Los cuentos de Lydia Cabrera." *Carteles* [La Habana] 28.41 (1936): 40.

Castellanos, Isabel Mercedes. "The Use of Language in Afro-American Religions." Diss. Georgetown University, 1976.

Castellanos, Isabel, and Josefina Inclán, Eds. *En torno a Lydia Cabrera*. Miami: Ediciones Universal, 1987.

Fernández, Wilfredo. "Puntos de vista." *Réplica* 30 Mar. 1970, 16.

Figueroa, Esperanza. "Lydia Cabrera: *Cuentos negros de Cuba*." *Sur* [Argentina] 349 July-Dec. 1981: 89-97.

Foster, David William. *Cuban Literature: A Research Guide*. New York: Garland Publishing, Inc., 1985. 122-24.

————. *A Dictionary of Contemporary Latin American Authors*. Tempe: Center for Latin American Studies, Arizona State University, 1975. 19-20.

García Vega, Lorenzo. "Entrevistando a Lydia Cabrera." *Escandalar* 4.4 (1981): 80-86.

González, Manuel Pedro. "Cuentos y recuentos de Lydia Cabrera." *Nueva Revista Cubana* [La Habana] 1.2 (1959): 153-61.

Gordo-Guarinos, Francisco. "El negrismo de Lydia Cabrera visto con perspectiva de España." Congreso de literatura afro-americana: Homenaje a Lydia Cabrera. Florida International University. Nov., 1976. Rpt. in *Homenaje a Lydia Cabrera*. Eds. Reinaldo Sánchez and José Antonio Madrigal. Miami: Ediciones Universal, 1978. 25-30.

Granda, Germán de. "Un caso más de influencia canaria en Hispanoamérica (Brujería isleña en Cuba)." *Revista de dialectología y tradiciones populares* [Madrid] 29.1-2 (1973): 155-62.

Gutiérrez, Mariela. *Los cuentos negros de Lydia Cabrera: estudio morfológico esquemático.* Miami: Universal, 1986.

Guzmán, Cristina. "Diálogo con Lydia Cabrera." *Zona Franca* 24 (1981): 34-38. Rpt. in *Repertorio Latinoamericano* Jan.- Mar. 1985: 7-10.

Hiriart, Rosario. "Algunos apuntes sobre *Cuentos negros.*" *Vida Universitaria* [Mexico] 25.1298 (1976): 5-16.

———. *Cartas a Lydia Cabrera (correspondencia inédita de Gabriela Mistral y Teresa de la Parra).* Madrid: Ediciones Torremozas, 1988.

———. "El tiempo y los símbolos en los *Cuentos negros de Cuba.*" Congreso de literatura afroamericana: Homenaje a Lydia Cabrera. Florida International University. Nov., 1976. Rpt. in *Homenaje a Lydia Cabrera*. Eds. Reinaldo Sánchez and José Antonio Madrigal. Miami: Ediciones Universal, 1978. 31-43.

———. "En torno al mundo negro de Lydia Cabrera." *Cuadernos Hispanoamericanos* 359 (1980): 433-40. Rpt. in *Américas* 32.3 (1980): 40-42.

———. "La experiencia viva en la ficción: Lydia Cabrera e Hilda Perera." *Círculo: Revista de Cultura* 8 (1979): 125-31.

———. *Lydia Cabrera: Vida hecha arte.* New York: Eliseo Torres & Sons, 1978. Rpt. in Miami: Ediciones Universal, 1983.

———. "Lydia Cabrera and the World of Cuba's Blacks." *Américas* 32.3 (1980): 40-42.

———. *Más cerca de Teresa de la Parra: diálogos con Lydia Cabrera.* Caracas: Monte Avila, 1983.

Inclán, Josefina. *Ayapá y Otán Iyebiyé de Lydia Cabrera.* Miami: Ediciones Universal, 1976.

Irizarry, Estelle, "Los hechos y la cultura en los Estados Unidos." *Nivel* [Mexico] Dec. 1976: 10.

———. "Lydia Cabrera, fabuladora surrealista." *The Contemporary Latin American Short Story.* Ed. Rose S. Minc. New York: Senda Nueva, 1979. 105-11.

———. "Review of *Lydia Cabrera: vida hecha arte* de Rosario Hiriart." *Nivel* 195 31 Mar. 1979: 10.

Jiménez, Julio. "Review of *Lo ancestral africano en la narrativa de Lydia Cabrera* de Rosa Valdés-Cruz." *Hispania* 59.1 (1976): 181.

Jiménez, Onilda A. "Dos cartas inéditas de Gabriela Mistral a Lydia Cabrera." *Revista Iberoamericana* 53.141 (1987): 1001-11. Rpt. in *Hispamérica* 12.34-35 (1983): 97-103.

Josephs, Allen. "Lydia and Federico: Towards a Historical Approach to Lorca Studies." *Journal of Spanish Studies: Twentieth Century* 6 (1978): 123-30.

Lama, Sonia de. "Review of *Homenaje a Lydia Cabrera*." *Hispania* 63.1 (1980): 159.

León, Argeliers. "*El monte*, de Lydia Cabrera." *Nuestro tiempo* 2.7 (1955): 15-16.

León, René. *Bibliografía sobre Lydia Cabrera*. N.p.: n.p., 1977.

Levine, Suzanne Jill, "A Conversation with Lydia Cabrera." *Review: Latin American Literature and Arts* [New York] 31 (1982): 13-15.

Lezama Lima, José. "El nombre de Lydia Cabrera." *Tratados en La Habana*. Ed. José Lezama Lima. La Habana: Universidad Central de las Villas, Departamento de Relaciones Culturales, 1958. 144-48. Rpt. in Buenos Aires: Ediciones de la Flor, 1969. 144-48.

Madrigal, José Antonio. "El mito paradisíaco y la poesía afrocubana contemporánea." *Homenaje a Lydia Cabrera*. Eds. Reinaldo Sánchez and José Antonio Madrigal. Miami: Ediciones Universal, 1978. 35-39.

Menton, Seymour. *Prose Fiction of the Cuban Revolution*. Austin: University of Texas Press, 1975. 243-44.

Miomandre, Francis de. Introduction. *Contes negres de Cuba de Lydia Cabrera*. Paris: Gallimard, 1936. 9-15.

———. "Sobre *El monte*, de Lydia Cabrera." *Orígenes* 39 (1955): 75-78.

Mistral, Gabriela. *Siete cartas de Gabriela Mistral a Lydia Cabrera*. Miami: Peninsular Printing, 1980.

Montes Huidobro, Matías. "Itinerario del ebo." *Círculo* 8 (1979): 105-14. Rpt. in *Studies in Afro-Hispanic Literature* 2-3 (1978-1979): 1-13.

———. "Lydia Cabrera: observaciones estructurales sobre su narrativa." Congreso de literatura afroamericana: Homenaje a Lydia Cabrera. Florida International University. Nov. 1976. Rpt. in *Homenaje a Lydia Cabrera*. Eds. Reinaldo Sánchez and José Antonio Madrigal. Miami: Ediciones Universal, 1978. 41-50.

Noulet, Edmond. "Lydia Cabrera." *La Nouvelle Revue Francaise* May 1936: 798.

Novás Calvo, Lino. "Los cuentos de Lydia Cabrera." *Exilio* [New York] 3.2 (1969): 17-20.

———. "*El monte*." *Papeles de Son Armadans* [Palma de Mallorca] 150 Sept. 1968: 298-304.

Ortiz, Fernando. "Dos nuevos libros del folklore afrocubano." *Revista Bimestre Cubana* 42 (1938): 307-19.

———. "Lydia Cabrera (una cubana afroamericanista)." *Crónica* [La Habana] 1.3 (1949): 7-8.

———. Prologue. *Cuentos negros de Cuba*. La Habana: Nuevo Mundo, 1961. 9-12.

Ortiz Aponte, Sally. "*La virtud del árbol Dagame*, de Lydia Cabrera." *La esoteria en la narrativa hispanoamericana*. Ed. Sally Ortiz Aponte. Puerto Rico: Editorial Universitaria, Universidad de Puerto Rico, 1977. 231-38.

Perera, Hilda. "La Habana intacta de Lydia Cabrera." *Circulo: Revista de Cultura* 13 (1984): 33-38.

————. *Idapo: el sincretismo en los cuentos negros de Lydia Cabrera*. Miami: Ediciones Universal, 1971.

————. "Recordando a Teresa de la Parra con Lydia Cabrera." *Romances* IV (1967): 64-98.

Perera Soto, Hilda. "El aché de Lydia Cabrera." Congreso de literatura afroamericana: Homenaje a Lydia Cabrera. Florida International University. Nov., 1976. Rpt. in *Homenaje a Lydia Cabrera*. Eds. Reinaldo Sánchez and José Antonio Madrigal. Miami: Ediciones Universal, 1978. 51-59.

Pita, Juana Rosa. *"Cuentos para adultos, niños y retrasados mentales* de Lydia Cabrera." *Vuelta* 8.86 (1984): 35-36.

R. B. "Los negros en Cuba." *Indice de artes y letras* 127 (1959): 24.

Rodríguez-Florido, Jorge. "La función del doble en los *Cuentos negros* y en *Porqué* . . ." Congreso de literatura afroamericana: Homenaje a Lydia Cabrera. Florida International University, 1976. Rpt. in *Homenaje a Lydia Cabrera*. Eds. Reinaldo Sánchez and José Antonio Madrigal. Miami: Ediciones Universal, 1978. 61-71.

Rodríguez Tomeu, Julia. *"Cuentos negros de Cuba." Cuadernos Americanos* [Mexico] 7.2 (1949): 279-81.

Ruiz del Vizo, Hortensia. "La función del monte en la obra de Lydia Cabrera." Congreso de literatura afroamericana: Homenaje a Lydia Cabrera. Florida International University. Nov., 1978. Rpt. in *Homenaje a Lydia Cabrera*. Eds. Reinaldo Sánchez and José Antonio Madrigal. Miami: Ediciones Universal, 1978. 73-82.

Sánchez, Reinaldo et al. *Homenaje a Lydia Cabrera*. Miami: Ediciones Universal, 1978.

Sánchez-Boudy, José. "La armonía universal en la obra de Lydia Cabrera." Congreso de literatura afroamericana: Homenaje a Lydia Cabrera. Florida International University. Nov., 1978. Rpt. in *Homenaje a Lydia Cabrera*. Eds. Reinaldo Sánchez and José Antonio Madrigal. Miami: Ediciones Universal, 1978. 83-92.

————. "Review of *Lo ancestral africano en la narrativa de Lydia Cabrera* by Rosa Valdés-Cruz." *Explicación de textos literarios* 5.1 (1976): 112.

Soto, Sara. "Magia e historia en los *Cuentos negros, Por qué* y *Ayapá* de Lydia Cabrera." *DAI* 46.12 (1986): 3732A-33A.

————. *Magia e historia en los "Cuentos negros", "Por qué", y "Ayapá" de Lydia Cabrera*. Miami: Universal, 1988.

Tarleton Kirbey, Marjorie. *A Literary History of the Cuban Short Story (1797-1959)*. Diss. University of North Carolina at Chapel Hill, 1971. University Microfilms, A XEROX Co., Ann Arbor, MI. 72-10, 738. 296-309.

Torre, Guillermo de. "Literatura de color." *El sol* [Madrid] 12 July 1936: 5-11. Rpt. in *Revista Bimestre Cubana* 38 (1936): 5-11.

Valdés-Cruz, Rosa. "African heritage in folktales." *Actes du VIIe. Congres de l'Association Internationale de Littérature Comparée* [Bieber, Stuttgart] (1979): 327-30.

————. *Lo ancestral africano en la narrativa de Lydia Cabrera* Barcelona: Editorial Vosgos, 1974.

————. "Los cuentos de Lydia Cabrera: ¿transposiciones o creaciones?" Congreso de literatura afroamericana: Homenaje a Lydia Cabrera. Florida International University. Nov. 1978. Rpt. in *Homenaje a Lydia Cabrera*. Eds. Reinaldo Sánchez and José Antonio Madrigal. Miami: Ediciones Universal, 1978. 93-99.

———. "Mitos africanos conservados en Cuba y su tratamiento literario por Lydia Cabrera." *Chasqui* 3.1 (1973): 31-36.

———. "El realismo mágico en los cuentos negros de Lydia Cabrera." *Otros mundos otros fuegos: fantasía y realismo mágico en Iberoamérica*. Ed. Donald A. Yates. Memoria del 16 Congreso Internacional de Literatura Iberoamericana. East Lansing: Michigan State University Latin American Studies Center, 1975. 206-09.

———. "The Short Stories of Lydia Cabrera: Transpositions or Creations?" Eds. Charles Tatum and Yvette Miller. *Latin American Women Writers: Yesterday and Today*. Pittsburgh: Latin American Literary Review, 1977. 148-54.

Verger, Pierre. *Cuba: 196 photos de Pierre Verger*. [Preface and notes by Lydia Cabrera]. Paris: P. Hartmann, 1958.

Viera, Ricardo. "Arte visual en la palabra de Lydia Cabrera." Congreso de literatura afroamericana: Homenaje a Lydia Cabrera. Florida International University. Nov., 1978. Rpt. in *Homenaje a Lydia Cabrera*. Eds. Reinaldo Sánchez and José Antonio Madrigal. Miami: Ediciones Universal, 1978. 101-08.

Willis, Miriam DeCosta. "Folklore and the Creative Artist: Lydia Cabrera and Zora Neale Hurston." *College Language Association Journal*. 27.1 (1983): 81-90.

Zambrano, María. "Lydia Cabrera, poeta de la metamorfosis." *Orígenes* [La Habana] 7.25 (1950): 11-13.

AÍDA CARTAGENA PORTALATÍN
Dominican Republic

Aída Cartagena Portalatín was born in Moca, Dominican Republic, in 1918. She graduated from the Faculty of Humanities at the Autonomous University of Santo Domingo and did post-graduate studies in music and theory of fine arts in Paris. She teaches history of art, colonial art, and history of civilization at her alma mater, and serves as director of the Museum of Anthropology in the Dominican Republic.

Cartagena Portalatín has edited numerous literary journals and collections. Among the most important are *Revista de la Facultad de Humanidades* (Journal of the Faculty of Humanities) and *Cuaderno Brigadas Dominicanas* (Dominican Brigades Notebooks), which published much of the clandestine literature produced during the dictatorship of Rafael Trujillo. She has also published original research in anthropology. A well-known critic, she traveled extensively in Central America representing her country. In 1977 she was invited to be a juror in the Casa de las Americas Prize in Cuba and in 1980 she represented the Dominican Republic in the Congress of Women Writers in Puerto Rico.

She has written one novel, short stories, poetry and literary essays. Her novel *Escalera para Electra* (A Ladder for Electra, 1970) was a finalist in the prestigious literary contest Biblioteca Breve of Seix Barral in 1969. Her writing is characterized by innovative use of language, cinematographic techniques and symbolism.

A PASSION FOR
DONNA SUMMER

Mommy used to call me "Colita," Colita García. But Mrs. Sarah registered me in public school as "Dawn."

"There will be no such thing as 'Colita,'" she screamed. I felt like 'Colita' to me even if I was 'Dawn' to her. I'll never forgive Mrs. Sarah for giving me Dawn as a nickname so that she can discriminate against me whenever she calls me laughingly and teasingly. No. Noo. And Noo! I am not going to stay here with her, in her house, even though it is true that she pays for my studies, that she tells everyone that I am very talented. I'm fed up with her and the nuns at the school, Sister Tantina, long and skinny like Twiggy from T.V., and Mother Superior, wise but with the looks of Aldonza, Sancho Panza's wife. They carry on about those theorems, and about the triangle and rectangle and what are parallel lines, and screw Colita-Dawn with punishments and telephone calls so that Mrs. Sarah attacks me like a machine gun. No. Noo. And Nooo, NO!

I said no. I don't like Mrs. Sarah nor do I care about her beautiful house, nor am I going to get old inside her four walls like a tree destined for charcoal. No, I am not going to stay with her like a tree burning under a dog day sun. No, I'm not going to remain sad, head bowed, like the leaves beaten by the thunder-rain storms, within these walls surrounded by an evergreen lawn and some fruit trees. Nor do I accept that Dawn is "an intelligent little black girl," nor that blacks amuse people, nor that blacks with their jazz and rhythm make the world happy. I don't like it either when she tells me to go to the store and bring her Donna Summer's latest record. I hate when she says blacks ought to be good for something, that it's good they amuse whites. No, Noo. And noo. I like the unending music of Donna Summer, scratching, howling without stopping, falling like a vibrant exciting cascade. But it's for sure that Mrs. Sarah is not going to keep me forever inside her exciting music box. What about the jazz, what about the boogaloo, what about the ragtime or the beguine? That stuff is not for the old bag. She thinks I could never leave. I'd love for her to see how fast I'm walking to the bus stop, dragging this heavy bundle with my clothes and books. Here, driver, I'm getting off in Haina.

I walk around a bit, smelling the air of the sugar refineries. I sit in Candita's restaurant where I have a very cold 7-Up. Hungry, that's what I am, and I move to The Dwarf's where I drink a Pepsi and eat two rolls. I leave quickly. Donna Summer's music fills the shack and extends itself through the whole neighborhood. How I remember now that little unending cascade meows of years ago. Donna's music and singing extend beyond the shack, the neighborhood; it is the same tune that excites and shakes Mrs. Sarah.

The hell with everything, here I am again exactly fourteen kilometers from the capital and away from Mrs. Sarah's house. It is seven o'clock at night. I enter the church and hide behind Saint Isidro's altar, the saint who takes away the rain and brings the sunshine. Let the saint hide me, that I shouldn't be found. Saint, Saint, Saint, the streets are full of job-seekers and beggars. La la la la laaa, ya ya ya ya yaaa.

Next to a wall of The Dwarf Bar a girl is rocking. Donna's voice gets louder as a lottery vendor turns up the volume on his radio. Donna's voice again fills the bar, the neighborhood, the town. I try to gather up my kinky hair. If I was born with it this way, this is how I will keep it. What is really absurd is that they discriminate against me and show off my intelligence because I am almost a high school graduate. No. Noo. And noo. No! It infuriates me to see how so many millions of whites are enjoying Donna Summer, the little black girl who sings excitingly. They got into a frenzied pitch over the music of Armstrong, later that of Makeba. They chose to ignore our history. What about jazz and all that rhythm that's born so happily? Congratulations! No, if I were Donna Summer I would recall all the records from the stores' shelves, dance floors, cabarets, hotels, motels and the high class houses.

I am persuaded to start out as a housekeeper by the sugar technician's wife from Ohio who advised me to come to New York. Here, in their apartment, on the eleventh floor, I cook, wash, iron, and shop for them. I put up with the nonsense of the grocery keeper, that Italian son of a bitch, who pulls my hair and calls me "ugly black girl," asking where I'm from and this and that. I put up with my gringo Mrs. who asks me: "Colita, why do you take so long?" Sometimes I explain to her that the son of a bitch detained me, or that I stopped and saw Giordano knife Manfredi (because both wanted a dead neighbor who both think should be taken to his respective funeral parlor, and the police very calmly declare: Giordano is dead).

I am going to have to organize myself mentally like in a sequence of classified ads:

1. I have been told that this was the Free World and yet here I find out that the gringo Mrs. exploits me like a slave.

2. I don't understand how come the Free World agrees with Exploitation.

3. "Colita, how ignorant you are!"

4. I didn't know anything about monopolies but now I find out that they control everything I buy.

Policemen, policemen, policemen everywhere! One of them grabs my breast and I scream "fresh." I am tired of seeing drunks, drug addicts, cops and CIA agents all over the world. I am tired of seeing unemployed classless guys allowing tough cops to beat them up like in the westerns. This is not being manly, Dominican-style. Is this the Free World, overexploited, overdone? I'm going to go crazy. And no. Noo. And no!

I'm back at Mrs. Sarah's house, with her continuous music, the Donna Summer music, with the same calamities, screaming at me all the time. And she screams and howls in anger when I read in the newspaper about the injustices that are committed against the blacks in South Africa. When I read about the lynchings of Soweto and Johannesburg, Steve Biko imprisoned in Pretoria. Mrs. Sarah grabs me by the hair and she screams "nonsense." Then she drags me by the hair to the record player where she raises the volume as far as it will go. I can't even hear myself cry now. Donna Summer, my dear little black girl, fill Mrs. Sarah's house with your voice and excite it with your rhythm.

Translated by Nora Erro-Peralta and Caridad Silva-Núñez.

Bibliography: Aída Cartagena Portalatín

Fiction

Cartagena Portalatín, Aída. *Víspera del sueño*. N.p., n.p., 1944.

———. *Del sueño al mundo*. N.p., n.p., 1944.

———. *Una mujer está sola*. N.p., n.p., 1955.

———. *Mi mundo, el mar*. N.p., n.p., 1955.

———. *La voz desatada*. N.p., n.p., 1961.

———. *La máscara*. N.p., n.p., 1968.

———. *Escalera para Electra*. Santo Domingo: Universidad Autónoma de Santo Domingo, 1970. Rpt. in Santo Domingo: Taller, 1975.

———. *Tablero*. Santo Domingo, República Dominicana: Editorial Taller, 1978.

———. *La tarde en que murió Estefanía*. Santo Domingo, Dominican Republic: Taller, 1983.

———. "La autopsia." *La cuentista dominicana*. Ed. Jenny Montero. Santo Domingo, República Dominicana: Biblioteca Nacional, 1986. 174-77.

———. "Colita." *Anthology of Contemporary Latin American Literature 1960-1984*. Ed. Barry J. Luby and Wayne H. Finke. London-Toronto: Associated University Press, 1986. 91-93.

————. "La llamaban Aurora." (Pasión por Donna Summer). *Puerta abierta: la nueva escritora latinoamericana.* Ed. Caridad L. Silva-Velázquez and Nora Erro-Orthmann. Mexico City: Joaquín Mortiz, 1986. 75-77.

Essays

Cartagena Portalatín, Aída. "El cuento dominicano." *Narradores dominicanos: antología.* Ed. Aída Cartagena Portalatín. Caracas: Monte Avila Editores, 1969. 7-12.

————. *Culturas africanas: rebeldes con causa.* Santo Domingo, Dominican Republic: Taller, 1986.

Criticism On the Works of Aída Cartagena Portalatín

Figueroa, Ramón. "Nacionalismo y el universalismo en *Escalera para Electra*." *Areito* 10.38 (1984): 41-43.

Guzmán, Catherine. "Onomatology in Aída Cartagena Portalatín's Fiction." *Literary Onomastics Studies* 10 (1983): 75-86.

Montero, Jenny. *La cuentista dominicana.* Santo Domingo, República Dominicana: Biblioteca Nacional, 1986. 79-82.

LYGIA FAGUNDES TELLES
Brazil

Lygia Fagundes Telles was born in São Paulo, Brazil, in 1923 and spent her childhood in small towns, where her father was posted as district attorney, police commissioner, and judge. Although she has led a fruitful legal and public service career, she has devoted most of her life to cultural and literary activities. Fagundes Telles has served as vice-president of the Brazilian Writers' Union and as president of the Brazilian Cinematique. She was recently elected to the Brazilian Academy of Letters.

She has written three novels and twelve collections of short stories. Since the publication of her first volume of short stories, *Praia viva* (Living Beach, 1944), and through all her long, steady production over the years, Fagundes Telles has collected numerous honors and prizes at home and abroad. Her literary career has been marked by a rare set of circumstances for a woman writer: the official recognition of intellectual and literary critics and the sustained interest in her works of the general public, which makes her one of the most popular serious writers of Brazil today.

Lygia Fagundes Telles' short stories exhibit tightly-knit structures and a commitment to realism and aesthetic values, in combination with an indirect style and a frequent use of myth, evocation, and ambiguity. While her short stories often deal with the complex corners of the human mind and with experiences that go beyond rational order, her novels portray women characters caught in conflict between the pursuit of self-fulfillment and the reality of established social codes.

THE HUNT

The antique shop with its mildewed clothes and moth-eaten books smelled like a coffer in a sacristy. With his fingertips the man touched a pile of paintings. A moth took off and collided with a statue with chopped-off hands.

"A beautiful statue," the man said.

The old woman removed a hairpin from her bun and cleaned her thumbnail. She replaced the pin in her hair.

"It's a Saint Francis."

Then the man turned slowly to face the tapestry that covered most of the wall at the back of the shop. He drew closer. The old woman also drew closer.

"I see that you're really interested in it. A pity it's in such a condition."

The man's hand reached for the tapestry, but he didn't touch it.

"It looks much sharper today."

"Sharper?" replied the old woman, putting on her glasses. Her hand slid along its threadbare surface. "What do you mean—sharper?"

"The colors look brighter. Have you treated the tapestry with something?"

The old woman stared at him. Then, evasively, she turned her gaze on St. Francis with the chopped-off hands. The man looked as pale and bewildered as the statue.

"No, of course not. Why do you ask?"

"I notice some difference."

"No, I didn't treat it with anything. This tapestry wouldn't bear even the slightest brushing, can't you see? I think the dust is what's holding the fabric together," she added, once more removing the hairpin from her head. She turned it in her fingers, her expression thoughtful. She pouted. "A stranger brought it here. He needed the money very badly. I told him that the fabric was much too damaged, that it wouldn't be easy to find a buyer, but he kept persisting. I hung it on the wall, and there it has remained. But it's been many years. And that young man has never shown up again."

"Extraordinary . . ."

The old woman couldn't tell whether the man was referring to the tapestry or to the incident she had just told him. She shrugged. She started cleaning her fingernails with the hairpin.

"I could sell it to you, but quite frankly, I don't think it's worth anything. The moment we remove it, it will probably fall apart."

The man lit a cigarette. His hands shook. When, oh God, when had he witnessed this same scene? And where?

The tapestry depicted a hunt. In the foreground was a hunter with a taut bow aimed at a large clump of bushes. In the background, a second hunter peered into the trees of the thicket, but he was merely a blurred silhouette whose face was reduced to a faded contour. The first hunter looked powerful and independent, his beard turbulent like entangled serpents, his muscles tense, waiting for his prey to emerge before shooting the arrow.

The man was breathing with difficulty. His gaze roamed over the tapestry, which was the greenish color of a stormy sky. Defiling the moss-green of the fabric were some purplish-black blots, which seemed to ooze out of the foliage, slide down the hunter's boots, and spread over the ground like some malignant liquid. The clump of bushes where the animal was hidden also displayed the same blots, which could have been either part of the design itself, or else the mere effect of time eating up the fabric.

"Today everything seems closer together," the man said in a lower voice. "It's as if . . . Don't you think it looks different?"

The old woman narrowed her eyes. She took off her glasses and put them on again.

"I can't see any difference."

"Yesterday it was impossible to tell whether or not he had shot the arrow."

"What arrow? Can you see any arrow?"

"That tiny dot on the bow."

The old woman sighed.

"But isn't that a moth-eaten hole? See how the wall already shows through; these moths just put an end to everything," she complained, stifling a yawn. Noiselessly she moved away in her woolen slippers. She gestured vaguely, "Make yourself at home; I'm having my tea."

The man dropped his cigarette. He slowly stubbed it out with the sole of his shoe. His jaws tightened painfully. He knew that thicket, that hunter, that sky—how well he knew them all, ah, how well! He could almost smell the scent of the eucalyptus trees, could almost feel the damp cold of the dawn nipping his skin; ah, that dawn such a long, long time ago. Oh God, when had he traversed that same path, when had he breathed in that same mist that descended densely from the green sky? Or did it rise from the ground? The hunter with the curly beard seemed to smile, perversely cunning. Could he have been that same hunter? Or had he been the companion over there, that faceless man peering into the trees? A tapestry character. But which one? He stared at the clump of bushes where the game hid. Nothing but leaves, silence and leaves plastered down in the shadows. But behind the leaves, behind the blots, he thought he could see the arched shape of the animal. He felt compassion for that panicky being waiting for an opportunity to proceed in its flight. Death so close! The slightest movement and the ruthless arrow . . . The old woman hadn't seen it. Nobody would be able to see the arrow reduced to a tiny worm-eaten dot, paler than a speck of dust suspended over the bow.

Wiping the sweat off his chin with the back of his hand, the man stepped backward. A certain peacefulness invaded him now that he knew he had participated in that hunt. But his was a lifeless peacefulness, one impregnated with those treacherous blots in the foliage. He closed his eyes. Could he have been the painter of the picture? Most of the ancient tapestries were reproductions of paintings, weren't they? He had painted the original picture and therefore could reproduce with his eyes closed the entire scene in its finest details: the configuration of the trees, the dark sky, the hunter with his unkempt beard, all muscles and sinews, aiming at the clump.

"But I hate hunting! Why do I have to be in there?"

He pressed the handkerchief to his mouth. The nausea. Ah, if only he could explain all this frightening familiarity, if he could at least . . . Could he have been a mere casual spectator, one of those people that watch and then move on? A likely hypothesis. Or else he might have seen the original painting; the hunt was nothing but a figment of his mind. "Before making use of the tapestry . . ." he murmured, drying the spaces between his fingers with the handkerchief.

His head jerked backward as if someone were pulling him by his hair; no, he hadn't stayed outside. He had been in there, nailed to the scenario. And why did everything look sharper than yesterday, why were the colors stronger despite the dusk? Why was the fascination, now coming out from the landscape, becoming so vigorous and rejuvenated?

He left with his head bowed, his hands clenched into a fist inside his pockets. Almost panting, he stopped at the street corner. His body ached, his eyelids felt heavy. And if he tried to sleep? But he knew that he wouldn't be able to sleep, and he already felt sleeplessness following him in step with his shadow. He turned up the collar of his jacket. Was this cold real? Or was it the remembrance of the cold in the tapestry?

"How crazy! But I'm not crazy," and he smiled helplessly. That would have been the easy way out. "But I'm not crazy."

He wandered through the streets, went to a movie and soon left, then realized that he was standing before the secondhand shop, his nose flattened against the show window in his attempt to catch a glimpse of the tapestry way back in the room.

When he got home he threw himself on the bed and there he remained, his eyes wide open, staring at the darkness. The old woman's tremulous voice seemed to come from the pillow, a disembodied voice wearing woolen slippers: "What arrow? I can't see any arrow." Intermingled with her voice, the murmuring of the moths, amidst giggles, was rising in a *crescendo*. The cotton in the pillow muffled the peals of laughter, interwoven into a greenish, tightly-knit net, which became enmeshed in a fabric that had blots trickling down to the ornamental borders. He became entangled in the filaments and wanted to escape, but the ornamental border arrested him in its arms. Down, deep down in the pit he could see the serpents entangled into one greenish-black ball. He touched his chin. "Am I the hunter?" But instead of a beard he felt a gory clamminess.

He woke up with his own scream reverberating in the dawn. He dried his sweat-drenched face. Ah, that heat and that cold! He wrapped the sheets around him. And if he had been the craftsman who wove the tapestry? Again he could see it, so sharp and so near that if he reached out his hand he would awaken the foliage. He clenched his fists. He would destroy it. It wasn't true that there was anything else in that abhorrent rag; it was nothing but a rectangle of cloth held together by dust. It would be enough to blow upon it, to blow upon it!

He met the old woman at the door of her shop. She smiled ironically.

"You made an early start today!"

"You might think it strange, but . . ."

"I don't think anything strange anymore. Come in, come in, you know the way."

"I know the way," he murmured, following her between the furniture. He stopped, nostrils flared. That smell of foliage and earth—where did that smell come from? And why was the shop becoming blurred and distant? Growing larger, only the tapestry was real, creeping down to the floor, up to the ceiling, its greenish blots swallowing up everything. He wanted to turn back, he clutched at a cupboard, he staggered, still resisting, and extended his arms toward the pillar. His fingers disappeared amidst the branches and slid down the trunk of a tree; it wasn't a pillar, it was a tree! He stared wildly about him: he had entered the tapestry, he was in the thicket, his feet heavy with mud, his hair soaked with dew. Around him everything was motionless, spellbound. In the silence of the dawn, not even the chirp of a bird or the rustle of a leaf. He bent over, gasping. Was he the hunter? Or the hunted? It didn't matter, it didn't matter. He only knew that he had to go on running without stopping through the maze of trees, hunting or being hunted. Or being hunted? He pressed the palms of his hands to his flushed face, and in the cuffs of his shirt he dried the sweat that was trickling down his neck. His cracked lips were bleeding.

He opened his mouth. He remembered. "No!" he cried out, plunging into a clump of bushes. He heard the arrow hiss as it penetrated the foliage.

"No," he moaned, falling to his knees, still trying to hold on to the tapestry. He rolled down, huddled up and livid, his hands firmly clutching at his heart.

Translated by Eloah F. Giacomelli

Bibliography: Lygia Fagundes Telles

Fiction

Fagundes Telles, Lygia. *Praia Viva*. São Paulo: n.p., 1944.

———. *O Cacto Vermelho*. Río de Janeiro: Editora Mérito, 1949.

———. *Gaby. Os Sete Pecados Capitais*. Río de Janeiro: n.p., 1954.

———. *Ciranda de Pedra*. Lisboa: Editorial Minerva, 1954. Rpt. in Río de Janeiro: José Olympio, 1983.

———. *Histórias do Desencontro*. Río de Janeiro: José Olympio, 1958.

———. *Os Mortos*. Lisboa: Casa Portuguesa, 1963.

———. *Verão no Aquário*. São Paulo: Martins, 1963. Rpt. in Río de Janeiro: José Olympio, 1980.

———. *Histórias Escolhidas*. São Paulo: Boa Leitura, 1964.

———. *O Jardim Selvagem*. São Paulo: Martins, 1965. Rpt. in Río de Janeiro: José Olympio: Civilizacao Brasileira Editora Tres, 1974.

———. "Trilogia da Confissão." *Os Dezoito Melhores Contos do Brasil*. Río de Janeiro: n.p., 1968.

———. *Antes do Bailes Verde*. Río de Janeiro: Edicoes Bloch, 1970. Rpt. in Río de Janeiro: Livraria J. Olympio Editora, 1982.

———. *Selecta de Lygia Fagundes Telles*. Ed. Nelly Novaes Coelho. Río de Janeiro: José Olympio, 1971. Rpt. in Río de Janeiro: José Olympio, 1978.

———. *As Meninas*. Río de Janeiro: José Olympio, 1973. Rpt. in Río de Janeiro: José Olympio, 1981.

———. "Before the Green Ball." *Short Stories of the Americas*. Ed. Lygia Johnson. San Francisco: Compile-a-Text, 1974. Rpt. in *Women of Latin America: A Collection of Twentieth Century Short Stories*. Ed. Lygia Johnson. *Latin American Literary Review* IV.7 Fall-Winter 1975: 121-25.

———. "The Window." Trans. Eloah F. Giacomelli. *Branching Out* Feb-March (1976): 26-27, 47.

———. *Seminário dos Ratos*. Río de Janeiro: Livraria J. Olympio Editora, 1977.

———. "Tigrela." Trans. Eloah F. Giacomelli. *Seminario dos Ratos*. 1977. Rpt. in *Mundus Artium* XI.1 (1979): 72-27. Rpt. in *Other Fires: Short Fiction by Latin American Women*. Ed. Alberto Manguel. Toronto: Lester & Orpen Dennis, 1986. 179-87.

———. *Filhos Pródigos*. São Paulo: Livraria Cultura Editora, 1978.

———. "Depoimento." *Prismal/Cabral* 3-4 (1979): 135-139. Rpt. in *Journal de Letras* Lisbon 2.30 (1982): 7.

———. *Lygia Fagundes Telles: Seleção de Textos, Notas, Estudos Biográfico, Histórico e Crítico e Exercícios*. Montfeiro, Leonardo, São Paulo: Abril Educacao, 1980.

———. *A Disciplina do Amor; Fragmentos*. Río de Janeiro: Editora Nova Fronteira, 1980. Rpt. in Río de Janeiro: Editora Nova Fronteira, 1981.

———. *Mistério ficcoes*. Río de Janeiro: Editora Nova Fronteira, 1981. Rpt. in Río de Janeiro: Editora Nova Fronteira, 1981.

————. "New Fiction, Lygia Fagundes Telles." Trans. Jon M. Tolman and Margaret Abigail Neves. *Review: Latin American Literature and Arts* 30 (1981): 65-70.

————. *The Girl in the Photograph*. Trans. Margaret Neves. New York: Avon Books, 1982.

————. "La cacería." *Revista de la Universidad Mexicana*. Trans. Lilia Osorio. *Nueva Epoca* 39.25 (1983): 14-15.

————. "The Objects." Trans. Eloah Giacomelli. *Mundus Artium* XIV. 1 (1983): 38-43.

————. *Dez Contos Escolhidos*. São Paulo: n.p., 1984.

————. *Os Melhores Contos de Lygia Fagundes Telles*. Ed. Eduardo Portella. São Paulo: Global Editora, 1984.

————. "La estructura de la pompa de jabón." Trans. Manuel Rodríguez Ramos. *Casa de las Américas* 27.159 (1986): 46-49.

————. *The Marble Dance*. Trans. Margaret A. Neves. New York: Avon Books, 1986.

————. *Tigrela and Other Stories*. Trans. Margaret A. Neves. New York: Avon Books, 1986.

————. "The Wild Garden." Trans. Eloah F. Giacomelli. *Review* 36 (1986): 34-37.

————. "The Truth of Invention." *Lives on the Line: The Testimony of Contemporary Latin American Authors*. Ed. Doris Meyer. Berkeley: University of California Press, 1988. 265-71.

Essays

Telles, Lygia Fagundes. "Depoiment." *Jornal de Letras* 2.30 (1982): 7.

Criticism on the Works of Lygia Fagundes Telles

Angelini, Paulo Roberto Escudero. "A Intertextualidade em Dois Contos Femeninos." *Cuadernos de Lingüistica e Teoria da Literatura* 8 (1982): 107-15.

Araujo, Vagner Correia de. "Antes do baile verde." *Minas Gerais* [Literary Supplement.] 230 (1971): 7.

"As meninas, o novo romance de Lygia Fagundes Telles." *O Estado de São Paulo* [Literary Supplement] 9 (1973): 1.

Ataide, Vincente de Paula. "Criaçao e técnica." *Minas Gerais* [Literary Supplement] 312 (1972): 3.

————. *A narrativa de Lygia Fagundes Telles*. Curitiva: Escola Estrutural, 1969.

————. "Noticias sobre Lygia Fagundes Telles." *Minas Gerais* [Literary Supplement] 243 (1971): 11.

Barbosa, Rolmes. "O drama da solidao humana." *Estado São Paulo* [Literary Supplement] 771 (1972): 2.

Bella, Josef. "El arte de Lygia Fagundes Telles." *Nueva Narrativa Hispanoamericana* 5.1-11 (1975): 185-88. Rpt. in *Minas Gerais* [Literary Supplement] 2 (1974): 12.

Bins, Patricia. "Lygia Fagundes Telles Ontem, Hoje e Sempre: A Imortal." *Minas Gerais* [Literary Supplement] 20.1002 (1985): 4.

Burgin, Richard. *"Tigrela and Other Stories."* *New York Times Book Review* 4 May 1986: 40.

Carvalho, Alfredo Leme Coelho de. "A Densidade Simbolica e Sugestiva em Dois Contos de Lygia Fagundes Telles." *Mimesis: Revista de Letras* 3 (1977): 81-88.

Coelho, Neli Novais. "Antes do baile verde." *Estado São Paulo* [Literary Supplement] 688 19 Sept. 1970: 1. Rpt. in *Minas Gerais* [Literary Supplement] 688 21 Nov. 1970: 1.

————. "Lygia Fagundes Telles." *Estado São Paulo* 15 Jan. 1966: 1.

————. "A linguagem criativa de Lygia Fagundes Telles." *J Letras* 22 (1970): 44.

Coelho, Nelly Novaes. "Lygia Fagundes Telles: Romancista." *Coloquio/Letras* 27 (1964): 44-47.

Coronado, Guilhermo de la Cruz. "O ódio caímico em Lygia e Unamuno." *C. Povo, 4* 191, 192 (1971): 10.

Coutinho, Edilberto. "Lygia Fagundes Telles: O aspero casco de uma arvore." *Correio da Manha* 2 June 1970: 3.

Dantas, Raimundo Sousa. "Lygia, no conto o itinerário de uma ficcionista." *J. Brasil* 30 Jan. 1971: 9.

————. "Originalidade de ficcionista." *Leitura* 17 (1950): 20.

Duarte, José Afranio Moreira. "Antes do baile verde e Fundador (os contos de Lygia e a ficcao de Nélida)." *J. Letras* 22 (1970): 41.

Faria, Otávio de. "A ficcionista Lygia Fagundes Telles." *Estado São Paulo* 30 Apr. 1966: 6.

Ferreira, Edda. "As Meninas e a Maestria Tecnica de Lygia Fagundes Telles." *Minas Gerais* [Literary Supplement] 13 (1976): 8-9.

Fischer, Almeida. "Contistas muitos e bons." *C. Povo* 142 15 Aug. 1970: 11.

Gomes, Duílio. "Antes do baile verde." *Minas Gerais* [Literary Supplement] 15 Apr. 1972: 11.

Gorga Filho, Remi. "Lygia Fagundes Telles." *C. Povo* 88 12 July 1969: 15.

Linhares, Temístocles. "Lygia Fagundes Telles e as duas edicoes de Antes do baile verde. A última fase da escritora." *22 diálogos sobre o conto brasileiro atual.* Río de Janeiro: J. Olympio, 1973. 109-16.

Lucas, Fábio. "Contos fortes." *Temas literários e juizes críticos.* Belo Horizonte: Tendencia, 1963. 149-152. Rpt. in *Est.S. Paulo* 27 June 1959: 3.

————. "O Conto no Brasil Moderno." *O Livro do Seminário.* São Paulo, 1983. 103-64.

————. "Mistério e magia: contos de Lygia Fagundes Telles." *Est. S. Paulo.* [Literary Supplement] 5 Sept. 1970: 686. Rpt. in *A face visível.* Río de Janeiro: J Olympio; São Paulo, Cons. Est. de Cultura, 1973. 143-46.

Magalhaes Junior, Raimundo. *Panorama do Conto Brasileiro.* 10 vols. Río de Janeiro: n.p., 1959-1961.

Malard, Letícia. *Escritores de Literatura Brasileira.* Belo Horizonte, Brazil: n.p., 1981.

Mautner, Wasserman, Renata R. "The *Guerrilla* in the Bathtub: Telles's *As Meninas* and the Irruption of Politics." *Modern Language Studies* 19.1 (1989): 50-65.

Medina, Cremilda. "Lygia Fagundes Telles na Eter na Aventura do Morro de Duro." *Minas Gerais* [Literary Supplement] 9 Feb. 1985: 8.

Melillo Reali, Erilde. "Missa do Galo e variazioni sul tema: Sei riscritture di un racconto machadiano." *Annali Istituto Universitario Orientale* 25.1 (1983): 69-124.

Monfeiro, Leonardo. *Lygia Fagundes Telles: Seleçao de textos, notas, estudos biográficos e crítico e exercicios*. São Paulo: Abril Educaçao, 1980.

Nascimento, Bráulio do. "Histórias do desencontro." *J. Letras* 11 5 Jan. 1959: 114.

Pólvora, Hélio. "A intensidade do conto." *J. Brasil* 20 May 1970: 2. Cad. B. Livros.

Pontes, Joel. "Unidade nas Historias do desencontro." *Est. S. Paulo* 29 Aug 1959. Rpt. in *O aprendiz de crítica*. Río de Janeiro: INL, 1960. 108-115.

Rodrígues, Urbano Tavares. "Uma obra reflete São Paulo." *Estado São Paulo* 28 May 1972: 3.

Silva, Arguinaldo. "Um tratado sobre plantas carnívoras." *Globo* 28 July 1974: 7.

Silva, Vera Maria Tietzmann. *Metamorfose nos Contos de Lygia Fagundes Telles*. Río de Janeiro: n.p., 1985.

Silverman, Malcolm. "O Mundo Ficcional de Lygia Fagundes Telles." *Moderna Ficçao Brasileira 2* Río: Civilizaçao Brasileira, 1981. 162-84.

Steen, Edla van. "The Baroness of Tatui." Trans. Irene Matthews. *Review* 36 (1986): 30-33.

Stern, Irwin, ed. *Dictionary of Brazilian Literature*. New York: Greenwood Press, 1988. 337-38.

Tolman, Jon M. "New Fiction: Lygia Fagundes Telles." *Review 30* (1981): 65-70.

Xavier, Raul. "Uma contista maior. Antes do baile verdo." *J. Letras* 22 2 June 1970: 239.

ROSARIO FERRÉ
Puerto Rico

Rosario Ferré was born in Ponce, Puerto Rico, in 1942. She was raised in a traditional upper-class family. Her father, Luis Ferré, is a former governor of Puerto Rico. She married, had three children, divorced, and moved to Washington, D.C., where her life centers around her literary career and her feminist and social commitments. Ferré received her bachelor's degree from Manhattanville College, her master's from the University of Puerto Rico, and her doctorate from the University of Maryland.

In the early 1970s Ferré began her career as the co-founder and editor of the literary magazine *Zona de carga y descarga* (Loading and Unloading Zone), which promoted literary and social reforms. She has published a novel, short stories and numerous articles and feminist essays.

The major focus of Ferré's work is contemporary Puerto Rican women caught in an empty, materialistic world. In a society divided by class and gender, her characters' only hope of escape is through rebellion. This insight is implemented by Ferré in her own writing. Her complex narrative structures and provocative use of language, employed in combination with fantasy and social criticism, make Rosario Ferré one of Puerto Rico's most innovative and accomplished writers.

MERCEDES BENZ 220 SL

The Mercedes is fantastic, Mom, don't you think so, look how it fields the curves and sticks to the asphalt *vrroom* powerful the steering wheel responds to the touch of my fingertips through pigskin gloves they were a present from you so I could take the car out on its first spin, so my hands wouldn't slip over the grooves of the wheel that turn right and left at the slightest pressure from my fingers, the crossed lances on the hood flash chrome every-which-way see the passersby in the rain looking at us Mom what a car, it feels like a tank the mudguards up ahead rolling rhinoceros my family's always had big cars, Mom, the first Rolls Royce in San Juan was theirs, big as hope and poor as black we've got to show them who runs this country, Mom, we've got too many people living on this island, crowded together like monkeys they like to smell each other's sweat, rub each other like bedbugs, that's what they like, a riot, how amusing, Mom, I never thought of our overpopulation problem that way before, that man's coming our way, Dad, he's right in front of us, careful, you'll hit him, a man was walking with his back to the car along the shoulder of the road, pressing with his thumb the golden disc of the horn that shone in the center of the elegant beige leather steering wheel, I love the touch of this wheel, squeezing the golden disc, it sounds just like the first trumpet in Das Reingold, Mom, but the man doesn't hear, doesn't get off the road until the last minute when he leapt sideways, the mudguards spared his head by an inch, he fell flat on his face in the ditch, I'll pick you off next time, you long-tailed monkey, next time you'll drop out of the trees, you're frightened, Mom, you're white as a sheet, it's because I'm thinking of the patrol car, Dad, it's for your sake, the hell with patrol cars, Mom, it's incredible that you should worry about them now, you still don't know who your husband is, this car is like a fortress, wherever we go it'll put us in the right, that's what I bought it for, Mom, what nonsense, do you think I work from eight to eight just to put fat on my ass, in this country power is the only thing that counts, Mom, don't you forget it.

He floored the pedal and shot off in a straight line, at least there's no traffic at this hour, Sunday morning is the best time to drive on this island's roads, the woman silently rubs the last beads of her rosary, I'm going to put the seat back to see if I can sleep a little, Dad, it's still dark and I'm a bit sleepy, these seats are really sexy, Mom, slipping his hand over the short, grey pile that yields to his fingertips, dolled up in your three hundred dollar alligator shoes and your nine carat emerald cut diamond ring, when I bought it you said it looked like an ice rink and I wanted to laugh, Mom, that's a good one, a ring as big as a skating rink, how you love to squander money, the stores and the church have me in the poor house, but I don't complain, Mom, it's fine with me, you're every inch a lady and I couldn't manage without you.

He took his hand from the steering wheel and reached into the darkness to caress the forehead of the woman who slept at his side, I love you Dad, I said when I felt his hand on my face as I prayed again to the Holy Mother, you're like a little boy with a new toy, the truth is you work too hard, poor dear, you deserve a reward, it's not right to kill yourself working, only sometimes you make me suffer so with your lack of consideration like right now don't go so fast, Dad, the road is wet, the car could skid, you never pay attention, you never listen, it's just as if I were talking to myself, rubbing my arms because suddenly I feel cold, the trees shoot out from the sides forming a tunnel that is gobbling us up narrow-and-dark up ahead, wide-and-falling-on-us be-hind, we must be doing ninety, please, Dad, God forgive us and the Virgin protect us the wipers won't go fast enough to clear the huge raindrops, it's always been like this, since we got married twenty years ago he buys me everything, he's a good provider, but always the same deafness, I'm always at his side and always alone, eating alone, sleeping alone, once I looked at myself in the mirror, I opened my mouth, touched my palate with my finger to see if any sound came out, testing, one, two, three, my mouth formed the words for things, wood and hair, eye and lip, checking, the flow of breath, testing, one two three, but nothing came out, it was clogged up in there as if the opening were too small or the words too large, edges painfully jammed into the gums. I forced the words upward from the back of my throat but to no avail, it felt like I was touching a mute hole, I put my finger in deeper every time and then I looked at myself in the mirror and thought I was going crazy. Then my son was born and I could speak again.

She lay back in the seat and watched his profile outlined in darkness. The dashboard lights lit up his heavy features, his childlike smile. She closed her eyes and crossed her arms over her chest to rub her shoulders. And now she was alone again, because her son had left home after many angry disputes with his father. He said the business made him want to vomit, he was fed up with Dad's threatening to disinherit him, one morning I found a note on his bed don't look for me I'll come see you on Sundays. Of course we searched but he was always changing addresses until at last Dad got tired of shelling out money for private detectives and let him go to hell, he said, I'm not going to work my hide off just to waste thousands of dollars on detectives tracking out the likes of a prima donna who doesn't give a damn about money, raise crows and they'll pick out your eyes I've always said, and I wept but it was no use because deep down I knew Dad was right. Look at that road ahead of us, Mom, it's all ours, if it weren't six o'clock Sunday morning it'd be packed full of cars, one on top of the other like monkeys, that's what they're like, the stink of apes, the stench of chimps, smooth, so smooth, the gas pedal to the floor, these Germans make cars as if they were tanks, Mom, no matter what it knocks off the steel body won't even dent, if it hits you it means a one-way ticket to kingdom come.

Standing before the kitchen sink, the girl picked up the cup from which she had just drunk coffee, and slid her finger over the blue roses of the porcelain. She turned on the hot water tap, squeezed the plastic bottle and let three sluggish drops fall. She watched them slide slowly down the cup. The liquid, a raw green, reminded her of her fear, but when she let the water fill the cup it dissolved harmlessly in suds, spilling over the edge. She wiped the cup and dried it, feeling the glaze squeak clean under her fingertips, and then put it, still warm, on the table. She dried her reddened hands on her skirt and looked out through the kitchen window at the patio. In the grey light of dawn, the plants nodded at her under the rain as if they were wanderers that had lost their way. A mist was rising from the wet earth and the smell reminded her of when she was a child and used to bury things nobody wanted in the garden: a comb with missing teeth; a plastic swan with a ribbon around its neck, "Fernando and María, Happiness Always," that her mother had brought back as a keepsake from a wedding; a half-used lipstick; a thimble. I always enjoyed burying things nobody wanted so only I knew where they were. When it rains hard like now I remember it clearly, I see myself breathing the smell of the clods of earth that crumble between my fingers. Then when I went out for a spell in the garden, I'd walk over the buried things that only I knew were there. Now I stand over the little comb, I'd say to myself in a low voice, now I'm stepping over the wings of the swan, now over my old Easter bonnet, as if the power to remember every detail of the hidden objects somehow made me different from everyone else.

She left the kitchen sink and looked around at the half-furnished room. She had nothing to do so she began to pull out the bureau's half empty drawers. She opened the almost empty closet and rattled the wire hangers together. It didn't bother her at all to have so few belongings; on the contrary, she welcomed the peace that an empty room brings. They usually sat on the floor at dinner and ate on a straw tatami which she kept scrupulously clean. In the mornings, before six o'clock, they would both do their zen meditation together, sitting in lotus position with pistil straight backs and warbling like birds the mantra's sacred words. Then a soft ray of light fell on her hand and made her think of him. She realized she couldn't picture his face away from this place; he was part of the room itself, of the books, orderly, aligned on the table, of the little gas stove, of the faded bedspread covering the thin mattress which lay on the floor, of the bronze fish mobile that tinkled to the comforting beat of the rain against the window. Then she heard his knock on the door, ran to meet him and embraced him. Should you go today she asked, because look how it's raining, you're drenched. Yes; I agreed to go every Sunday.

If you go early we'll have Sunday to ourselves, I tell him. You should come with me, Mom has never met you and perhaps she'd come to like you, Dad might even forgive us both. No, it's better they don't meet me, let's leave it for now, I'll go with you as far as the house, as usual, and then I'll go. She looked out the window again, everything's so dark and still, the rain makes it seem like nighttime. Sunday mornings always seem endless, people sleep forever behind closed doors. It's as though they grew roots under their sheets, or as if they lay with ears pressed against the windows, listening to the dry rasp of sunlight as it slowly climbs the walls.

The woman sat up in the car seat and tried to make out the silhouette of houses through the raindrops that spread a thick, transparent skin down the windshield. As they neared their own street she gave a sigh of relief, feeling the end of her travail near. She put away her rosary, shut her handbag and let her body relax little by little, anticipating the moment when they would slow down, her hand on the handle to open the door, the car before their house at last. She saw him first, the dark figure zigzagging in the half-light of dawn trying to get out of the way of the car but trapped by the side of the building, it all happened in a fraction of a second. He came out of nowhere, his body swept by the curtain of rain which smothered everything. The mudguard hit with a thud and all of a sudden he was stuck to the hood, how awful, Dad, please stop, I told you we were going too fast, I begged you a hundred times, the body splayed across the hood, you have to get out and do something, Dad, you have to get out, shut up, for God's sake, you're driving me crazy, sitting side by side unable to think, looking at the rain that kept on falling as if nothing had happened, as if it wanted to rinse out the blood from the platinum surface, the grotesque shadow sprawled over the chrome trim like a mashed-up doll.

The low voice began again its endless string of swear words, crowded together like monkeys the better to smell the stink, the better to rut the stench, you can't even drive out at dawn on Sunday morning on this island without there being that thing crushed on top of the car, wiping the windshield from the inside as though nothing had happened, after all the world goes on perfectly ordered on this side of the glass, sitting comfortably on the grey pile, eyes glued to the windshield, telling himself that it was all right, nothing had happened which couldn't be fixed, his hand on the latch but unable to open the door.

The girl approached the car in the downpour, hair plastered to her face. She paused before the lighted headlights, useless now in the early morning light. They watched her from behind the windshield slide the body over the hood, struggling to support his weight against hers. Then she let the boy down slowly over the side, before stretching him out on the pavement. I lowered the window halfway and the rain splashed on my face, my mouth filled with water, what's going on, I screamed, what should we do, Dad, he lowered his window an inch and peered out, shut up you idiot, the whole neighborhood will hear you, that woman has taken charge of him now, she's sat him on the ground with his head on her lap, we'd better go, I'll leave her our name and address, how can we leave, Dad, the man is hurt, we can't leave him lying on the road in this downpour, don't argue with me, you're hysterical, we're not going to put him in the car and stain the new upholstery with all that blood. And so Dad scribbled something on a piece of paper lowered his window an inch more to put out his hand and let go of the note so that it fluttered to the side of the road.

He started the engine and backed up, the screeching tires began bearing down on the asphalt. Mom caressed the grey pile gently, as if trying to appease it. The upholstery, of course, how stupid of me not to think of it, so new, so soft, so alien to anything as disagreeable as a smear of blood, and she curled up in her bucket seat and began to pray. Thank you, oh God, for the protection, for the security, for the wonderful armor of a car around us, God forgive us and the Virgin protect us, one can't live without money, calming down little by little as they drove closer to home. She wiped her forehead, a nightmare, maybe it never happened, exhausted, anxious to lower herself into a hot tub, not to think about anything but the peaceful white ceiling over her room.

It had been raining all through lunchtime when the doorbell rang. I opened the door and recognized her immediately, she held the crumpled piece of paper in her hand. It fell apart as I tried to read it, "Contact us if we can be of help," next to the address of our house. She opened the door and I showed her the note. She turned white, as I knew she would when she saw me. Please wait here, Miss, I'll be right back. She half-closed the door and went in. My hands were in a sweat, Dad, I dried them on my skirt as I went to find you. I looked for you all over the house but you'd already left for the office. My husband's not here, Miss, can I be of help, please come in. I walked over the doorstep, let my feet sink in the carpet and saw the stairway you had talked to me so much about, the handrail you used to slide down as a child as you burst through the door of the patio, the panes of glass in the living room window were blue and pink, just as you'd told me. Have a seat, Miss, please sit down. No Ma'am I'm not going to stay long. I looked out through the blue pane and saw you sitting next to the fountain in the garden, it's not fair, it's just not fair to see you all tinted in blue in the middle of the patio, playing a different game now where I can't reach you, where I can't be with you, swaying blue on the other side of the pane of glass, the water flowing hard and blue against your hands, your white face on my lap bleeding, stained by the rain that now gushes out of me too and I can't stop it, what's the matter, Miss, why, you're crying.

Are you the young lady who was with the stranger that awful night, I asked her, my hand trembling on the goosedown pillow as I leaned curiously towards her. I wasn't sure it had really happened, it seemed like a nightmare, tell me, how is the boy, I've been so concerned about him. I felt terribly guilty for not having gotten out of the car to help you, for not having shared the unpleasantness, that's why my husband left that piece of paper with you, so you could get in touch with us and wouldn't think we were just common hit-and-runs. I'm sorry that at the moment my husband wasn't much help, he was so upset by the whole thing I almost had to take him to the hospital later he was in such a state. He's a good man, Miss, I love him very much, and he suffers from terribly high blood pressure, I was afraid he'd have a heart attack that night. But it's different now, I'm sure we can help that poor boy Miss, were there hospital bills, were there drug expenses, we'll pay for everything, I assure you. Only I'm curious to know why it took you so long to reach us, to get in contact with us, why didn't you come to see us the very next day, you'd have found friends to help you out, to take the boy to the best specialists, believe me, Miss, we want to help.

Thank you Ma'am, but I didn't come here to talk about that. Then the accident wasn't serious, what a relief, Miss, thank God. My friend is dead, Ma'am, I wanted you to know that. He was buried two weeks ago; I took care of the arrangements myself. A simple coffin, a simple grave. There was no funeral that you may call as such; only a few friends and myself. He had no family. That's all. But it was my duty to tell you. The boy is dead and buried. Good-bye, Ma'am. You mean you're leaving, don't you want to explain what happened, Miss, please wait until my husband returns, I'm sure he'll want to give you something, at least help out with some of the expenses of the burial, you can't leave like this without even telling us his name, Miss, we'd like to know that poor boy's name.

A few days later the girl stood once again in front of the kitchen window and turned on the hot water tap. It was Sunday, so she didn't have to go to work. She could spend the whole day thinking, remembering about things. She squeezed the plastic bottle and let three drops of green liquid fall on her empty coffee cup. She watched the blue rose of the porcelain disappear under the soapsuds that rose to the edge. She knew that today the woman would wait again all day for her son, to no avail. She could almost see her leaning out the front door for the hundredth time, looking down the empty street at the short row of houses as the sun rose in the sky, making the walls seem more solid and heavily shadowed. She put her hand in the water and carefully rinsed out the cup and saucer. She could almost hear her say, I musn't worry, this Sunday is like any other Sunday, he's just later than usual. For a while the girl went on looking through the window at the lush garden. The woman left the doorway and sat on the edge of her bed. There's no reason to get upset, he'll come next week if he doesn't come today, she said to herself out loud, as her eyes wandered to the bedspread. She patted the silk coverlet tenderly and thought of the expense of keeping a nice house. I just bought this coverlet a year ago and it already looks worn, there's no end to what a house will require, the redecorating is endless. After all, I made the right decision not to leave Dad, he keeps doing foolish things to scare me, like driving a hundred miles an hour down a highway, but it's not that he doesn't love me, it's just his way. All my friends envy me my husband because he's such a financial success, and this year, God willing, we'll make our usual trip to Europe. In Madrid I'll buy a Loewe suede coat for a bargain; and in Paris I'll visit Michel Swiss on the Rue de la Paix and Dior and Guerlain on the Place de la Victoire. And in addition to all that, I have him and he has me and we'll grow old together and never be alone. Young people want to be free and at the same time feel loved but they won't pay the price, life is hard, it's not a bowl of cherries, no, those who think life is a bowl of cherries have it all wrong. The girl opened the kitchen door and went out into the garden. She felt the ground with her feet and crouched down, burying her hands in the wet earth. She then began to reconstruct the memory of his face, his hands, his arms. She felt at peace. Now she was sure no one would ever discover where he had been buried.

Isn't it a splendid Sunday morning to go for a ride in our Mercedes, Mom, we haven't done this for a while and I just had it specially waxed. I had new hubcaps put on it and now it's sexier than ever, it shines in the dark like a chromium rhinoceros, just look at that highway up ahead, empty of cars and leading to kingdom come, it's just waiting for us, Mom, in this country there are so many people on the road you can't go for a ride any more except at dawn on Sundays, that's the only time one can put one's head out the door and breathe. Now we can plan our trip to Europe in peace, Mom, tell me where you want to go.

First I have to tell you something, Dad, the strangest thing happened yesterday afternoon, a girl came to the house, she had a piece of paper in her hand, the very one you scribbled our address on under the rain the day that man threw himself under our car, it was definitely the same, I'm sure of it, I recognized your handwriting. You can't imagine what a time I had; she didn't complain, she didn't say more than ten words.

She stood in the middle of the room and just stared at me for what must have been like fifteen minutes, until I began to think she was out of her mind. This girl wants something, I told myself. But I couldn't say anything, I just stood there in the middle of the room and stared back at her, begging all the saints to make you come back early from the office so you'd deal with her and let her know she couldn't blackmail us, that sort of thing doesn't go over with us because we have all the right friends in the right places. Still, I tried to be as civil to her as possible and kept asking her about the fellow, I was truly concerned and tried to learn all I could about the accident to see how we could help when the wretch cuts me short and tells me in an angry voice, the boy is dead, Ma'am. I buried him, just like that and nothing else, the boy is dead, I buried him, as if it were the most natural thing in the world to bury the dead yourself. I was struck absolutely dumb, unable to say a word. I felt as if a corkscrew or something were twisting into my left side and then was pulling hard. I had to sit down on the sofa I felt so faint. She went on looking at me without a word for I don't know how long, and all I could do was sit there with that terrible pain in my chest.

But thank God I finally came to. I sat up on the sofa and told myself you're a fool, Mom, if you're going to let yourself be upset by what a stranger tells you. Life is always tragic and if you put it into your mind to save humanity you're sunk, give away what you have and you'll end up begging, we must all stand up and bear our cross. And just then I realized what the wretch was saying. That you had run over the fellow and killed him, that you were totally to blame. I flew at her in a rage how dare you, you insolent wimp, you know me, Dad, I may complain and grumble, gripe and fume, but when I see you under fire I turn into a fiend. I could already see her coming at you with a charge of first-degree murder and a million dollar lawsuit, my God, this world is full of swine. Your friend threw himself under the car, I was there, I saw it, I screamed back at her. I'll testify in any court and swear on any Bible to that fact. And I was still talking, setting things straight for her, when she turned her back on me and began walking towards the door and all I could do was stand there, watch her open it calmly and step out, with my mouth open and the words stuck in my throat. And then I sat down on the sofa with that thing twisting into my chest and thought I was going to die.

Don't let it bother you, Mom, you should have told me about it sooner, I would have made inquiries last night. If she shows up again at the house you mustn't open the door, if I'm not in tell the maid you can't talk to her, she can come see me at the office, I'll know how to deal with her. Forget about it for now, Mom, just look at the Mercedes go, watch it glide along the empty road purring like a car, its fenders shinning in the dark like a chromium rhinoceros' . . .

Translated by Rosario Ferré

Bibliography: Rosario Ferré

Fiction

Ferré, Rosario. *Papeles de Pandora*. Mexico City: Joaquín Mortiz, 1976. 2nd. ed. [Corrected and expanded]. Mexico City: Joaquín Mortiz, 1979.

――――. *El medio pollito: Siete cuentos infantiles*. Puerto Rico: Huracán, 1976. Rpt. in Puerto Rico: Huracán, 1977.

――――. *La caja de cristal*. Mexico City: La Máquina de Escribir, 1978.

――――. *La muñeca menor*. Puerto Rico: Huracán, 1980.

――――. "Juan Bobo va a oír misa." *Sin Nombre* [San Juan, Puerto Rico] 11.2 (1980): 41-42.

――――. "El cuento de hadas." *Sin Nombre* [San Juan, Puerto Rico] 11.2 (1980): 36-40.

――――. *Los cuentos de Juan Bobo*. Puerto Rico: Ediciones Huracán, 1981.

――――. *La mona que le pisaron la cola*. Puerto Rico: Ediciones Huracán, 1981.

――――. *Fábulas de la garza desangrada*. Mexico City: Editorial Joaquín Mortiz, 1982.

――――. "Maldito amor." *Novísimos narradores hispanoamericanos en Marcha 1964-1980*. Ed. Angel Rama. Montevideo: Marcha Editores, 1981. 307-18.

――――. "Pico Rico Mandorico. *"Apalabramiento: Diez cuentistas puertorriqueños de hoy*. Ed. Efraín Barradas. Hanover, NH: Ediciones del Norte, 1983. 73-84. Rpt. in *Reclaiming Medusa: Short Stories by Contemporary Puerto Rican Women*. Ed. Diana Vélez. San Francisco: Spinster/Aunt Lute Book Company, 1988. 73-82.

――――. "El regalo. *"Apalabramiento: Diez cuentistas puertorriqueños de hoy*. Ed. Efraín Barradas. Hanover, NH: Ediciones del Norte, 1983. 85-119.

――――. "When Women Love Men." Trans. Cynthia Ventura. *Contemporary Women Authors of Latin America: New Translations*. Ed. Doris Meyer and Margarite Fernández Olmos. Brooklyn: Brooklyn College, 1983. 176-85.

――――. "El desengaño." *Hispamérica* 13.38 (1984): 67-72.

――――. "The Glass Box." Trans. Rosario Ferré and Kathy Taylor. *The Massachusetts Review* 3.4 (1986): 699-711.

――――. *Maldito amor*. Mexico City: Joaquín Mortiz, 1986.

――――. "El abrigo de zorro azul/The Fox Skin Coat." Trans. Rosario Ferré. *Mester* 15.2 (1986): 46-50.

――――. "La bella durmiente." *Ritos de iniciación*. Ed. Grínor Rojo and Cynthia Steele. Boston: Houghton Mifflin Company, 1986. 147-211.

――――. "Mercedes Benz 220 SL." *Puerta abierta: la nueva escritora latinoamericana*. Ed. Caridad L. Silva-Velázquez and Nora Erro-Orthmann. Mexico City: Joaquín Mortiz, 1986. 109-121.

――――. "Pico Rico, Mandorico." *Reclaiming Medusa: Short Stories by Contemporary Puerto Rican Women*. Ed. and Trans. Diana Vélez. San Francisco: Spinster/Aunt Lute Book Company, 1988. 64-72.

———. "Sleeping Beauty." *Reclaiming Medusa: Short Stories by Contemporary Puerto Rican Women*. Ed. Diana Vélez. Trans. Rosario Ferré and Diana Vélez. San Francisco: Spinster/Aunt Lute Book Company, 1988. 34-63.

———. *Sweet Diamond Dust*. Trans. Rosario Ferré. New York: Ballantine Books, 1988.

———. *La muñeca menor/The Youngest Doll*. Trans. Rosario Ferré. Puerto Rico: Huracán, 1980.

———. "The Youngest Doll." Trans. Gregory Rabassa. *The Kenyan Review* 2.1 (1980): 163. *Reclaiming Medusa: Short Stories by Contemporary Puerto Rican Women*. Ed. Diana Vélez. Trans. Rosario Ferré and Diana Vélez. San Francisco: Spinster/Aunt Lute Book Company, 1988. 27-22. Rpt. in *Longman Anthology of World Literature by Women 1875-1975*. Eds. Marian Arkin and Barbara Shollar. New York: Longman, 1989. 1055-1058.

———. *Sonatinas*. Puerto Rico: Huracán, 1989.

Essays

Ferré, Rosario. *Sitio a Eros: Trece ensayos*. Mexico City: Joaquín Mortiz, 1980.

———. "La cocina de la escritura: In." *Literatures in Transition: The Many Voices of the Caribbean Area: A Symposium*. Ed. Rose S. Minc. Gaithersburg, MD: Hispamérica, 1982. 37-51. Rpt. in *Fem* 49 (1986-1987): 36-42.

———. "El acomodador - autor." *Escritura* 7.13-14 (1982): 189-209.

———. "S/Z: una pregunta que responde y una respuesta que pregunta." *Texto Crítico* 30 (1984): 7-12.

———. *El acomodador. Una lectura fantástica de Felisberto Hernández*. Mexico City: Fondo de Cultura Económica, 1986.

———. "Felisberto Hernández: La vanguardia de un hombre solo." *La Gaceta del Fondo de Cultura Económica* 185 (1986): 17-19.

———. "Entre Clara y Julieta: dos poetas puertorriqueñas." *Revista Iberoamericana* 52.137 (1986): 999-1006.

———. "The Writers Kitchen." Trans. Diana L. Vélez. *Lives on the Line: The Testimony of Contemporary Latin American Authors*. Ed. Doris Meyer. Berkeley: University of California Press, 1988. 214-227.

———. *El árbol y sus sombras*. Mexico City: Fondo de Cultura Económica, 1989.

Criticism on the Works of Rosario Ferré

Agosín, Marjorie. "Génesis de 'La bailarina', un poema de Rosario Ferré." *Mairena* 13 (1983): 19-28.

Bush, Andrew. "Señalar las discrepancias: Rosario Ferré y Antonio Skarmeta hablan de Cortázar."*Revista de Estudios Hispánicos* 21.2 (1987): 73-87.

Chaves, María José. "La alegoría como método en los cuentos y ensayos de Rosario Ferré." *Third Woman* 2.2 (1984): 64-76.

Davis, Lisa E. "La puertorriqueña dócil y rebelde en los cuentos de Rosario Ferré." *Sin Nombre* 9.4 (1980): 82-88.

Escalera Ortiz, Juan. "Perspectiva del cuento Mercedes Benz 220SL'." *Revista/Review Interamericana* 12.3 (1982): 407-17.

Fernández Olmos, Margarite. "Desde una perspectiva femenina: La cuentística de Rosario Ferré y Ana Lydia Vega." *Homines* 8.2 (1984-1985): 303-11.

———. "From a Woman's Perspective: The Short Stories of Rosario Ferré and Ana Lydia Vega." *Contemporary Women Authors of Latin America: Introductory Essays*. Eds. Doris Meyer and Margarite Fernández Olmos. Brooklyn: Brooklyn College Press, 1983. 78-90.

———. "Rafael Sánchez and Rosario Ferré: Sexual Politics and Contemporary Puerto Rican Narrative." *Hispania* 70.1 (1987): 40-46.

———. "Sex, Color, and Class in Contemporary Puerto Rican Women Authors." *Heresies* 4.3.15 (1982): 46-47.

———. "Survival, Growth and Change in the Prose Fiction of Contemporary Puerto Rican Women Writers." *Images and Identities: The Puerto Rican in Two World Contexts*. Ed. Asela Rodríguez de Laguna. New Brunswick, N.J.: Transaction Press, 1987. 76-88.

Flores, Angel. *Narrativa hispanoamericana 1968-1981: historia y antología: Vol. V la generación de 1939 en adelante*. Mexico City: Siglo XXI Editores, 1983. 221.

Franco, Jean. "Self-destructing Heroines." *The Minnesota Review* 22 (1984): 105-15.

García Pinto, Magdalena. *Historias íntimas: conversaciones con 10 escritoras latinoamericanas*. Hanover, NH: Ediciones del Norte, 1988. 67-96.

Gazarian Gautier, Marie-Lise. "Rosario Ferré." *Interviews with Latin American Writers*. Elmwood Park, Ill.: Dalkey Archive Press, 1989. 79-92.

Gelpi, Juan. "Especulación, especularidad y remotivación en *Fábulas de la garza desangrada* de Rosario Ferré." *La Chispa '85: Selected Proceedings*. Ed. Gilbert Paolini. New Orleans: Tulane Univ., 1985. 125-32.

Guerra Cunningham, Lucía. "Tensiones paradójicas de la femineidad en la narrativa de Rosario Ferré." *Chasqui* 13.2-3 (1984): 13-25.

Heinrich, María Elena. "Entrevista a Rosario Ferré." *Prismal/Cabral* 7-8 (1982): 98-103.

Lagos-Pope, María Inés. "Sumisión rebeldía: El doble o la representación de la alienación femenina en narraciones de Marta Brunet y Rosario Ferré." *Revista Iberoamericana* 51.132-133 (1985): 731-49.

Levine, Linda Gould. "No más máscaras: Un diálogo entre tres escritoras del Caribe: Belkis Cuza Male - Cuba, Matilde Daviu - Venezuela, Rosario Ferré - Puerto Rico." *Literatures in Transition: The Many Voices of the Carribean Area: A Symposium*. Gaithersburg, MD; Upper Montclair, NJ: Hispamérica Montclair State College, 1982. 189-97.

Long, Sheri Spaine. "Entrevista breve con Rosario Ferré." *Mester* 15.2 (1986): 43-45.

López, Yvette. "'La muñeca menor': Ceremonias y transformaciones en un cuento de Rosario Ferré." *Explicación de Textos Literarios* 11.1 (1982-1983): 49-58.

López Jimenez, Yvette. "*Papeles de Pandora*: Devastación y ruptura." *Sin Nombre* 14.1 (1983): 41-52.

Méndez-Clark, Ronald. "La pasión y la marginalidad en (de) la escritura: Rosario Ferré." *La sartén por el mango*. Eds. Patricia Elena González and Eliana Ortega. Puerto Rico: Huracán, 1984. 119-30.

Rivera de Alvarez, Josefina. *Literatura puertorriqueña: su proceso en el tiempo*. Madrid: Ediciones Partenón, S.A., 1983. 731.

Solá, María. "Habla femenina e ideología feminista en *Papeles de Pandora* de Rosario Ferré." *Alero* 1 (1982): 19-26.

Umpierre, Luz María. "Los cuentos ¿infantiles? de Rosario Ferré - estrategias subversivas." *Nuevas aproximaciones críticas a la literatura puertorriqueña contemporánea*. Ed. Luz María Umpierre-Herrera. Puerto Rico: Editorial Cultural, 1983. 89-101.

————. "De la protesta a la creación: Una nueva visión de la mujer puertorriqueña en la poesía." *Imagine: International Chicano Poetry Journal* 2.1 (1985): 134-42.

————. "Un manifiesto literario: *Papeles de Pandora* de Rosario Ferré." *The Bilingual Review: la revista bilingüe* 9.2 (1982): 121-28.

————. *Nuevas aproximaciones críticas a la literatura puertorriqueña contemporánea*. Puerto Rico: Editorial Cultural, 1983.

————. "Rosario Ferré, *Sitio a eros: trece ensayos literarios*." *Revista Iberoamericana* 49.123-123 (1983): 678-80.

Vélez, Diana L. "Power and the Text: Rebellion in Rosario Ferré's *Papeles de Pandora*." *MMLA: The Journal of the Midwest Modern Language Association*. 17.1 (1984): 70-80.

LUCÍA FOX
Perú

Lucía Fox was born in Perú and studied at San Marcos University (Perú), Washington University, and the University of Illinois, where she received her doctorate. She is now a professor at Michigan State University, where she teaches courses in Latin American culture, and in Chicano and women's literature.

A Peruvian writer of great originality and versatility, Fox has written poetry, drama, short stories and literary essays. Her work has been characterized by an ardent defense of women. Her work has appeared in several important European and American journals and has received important awards such as a Rockefeller Grant (1989) and a Michigan State Award (1990).

Fox is also a renowned critic who has published numerous essays on women writers. Her book *Women Novelists in Spain and Spanish America* (1979) is a key work in feminist literary criticism. She has devoted much of her scholarly research to Chicano issues and Hispanic women. The result of some of this investigation is *Chicanas, Their Voices, Their Lives* (1989), an oral history of several Chicana women.

THE WEDDING

The twelve photographs were arranged in a circle on the floor of Otilia's room. She was sitting in the middle, moving them as if they were tarot cards, repeating phrases that could have been an invocation, but that did not belong to any language which Fernanda, who was spying on her from the balcony, could understand. Fernanda had come to the wedding of Elsa, Otilia's daughter. Feeling a little dizzy from the champagne, Fernanda had gone to look for a bathroom in the enormous house. She had entered this room, and on seeing the lovely balcony that opened onto the garden, had stopped to rest in a rocking chair.

"I must have fallen asleep . . . but what's the time?" she said to herself when she awoke. She hadn't worn her watch, preferring to wear bracelets. When she spotted Otilia engaged in her ritual with the photographs, she decided not to leave her hiding place. Fernanda had always been fascinated by Otilia's strange beauty, which stood out even when she was with Elsa's friends from school.

Otilia began to make a large doll out of clothing that she took from a dresser. She stuffed it, then went to the closet to take out one of her husband's three-piece suits. Now clothed, the doll was almost done; the only thing lacking was for it to talk. Otilia looked it over with what appeared to be restrained vehemence, then ran to get a red tie which she wrapped around the neck of the doll. Taking it to the center of the circle, she began the movements of a dance, her feet barely touching the photographs. As Otilia and the doll moved together, it seemed to Fernanda that a handsome head now adorned the rag doll.

"I must be seeing things," thought Fernanda, feeling as if she were contemplating a miracle.

Then Otilia carried the doll to the bed, and covered it and herself with the bedspread. The ferocious, rhythmic movements under the bedspread indicated that Otilia and the doll were taking part in a passionate sexual interlude. Taking advantage of this, Fernanda tried to make her getaway, but when she heard the voices and footsteps of a group of people in the hall, she hid on the balcony once again in order to avoid questions.

When Fernanda felt at last that she could leave, once Otilia was no longer in the room, she began to tiptoe away, but had to run and hide once more because Elsa in her bridal gown entered the room. Elsa went over to the bed, and when she discovered the doll began to tear it apart with a furious expression on her face, until there was nothing left of it but rags scattered across the bed. Then Elsa noticed the photographs and trampled them, kicking them in several directions. She went to the dressing table and, picking up a lipstick, wrote: "Mama, where are you?

I'm leaving. Elsa." She paused for a moment and with a sad expression looked at herself in the mirror. She dried the tears that her fury had caused her to shed and touched herself up a little before going out.

Although Fernanda had known Elsa for years—they had shared a desk during the last year of secondary school—this was the first time that Fernanda had had access to Elsa's personal life. She recalled one afternoon when the choir teacher, Miss Monone, had come to get some students, including Elsa, who were going to participate in the finals of the city choir contest. Since this was during study hall, nobody would bother the remaining students, who were expected to use the hour to catch up on their homework. Fernanda was counting on this fact to read Elsa's diary. With extreme care, trying to remember the exact details so as to be able to put it back again, Fernanda pulled out the diary and read: "I'm mama's baby and I'm ashamed of what's happening." Details followed but Fernanda concentrated more on the order of things. She found the entry in which Elsa first expressed anguish at her father's sexual intrusion into her body. "Yesterday Daddy got angry because I insisted on going with Mama on her monthly visit to the Romanian Center. He wanted me to stay home alone, but I knew what would happen . . . Daddy has threatened to kill himself if I talk."

Elsa's writing was scribbled, smudged perhaps by the tears that she must have shed in writing it. The entry was dated two years earlier. The most recent entries indicated the existence of young men whom Fernanda knew because they attended the neighboring boy's school. They would wait for the girls when school let out and accompany them to the city bus. These were the only moments that Elsa had met boys, since she was never permitted to attend her friends' parties nor leave the house after school without her mother.

Certain phrases of Elsa's diary stucked in Fernanda's mind:

"Daddy came looking for me at school and found out that Ricardo is my boyfriend. He's threatened to kill him if I keep seeing him . . ." Fernanda knew the details of this scene since she had been with Elsa, Tita and Ana that afternoon. The girls were with their respective boyfriends, but the couples never strayed too far from the group. Elsa had been dragged away by her father and shoved into his car. The next day Elsa had written, "He won't get away with this thing, even if it means that I have to kill him."

Fernanda felt that the diary simply confirmed what she had already suspected from bits and pieces of her conversations with Elsa. But now that she knew for sure, what should she do? Fernanda was paralyzed by confusion; she couldn't admit that she had read the diary because this would betray her friend's trust.

She could not tell Elsa about Otilia's strange ritual either.

Now, still in her hiding place, waiting for Elsa to leave her mother's room, Fernanda thought of her conversation with Elsa the day she had read her diary. Elsa had come back from choir practice. "It was a waste of time because we'll never win the contest. But we had a great time listening to the stories that Monone told us. She's not the greatest music teacher, but her stories are cute because they're so ridiculous."

"Haven't you ever wondered why Monone never got married?" asked Fernanda, trying to orient the conversation towards more confidential topics.

"Monone never got married because her parents wanted only the best for her, which is not the best," Elsa said, laughing. Fernanda noticed that Elsa made fun of the world; she, who was so pretty, had learned how to use irony.

"And aren't you afraid the same thing will happen to you? Your father is so protective that he doesn't let you come to our parties or even to our own class graduation," said Fernanda, knowing that Elsa would answer her directly.

"Daddy doesn't want to let me do certain things because he believes that he has power over me and over my Mama; but still, I'll find a boyfriend even more powerful than he is." Saying this, Elsa's face, normally beautiful, became sad and ugly.

Earlier on Elsa's wedding day, Tita said: "Who would believe that Elsa would get married before us? When I got the invitation I almost fainted. We've hardly seen each other during summer vacation, getting ready for the university entrance examinations."

"What a surprise!" agreed Ana, who always got wind of everything and who felt the most betrayed.

"And who *is* Roberto Gonzalez?" asked Fernanda, who believed that the whole group should go to the university and not get married until they had careers.

"He's a lawyer and he works for an international company, General Motors. He's as old as my father. My uncle Alfredo says that he's real rich," said Tita.

"What I don't understand is why her father hasn't stopped it," said Fernanda, remembering the strict vigilance that Elsa was subject to.

"Her father went to the United States for medical treatment and that's all the time Elsa needed. She is eighteen now," said Ana, who seemed to know more details, probably because she had already put out feelers through her network of friends.

Now on Elsa's wedding day, everything had taken place in the strictest intimacy. The groom had brought only his closest relatives and two of his best friends. On Elsa's side the only ones in attendance were Otilia who, having been a Romanian refugee, had no family in Lima, and two fellow refugees, who had been Elsa's godmothers at her baptism and confirmation. Elsa's three schoolmates were her only friends present.

But the one who was conspicuously absent was "El señor Arturo," Elsa's father.

Later when Fernanda returned from Otilia's room, Ana, who was Fernanda's best friend, asked, "Where have you been all this time?"

"We've looked for you everywhere, you really disappeared," said Tita. "Elsa seems to be madly in love. Listen, the groom was 'almost' blushing at Elsa's public display of affection," she added.

Tita seemed to have enjoyed herself, judging from her rosy cheeks and the bride's bouquet in her hands. Both Ana and Tita had danced with Roberto's friends. Roberto himself seemed to be a nice guy, although too old for them.

"The angels fly in silence," said Ana in a moment of inspired eloquence.

"And I hope Elsa's father is struck by lightning," said Fernanda suddenly, separating herself from the group.

Two weeks later when Elsa returned from her honeymoon, a detective-lieutenant asked her to identify a suicide. Elsa recognized her mother even though the body had been three days in the gorge that was called Paradise of the Suicides of San Miguel. Finally, the official notice of Otilia's death appeared in the paper. Fernanda went to express her condolences to Elsa, who seemed to have lost a lot of weight.

"Daddy abandoned Mama when he got back from the States and found out that my engagement to Roberto was serious. Poor Mama, she was so confused the day of my wedding. She must have felt like an accomplice. I could never explain to her what I was worried about."

"Maybe she guessed," said Fernanda in spite of herself. "Yes, but Daddy goes around telling everybody that she was crazy and that if he didn't say anything before, it was to protect the family name."

"Have you seen him?" asked Fernanda.

"I don't ever want to see him again. He says that I'm a disobedient disgrace. What do you think?" Elsa asked Fernanda, who was finally going to reveal everything that she knew.

Unfortunately, Roberto's presence in the room interrupted the conversation.

Translated by Lucía Fox

Bibliography: Lucía Fox

Fiction

Fox, Lucía. *Constelación*. East Lansing: Shamballa Publications, 1978.

―――. *Un cierto lugar*. Lima: Ed. Salesiano, 1980.

―――. "Detrás del telón." *Puerta abierta: la nueva escritora latinoamericana*. Mexico City: Joaquín Mortiz, 1986. 123-29.

―――. *Ruedas*. East Lansing: Superspace, 1988.

Essays

Fox-Lockert, Lucía. *Ensayos hispanoamericanos*. Caracas: García y Hermanos, 1965.

―――. *El rostro de la patria en la literatura peruana*. Buenos Aires: Ediciones Continente, 1970.

―――. *Women Novelists in Spain and Spanish America*. New Jersey: The Scarecrow Press, 1979.

―――. "Visión del paisaje andino peruano en José María Arguedas y Manuel Scorza." *Cuadernos de Aldeeu* 1.2-3 (1983): 337-45.

Poetry

Fox, Lucía. *Preludios íntimos*. Lima: Editorial Cóndor, 1945.

―――. *Imágenes de Caracas*. Caracas: García Hermanos, 1965.

―――. *Tragaluz*. Los Angeles: Ediciones la Frontera, 1967.

―――. *Redes*. Barcelona: Ediciones Carabela, 1968.

―――. *Tiempo atonal*. East Lansing: Ghost Dance, 1969.

―――. *Múltiples*. East Lansing: Ghost Dance, 1969.

―――. *Aceleración Múltiple*. Buenos Aires: Editorial Losada, 1969.

―――. *La odisea del pájaro*. Bilbao: Empresas Editoras, 1972.

―――. *Latinoamérica en evolución. Latin America in Evolution*. East Lansing: Superspace, 1974.

―――. *Latin America in Evolution*. East Lansing: Superspace, 1974.

―――. *Monstruos aéreos, terrestres y submarinos*. East Lansing: Superspace, 1974.

―――. *Mosaicos*. East Lansing: Old Marble Press, 1974.

―――. *Mosaics*. East Lansing: Argonauta, 1974.

―――. *Assemblage. Lucía Fox in Translation*. East Lansing: Superspace, 1977.

―――. *Leyendas de una princesa india - Legends of an Indian Princess*. East Lansing: Shamballa Publications, 1979.

―――. *Formas - Forms*. East Lansing: Shamballa Publications, 1985.

―――. *Lima en caos*. East Lansing: Nueva Crónica, 1990.

Theater

Fox, Lucía. *El perfil desnudo*. East Lansing: Shamballa Publications, 1978.

———. *Ayer es nunca jamás*. Lima: Ed. Salesiano, 1980.

———. *Sor Juana, the Tenth Muse*. East Lansing: Pachacamac, 1988.

Criticism on the Works of Lucía Fox

Agosín, Marjorie. "Lucía Fox: *Ayer es nunca jamás*." *Revista Iberoamericana* 48.120-121 (1982): 743-44.

———. "Review of *Women Novelists in Spain and Spanish America* by Lucía Fox-Lockert." *Revista Interamericana de Bibliografía/Inter-American Review of Bibliography* 30.4 (1980): 30.4 (1980): 437.

Cain, Joan. "Review of *Women Novelists in Spain and Spanish America* by Lucía Fox-Lockert." *Journal of Spanish Studies; Twentieth Century* 8.3 (1980): 317-18.

Werner, Flora M. "Introducción a la obra dramática de Lucía Fox." *Letras Femeninas* 5.1 (1979): 103-12.

ELENA GARRO
Mexico

Elena Garro was born in Puebla, Mexico, in 1920. She graduated from the Faculty of Philosophy at the National Autonomous University of Mexico, where she also distinguished herself as a choreographer. She married the famous Mexican writer Octavio Paz, with whom she had a daughter. They were divorced, and Garro now lives with her daughter in Paris.

In addition to her work as a journalist in Mexico and in the United States, Garro has produced a rich body of solid literature. By 1963 her plays were known in Mexico, many of which were published in a volume entitled *Un hogar sólido* (A Solid Home, 1958). Also in 1963 she published her novel *Recuerdos del porvenir* (*Recollections of Things to Come*), which won her the Xavier Villaurrutia Prize, and has been critically acclaimed because of its innovative use of narrative time.

Garro has written numerous short stories and essays that have appeared in magazines, journals, and anthologies. Some of her work has been translated into English, German, and Swedish. One of her most important collections is *La semana de colores* (The Week of Colors, 1964), in which she skillfully presents an atemporal approach to contemporary Mexican reality.

Elena Garro's use of poetic language, original themes, intriguing characters, and above all her brilliant handling of unconventional narrative and psychological time make her a master of Latin American fiction. Although she has lived most of her adult life in Spain and France, Garro's works always retain the illusive quality of the fantastic that so characterizes Mexican art.

PERFECTO LUNA

It must have been about eleven-thirty when Perfecto Luna passed the last houses in town. At that hour everyone was asleep and no one heard him go by. Everything, thank God, had been simple: lifting the bars on the warehouse door, squeezing through the crack in the door, and going out into the dark street.

"So long as no one robs the warehouse and makes them think: 'That bastard Perfecto, he went in and stole everything there was in the store.'"

But what else could he have done? He wasn't about to give up his life to a prankster! Especially not once he had seen that all there was in the other world were cold gusts of wind. Now the only thing left for him to do was to run, erase the tracks he had left in town and on the roads, throw away his name and look for another one. Leave no trace of Perfecto Luna.

But what name? It wasn't so easy to stop being himself. Since he was little they had called him that. He had always been Perfecto Luna, the mason, the peon, the boy who knew how to do anything, because that's the way the boss had taught him to be. Now he had to forget what he had known and start all over again, so he could be someone else. It made him feel sad for himself: he had been so good-natured and obliging! But that's how life is: each person has his own luck, good or bad. He remembered his friends' names. Crisóforo Flores: there was no way he could call himself that; he would be stealing his friend's soul. Still, maybe he would have to. Crisóforo always went around so sure of himself, so happy, so carefree; he went around like Perfecto Luna had before. Domingo Ibáñez was risky, because that guy had sad nights. So was Justo Montiel; he might take to killing his friends.

He left the path and headed across the fields, in the direction of Actipan. That way, when they were all looking for him around San Pedro, he would be going about his business in Acetepec. He liked the market at Acetepec. As soon as he got there he was going to buy himself a good silk handkerchief and start looking for work. After all, he could do anything. It would take him all night to cross the field of acacia trees, but he was feeling safer. Who would be able to find his tracks in all those *huizaches*? He started hurrying and tripped on a rock. "Now you've done it, Perfecto Luna, you've messed up your toe!" he told himself out loud, to scare away the round silence that was surrounding him at that moment. It was better not to look; the countryside had become enormous. What was starting to happen is what had always happened, for the last five months: the silence would start to grow so big that it was useless to try to say anything. There, for centuries and centuries, not a single noise had been made. He had just said, "Now you've done it, Perfecto Luna, you've messed up your toe!" and yet he hadn't said it. The words had come out silently and stayed there, hanging on the tip of his tongue. He had to get a long ways away from Amate Redondo and from the Perfecto Luna that they were looking for; that's why they had stuck him into those round nights that lasted longer than the days. He stepped up his pace again. The layers of air divided; his nose was trapped in the empty space between two of them, and he could barely breathe. On the other hand, around his eyes and hair, the wind was blowing without blowing, lifting up his hair and turning it cold, so cold that it felt like thousands and thousands of ice cubes were puncturing his head. When would he finally get past that strange territory?

"I'll be Crisóforo Flores. I won't hang around here anymore, and I'll start having a good time with my friends again."

There in front of him, he saw a man crouched down, looking for something in the *huizaches*. He was stooped over close to the ground, trying to see in the dark. Perfecto Luna was pleased to run into someone in that solitude. The man was right there, two steps away, blocking his path. Out of courtesy he said good evening.

"Good evening," replied the stranger, without stopping his search.

"Are you looking for something?" asked Perfecto Luna politely, thinking that's how Crisóforo Flores would say it.

"Yes," answered the stranger in a plaintive voice, "And I can't find it."

"Can I help you, Sir?" offered Perfecto Luna, feeling more and more like Crisóforo Flores.

"If you would be so kind," responded the other man weakly.

Perfecto Luna crouched down to look for the lost object. It must be money, and the white man didn't want to say so, for fear he would be robbed. He could barely see amid the shadows and the rocks. He peered curiously at the stranger's legs; it looked like he was wearing *huaraches* and a red cape. He seemed to move with difficulty, as if he were blind. He felt the ground around him laboriously, clinging to the rocks and bushes.

"Ay, Señor!" said Perfecto Luna, once again feeling as if the words were barely coming out of his mouth. The man paid no attention to him, but kept on searching, turning over rocks.

Perfecto Luna sat down on the ground, feeling discouraged.

"Ay Señor, you wouldn't believe the things that have happened to me!" he went on, forgetting to be Crisóforo Flores. "Look what's left of me, just a pile of skin and bones!"

The confession did not move the stranger, who did not change his position.

"You know, I was Perfecto Luna until tonight!"

"Damn, I'm getting tired of all this looking!" the stranger complained.

"I'll help you in a minute," Perfecto offered, remembering that he was supposed to be the good-natured Crisóforo. He energetically threw himself into the hunt again. The stranger was a long ways off now; he could barely make out his red-and-white form searching among the *huizaches*. Perfecto Luna felt calm in his company. He thought, *This is going to be my last unlucky night; starting tomorrow, when I'm Crisóforo Flores, no one will ever remember who I was.*

"Sir!" he shouted optimistically, feeling like it was already the next day. "Do you believe in the dead?"

"In the dead?" the other man asked, surprised. His voice came from deep down.

"Yes, Sir, but not the dead incarnate, the other ones . . ."

"The other ones?" the stranger asked, pausing in his search.

"Yes, the other ones," Perfecto answered with aplomb, becoming Crisóforo Flores more and more. "Just imagine, I used to be Perfecto Luna, and I had to stop being him, all because of a dead man!"

"Ah!" responded the stranger.

"Did you come through Amate Redondo? You must have met Don Celso, the owner of the warehouse. Everything that I was, I owe to him. He taught me how to work, when I was Perfecto Luna. I must have been about five years old when I started running errands for him. I grew up with him, because I was an orphan at birth. 'See, Perfecto, this is how you plane wood. Stay here, Perfecto. Now that you know how much a measure of corn costs, you can ring it up here, on the cash register.' Because Don Celso has the only cash register in Amate Redondo. He's the only one who has worked at it, even though they say he steals grams from the kilos. And that's how I made a living, working, until Don Celso decided to build the famous annexes."

Perfecto Luna grew quiet. He remembered that, until that day, he had been very self-confident. Don Celso told him to demolish the huts that were behind the warehouse so he could build some houses like the ones in Mexico City. He came back with the hoe and started tearing down those shacks. How long did it take him to do the job? Let's say a month; and at the end of that month everything was cleared away. Up until that day he had also been happy. What was missing? Nothing. He was treated well and had his friends' respect. No one wished him harm. It happened one April 4th, when Don Celso said to him, "Dig the ditches so we can lay the foundations." At about noon, as he was deepening the ditch, he found the dead man. It was an old dead body, because all that was left of him were bones. He could see him as if it was yesterday, glittering in the sun, with his arms crossed over his ribs. *He must have come to a bad end, because he doesn't have a head. Who could have killed him? Where can his head be?*

"Just imagine, Sir, his head was missing; someone must have chopped it off!" The stranger didn't say a word.

"The bad part, Sir, is that when I was Perfecto Luna I used to like to be wicked. 'Perfecto!' Don Celso's wife yelled at me, 'come eat.' I put my blanket in the dead man's hole and went to dinner. I remember that, while they were heating up the tortillas, I was laughing inside."

"'What are you laughing at?' they asked me.

"'The only one who knows is me,' I said.

"And the only one who knew was me. After dinner I wrapped up the little bones in my blanket and took them to my room. 'You'll see, you goddamn dead man!' I said to him. The day came when I found myself making the adobe bricks . . . ," and Perfecto could once again picture himself stirring the dry leaves into the mud and whistling.

"'Look at that guy enjoying himself; I wish everyone worked like that!' Don Celso would say. And it was true, because as long as I was Perfecto Luna, any old thing would make me happy. I remember that I was rolling a cigarette when the idea came to me. I went over to my room, took out a toe bone, and buried it in an adobe brick that I had put out in the sun to dry. 'Since they've done you the favor of burying you in pieces, I'm going to finish the job for you,' I said to him. I made a mark on the adobe, so I would know that a piece of his grave was there. Then I took out a rib and stuck it in another marked brick. And so on until I had used up all the little bones.

"'Hey, Don Celso, what happens to a dead man who's cut up in pieces?'

"'He goes crazy, boy, looking for his pieces.'

"'Ha, ha, ha.' And I went to see my little graves, content. How wonderful it is to be young and light-hearted, Sir!" Perfecto Luna said, sitting down again on the ground and looking around for the other man, who went about his business, paying no attention to him. Sadly, he thought that no one cared if he, Perfecto Luna, had been light-hearted, and that because of it, he had to stop being himself. He remembered how he began to build the houses: he carefully divided up the adobe bricks containing the bones among the different walls of the houses; not a space was left in the complex in which "the man with no head" wasn't buried. And he kept right on opening up windows, raising roofs, building doors, whistling and laughing to himself all the while.

"'Look, Perfecto, they turned out pretty; put a blue wash on them!' Don Celso said to me. I used the brightest blue, Sir, to cheer up the whitewashed burial site."

And he laughed again, in spite of himself, remembering. *I hope the Juárez family will come live here, and that during the night 'the man with no head' will grab their feet*, he had thought to himself, once the houses were finished. Don Celso told him to stand guard over them, so kids wouldn't go in there and write on the walls. They smelled new: like lime and mortar. The walls and the floor bricks were still damp; in all the rooms there was the presence of cleanliness, of something that hadn't been touched by people. Perfecto Luna took his shirts, his blanket and grass mat, and installed himself in one of the rooms. He was tired; he took off his *huaraches*, stretched out on the mat and watched the night through the window. The sky was calm and clear and, from where he lay, he could see two stars shining. He shut his eyes halfway. *Who would have thought that he would do all that work all by himself!* He opened his eyes and looked proudly at his work of art: his gaze ran over the roof, walls, door, and rested on the window again. Underneath it, a little protrusion marked one of the tombs of "the man with no head." *Who darkened the night?* He felt around for the candle that he had left next to the mat. He stretched out his arm, which felt like it had become very short; the room, on the other hand, had grown enormously and the candle was a long ways off, beyond his reach. He resigned himself to the darkness. He opened his eyes wide, trying to make something out, anything, but the shadows grew more and more dense. *I think that's how people get scared.* He kept still. All at once he saw that the marker he had put on the adobe was shining. *It's the man with no head!* His heart started beating so hard that it seemed like he was being carried away by a rushing river. He felt like he was going deaf. The only thing left for him to do was to wait for morning. But the night stretched out into many nights. When day broke, he saw that his grass mat was damp with sweat.

"What's wrong with you, Perfecto? You look wild-eyed."

He didn't know what to answer. He barely tasted his coffee, thinking that it was going to get dark any time. Sadly, he sat down in the courtyard of the annexes, to watch the sun beating against the roofs.

"The day's just about over . . ." he said with distress. He moved his mat and trinkets to the second room. Night returned and he went to bed, not daring to look out the window.

I'm not going to look at the night anymore. And he squeezed his eyes tightly shut. A whirr of wings filled the room, beating as they went up and down the walls. They passed over his forehead and his body. He began to freeze. Which goddamn bone could be making that noise that he couldn't hear? And, that night, it lasted longer than the night before. He wanted to think about how to satisfy the dead man, but the wings were beating so fast that he could not formulate his thoughts.

"You caught a chill, Perfecto," they told him.

And he could not tell them about what had happened the night before with those cold wings. The sun set, but his knees were still frozen stiff. He didn't have time to warm himself up, because that day the sun hardly lasted any time at all. It seemed like the rooster had barely crowed, when he heard the hens settling onto their roosts to go to sleep. Completely disheartened, he moved his mat, blanket and candle to the third room.

Goddamn dead man, rest in peace and stop making trouble for me; I never hurt anyone!

He wrapped himself up in his cape so he wouldn't get cold, and closed his eyes so he wouldn't see the shadows surrounding him. From a corner of the room a whirlwind started; it hummed violently and perched next to his left ear. It entered his ear at high speed, deafening him.

Tell me, you blasted dead man, what do you want me to do for you? he would have liked to say, but the words stuck to his tongue. Then they wrapped around it, like they had wrapped up Anselmo's leg after he was cut up in a fight. Immobile, with his tongue tied, he endured the whirlwind that filled his body with cramps.

"It's morning . . ." he said with difficulty, when he went into the kitchen to get some hot coffee.

"What's wrong with you, boy? Why are you talking that way? It sounds like the cat got your tongue."

And Perfecto Luna hung his head and thought that this day, too, would be over very soon.

"Don Celso, will you let Alambritos sleep with me?"

"What the hell, boy? What do you want him for? Is the bogy man after you?"

He barely had time to grab Alambritos before night had already fallen. He tied the dog up with a long twine rope attached to the door latch in the next room, and lay down on the mat. He was getting skinny and his laugh had died on him! The darkness began to descend from the roof, like a thick black cloud that was out to crush him. *What do you want me to do for you, dead man? I can't undo the annexes, to unite your bones again.* He had just finished thinking that when he saw Alambritos come dragging himself along the ground, staying close to the floor like a sticker, to lie down next to him. A howl came out of Alambritos' new shape smashed flat like a sheet of paper. *It's true that you're here*, Perfecto Luna thought. *What do you want? I'll give you whatever you want if you'll just go away.* At that moment the layers of shadow fell on top of him like a heavy blanket and left him without thoughts. It was him that it wanted! All night he lay there under that black cover.

"Look, boy, your nose is smashed!" they said when they saw him come out of the room. His legs could barely support him.

"Don Celso, how long does a night last?"

"As long as every night."

Now the days were barely a streak of light between two immense nights. He didn't even have time to put on his *huaraches* and take them off again. Clothes began to wear out his body. What chances were there that he could go trim his moustache and hair! As soon as it dawned, there was the night back already! He didn't even have time to eat, and he was turning into skin and bones. He went from one room to another until he had worked his way through them all, and in every one of them he found the presence of the dead man waiting to pull him out of his skin. From where he crouched in a corner of the courtyard, he could hear Crisóforo playing the harmonica and singing with his friends in the distance. They were in the *cantina*, for sure. This realization sunk him deeper into sadness, since it meant that night was out there waiting for him.

"What's wrong with you, boy? If you keep on like this, it won't be long before you give up the ghost."

"Don Celso, let me sleep in the warehouse!"

That way "the man with no head" would wander, furious, through all the rooms without finding him, since he would be sleeping amid the bunches of cinnamon and sacks of corn.

"Go ahead, but if you're doing it out of fear, you're not going to lose it there."

He moved his grass mat to the warehouse. It seemed like this night was falling more calmly. The warehouse was animated: the clients were having one last round of tequila; Don Celso was balancing his books; it smelled like alcohol and spices. He felt relieved. It struck ten o'clock and Crisóforo Flores, his friend, downed one last shot.

"See you around tomorrow, if you wake up, that is, 'cause you're looking more and more like a dead man . . ." And he went off confidently, with his hat cocked.

Don Celso told him good night. Perfecto Luna closed the warehouse doors, noting that they were well-greased, then put up the bar that stretched from wall to wall, and lay down on top of the counter, leaving the gas lamp burning. With the light on, "the man with no head" wouldn't dare. With delight he breathed in the smell of lard, mixed with dust from the beans, and, feeling safe, he stretched out. A noise arose in the backroom. He looked for the candle and matches, but they were in the pocket of his muslin shirt. The noise grew louder. It was wiser to not go see what was happening. Another noise echoed the first one: something was falling, falling endlessly, whistling softly. It sounded like two sacks of corn were emptying out their grain through a hole.

Now he's done it; the bastard is slitting open the sacks!

The whistling multiplied. All the sacks were spilling out at great speed. The backroom was filling up with corn, he was sure of it. Cautiously, he peered in that direction: the doorway, filled with grain, was overflowing, and the corn was advancing into the store. Stunned, he looked around him. He was surrounded by sacks. Up above the exit door there were boards piled high with agave-fiber bags. At that moment the first sack opened up and the grain began falling silently, in a golden stream, onto the ground. Then a second sack was perforated, then a third, then a fourth, then the whole store rained corn from every wall. The space of the counter grew narrower. He saw that the street door, which he had barred so carefully, was being blocked, since the sacks above it were also being pierced. He got up as best he could and, taking long strides, burying himself in grain up to his thighs, he reached the door. With difficulty he lifted the bar and, with great effort, he managed to open the door a crack, sniff the night, and go out into the street.

"Right about now, Sir, I'd be back there buried in corn, and 'the sonofabitch with no head' would have me by the hair for the rest of eternity. But I got away from him. And I got away not just from Amate Redondo, but from Perfecto Luna, because when he looks for him, he isn't going to find him anymore. Now I'm Crisóforo Flores. That's what you call having a little presence of mind! Don't you think, Sir? That's why I was asking you if you believed in dead men, because before 'the man with no head' I didn't believe either."

"Ah!" answered the stranger from deep down. And he began straightening himself up, with difficulty.

"I'm going to help you look, now that I've told you the sad story of the man who was Perfecto Luna."

"Never mind!" answered the stranger, on his feet beside the narrator. The latter barely had time to see the faceless face of his new friend: the stranger's body ended at his shoulders.

"He was possessed by the devil!" said Don Celso the next day. "He spilled out all my corn and went and died out in the middle of the *huizache* field. Goddamn! And that Perfecto Luna seemed like such a good boy!"

Translated by Cynthia Steele

Bibliography: Elena Garro

Fiction

Garro, Elena. "The Tiztla Robbery." *Americas* 7 July 1959: 21-25. Rpt. in *Mexican Life* 35.9 (1959): 20.

———. *Los recuerdos del porvenir*. Mexico City: Joaquín Mortiz, 1963. Rpt. in Mexico City: Joaquín Mortiz, 1977.

———. *La semana de colores*. Xalapa: Universidad Veracruzana, 1964.

———. "La culpa es de los Tlaxcaltecas." *Narrativa mexicana de hoy*. Madrid: Alianza Editorial, 1969. 75-93. Rpt. in *Cuentistas mexicanas siglo XX*. Ed. Aurora M. Ocampo. Mexico City: Universidad Nacional Autónoma de México, 1976. 109-22.

———. *Recollections of Things to Come*. Trans. Ruth L.C. Simms. Austin: University of Texas Press, 1969. Rpt. in Austin: University of Texas Press, 1987.

———. "¿Qué hora es?" *14 mujeres escriben cuentos*. Ed. Elsa de Llarena. México City: Federación Editorial Mexicana, 1975. 134-49.

———. *Andamos huyendo Lola*. Mexico City: Joaquín Mortiz, 1980.

———. *Testimonios sobre Mariana*. Mexico City: Grijalbo, 1981.

———. *Reencuentro de personajes*. Mexico City: Grijalbo, 1982.

———. *La casa junto al río*. Mexico City: Grijalbo, 1983.

———. "The Day We Were Dogs." Trans. Tona Wilson. *Contemporary Women Authors of Latin America: New Translations*. Ed. Doris Meyer and Margarite Fernández Olmos. New York: Brooklyn College Press, 1983. 186-91.

———. "It's the Fault of the Tlaxcaltecas." Trans. Alberto Manguel. *Other Fires: Short Fiction by Latin American Women*. Ed. Alberto Manguel. Toronto: Lester & Orpen Dennys, 1986. 159-78.

———. "Perfecto Luna." *Puerta abierta: la nueva escritora latinoamericana*. Ed. Caridad L. Silva-Velázquez and Nora Erro-Orthmann. Mexico City: Joaquín Mortiz, 1986. 131-39.

———. "The Tree." Trans. Evelyn Picón Garfield. *Women's Fiction From Latin America: Selections from Twelve Contemporary Authors*. Ed. Evelyn Picón Garfield. Detroit: Wayne State University Press, 1988. 69-86.

Essays

Garro, Elena. "Testimonios sobre Mariana." *Espejo* [Mexico City] 4 (1967).

Theater

Garro, Elena. *Un hogar sólido y otras piezas en un acto*. Xalapa: Universidad Veracruzana, 1958. Rpt. in Xalapa: Universidad Veracruzana, 1983.

———. "La mudanza." *La palabra y el hombre* 3.10 (1959): 263-74.

———. "A Solid House." *Evergreen Review* 2.7 (1959): 62-74. Rpt. in *Selected Latin American One Act Plays*. Ed. Francesca Colecchia and Julio Matas. Pittsburgh: University of Pittsburgh Press, 1973. 20.

———. "La señora en su balcón." *Tercera antología de obras en un acto*. Comp. Maruxa Vilalta. Mexico City: Colección Teatro Mexicano, 1960. 25-40.

———. "El árbol." *Revista Mexicana de Literatura*. 3-4 (1963): 10-31.

———. "Los perros." *Revista de la Universidad de México*. 21.7 (1965): 20-23.

———. "The Lady on Her Balcony." Trans. Beth Miller. *Shantih 3* 3 (1976): 36-44.

———. "The Dogs." Trans. Beth Miller. *Latin American Literary Review* 8.15 (1979): 68-85.

———. *Felipe Angeles*. Mexico City: Universidad Nacional Autónoma de México 1979.

Criticism on the Works of Elena Garro

Anderson, Robert K. "La cuentística-mágico-realista de Elena Garro." *Selecta* 3 (1982): 117-21.

———. "La realidad temporal en *Los recuerdos del porvenir.*" *Explicación de Textos Literarios* 9 (1980-81): 25-29.

———. "Myth and Archetype in *Recollections of Things to Come.*" *Studies in Twentieth Century Literature* 9.2 (1985): 213-27.

Anderson Imbert, Enrique. "Elena Garro." *Historia de la Literatura Hispano-americana. Época contemporánea.* Mexico City: Fondo de Cultura Económica, 1974. 408.

Avalos Facaci, Rafael. "El mundo maravilloso y alucinante de Elena Garro y Marcel Camus." *México en la Cultura* 748 21 Jul. 1963. 8.

Bárcenas, Angel. "*La dama boba.*" *Revista Mexicana de Cultura* 889 12 Apr. 1964. 15.

Batis, Huberto. "*Los recuerdos del porvenir.*" *La Cultura en México* 103 5 Feb. 1964. xviii.

———. "*La semana de colores.*" *La Cultura en México* 163 31 Mar. 1965. xvi.

Bermúdez, María Elvira. "Dramaturgas." *Diograma de la Cultura* [Literary Supplement to *Excelsior*] 5 Apr. 1959. 4.

———. "La novela mexicana en 1963." *Diograma de la Cultura* [Literary Supplement to *Excelsior*] 19 Jan. 1964. 8.

Beverido Duhalt, Francisco. "*Los perros* de Elena Garro" *Texto Crítico* 12.34-35 (1986): 118-35.

Bonfils, Alicia de. *La literatura Cristera.* Mexico City: Instituto de Antropología e Historia, 1970.

Bradú, Fabienne. "Testimonio sobre Elena Garro." *Señas particulares: escritora.* Mexico City: Fondo de Cultura Económica, 1987. 13-28.

Brushwood, John. *Mexico in its Novel.* Austin: University of Texas Press, 1966. 52-53.

Callan, Richard J. "Analytical Psychology and Garro's 'Los pilares de Doña Blanca.'" *Latin American Theater Review* 16.2 (1983): 31-35.

———. "El misterio femenino en *Los perros* de Elena Garro." *Revista Iberoamericana* 46.110-111 (1980): 225-31.

Cantón, Wilberto. "El teatro de Elena Garro: la poesía contra el absurdo." *La Cultura en México* 191 13 Oct. 1965. XV.

Carballo, Emmanuel. "Elena Garro." *Protagonistas de la literatura mexicana.* Mexico City: Consejo Nacional de Fomento Educativo, 1986. 490-518.

———. "El mundo mágico de Elena Garro" *Siempre.* [Mexico] 24 Feb. 1965. xv-xvi.

———. "La novela y el cuento." *La Cultura en México* 151 6 Jan. 1965. v.

———. "Todo es presente." *La Cultura en México* 109 18 Mar. 1964. xix.

———. "La vida y la obra de Elena Garro." *Sábado Uno más uno* 24 Jan. 1981. 2-5.

Castro, Dolores. "Los hechos y la cultura." *Nivel* 22 25 Oct. 1964. 12.

Catay. "Dos obras mexicanas . . ." *El Gallo Ilustrado* [Literary Supplement to *El Día*] 44 28 Apr. 1963. 4

Cypess, Sandra Messinger. "Titles as Signs in the Translation of Dramatic Texts." *Translation Perspectives II: Selected Papers, 1984-1985*. Ed. Marilyn Gaddis Rose. Binghamton: Tr. Research & Instruction Program, State Univ. of New York at Binghamton, 1985. 94-104.

———. "Visual and Verbal Distances in the Mexican Theater: The Plays of Elena Garro." *Woman as Myth and Metaphor in Latin American Literature*. Eds. Carmelo Virgilio and Naomi Lindstrom. Columbia: U of Missouri Press, 1985. 44-62.

Dallal, Alberto. "*Los recuerdos del porvenir.*" *Universidad de México* 18.6 (1964): 31.

Dauster, Frank. "Elena Garro." *Historia del Teatro Hispanoamericano Siglos XIX y XX*. 2 ed. Mexico City: Ediciones de Andrea, 1973. 104-05.

———. "Elena Garro y sus *Recuerdos del porvenir*" *Journal of Spanish Studies: Twentieth Century* 8 (1980): 57-65.

———. *Ensayos sobre teatro hispanoamericano*. Mexico City: Secretaría de Educación Pública, 1975.

———. "Success and the Latin American Writer." *Contemporary Women Authors of Latin America: Introductory Essays*. Eds. Doris Meyer and Margarite Fernández Olmos. Brooklyn: Brooklyn College Press, 1983. 16-21.

———. *Historia del teatro hispanoamericano: Siglos XIX y XX*. Mexico City: Ediciones de Andrea, 1966. 23, 84-85.

———. "El teatro de Elena Garro: Evasión e ilusión." *Revista Iberoamericana* 30.57 (1964): 81-89.

"Dos novelas mexicanas." *México en la Cultura* 768 8 Dec. 1963. 3.

Duncan, Cynthia. "*La culpa es de los tlaxcaltecas*: A Reevaluation of Mexico's Past Through Myth." *Crítica Hispánica* 7.2 (1985): 105-20.

Durán, Manuel. "El premio Villaurrutia y la novela mexicana contemporánea." *La Torre* 13.49 (1965): 233-38.

Durán Rosado, Esteban. "Memorias del pueblo de Ixtepec." *Revista Mexicana de Cultura* 879 2 Feb. 1964. 5.

Earle, Peter G. "*Los recuerdos del porvenir* y la fuerza de las palabras." *Homenaje a Luis Alberto Sánchez*. Ed. Robert G. Mead Jr. Madrid: Insula, 1983. 235-42.

Echeverría, Miriam B. "Texto y represión en 'Los perros' de Elena Garro." *De la crónica a la nueva narrativa mexicana*. Eds. Merlín H. Foster and Julio Ortega. Mexico City: Oasis, 1986. 423-29.

Fernández de Ciocca, María Inés. "*Los recuerdos del porvenir* o la novela del tiempo." *Revista Interamericana de Bibliografía/Inter-American Review of Bibliography* 36.1 (1986): 39-51.

Flynn, Susan Kingston. "The Alienated Hero in Contemporary Spanish American Drama." Diss. University of Illinois at Urban-Champaign, 1977.

Foster, David William. *Dictionary of Contemporary Latin American Authors*. Tempe: Center for Latin American Studies, Arizona State University, 1975. 45.

Fox-Lockert, Lucía. "Elena Garro: *Los recuerdos del porvenir* (1963)." *Women Novelists in Spain and Spanish America*. Metuchen, NJ: The Scarecrow Press, 1977. 228-40.

———. "The Meaning of Freedom in the Mexican Feminist Novel." *Sixth Conference of Ethnic Studies*. LaCrosse: University of Wisconsin-LaCrosse, 1978.

Francescato, Martha Paley. "Acción y reflexión en cuentos de Fuentes, Garro, y Pacheco." *Romance Quaterly* 33.1 (1986): 99-112.

Galván, Delia V. "Felipe Angeles de Elena Garro: Sacrificio heroico." *Latin American Theater Review* 20.2 (1987): 29-35.

———. "The Recent Writings of Elena Garro, 1979-83." *DAI* 47.6 (1986): 2173A-2174A.

———. *Las obras recientes de Elena Garro*. Querétaro, Mexico: Universidad Autonóma de Querétaro, 1988.

García, Kay Sauer. "Woman and Her Signs in the Novels of Elena Garro: A Feminist and Semiotic Analysis." *DAI* 48.3 (1987): 660A.

García Barragán, Guadalupe. "El tema del cacique y la cuestión religiosa en *Bramadero* y *Los recuerdos del porvenir*." Ed. Walter C. Kraft. *Proceedings: Pacific Northwest Conference on Foreign Languages*. Corvallis: Oregon University. 310-16.

García Ponce, Juan. "Poesía en voz alta." *Universidad de México* 11.12 (1957): 29.

Glantz, Margo. "'Andamos huyendo Lola': el niño y el adulto se vuelven expósitos." *Sábado* [Literary Supplement to *Uno más uno*] 23 May 1981. 21.

González Peña, Carlos. *History of Mexican Literature*. Trans. Gusta Barfield Nance and Florence Johnson Dunstan. Dallas: Southern Methodist University Press, 1968. 455.

———. *Historia de la literatura mexicana: desde los orígenes hasta nuestros días*. Mexico City: Editorial Porrúa, S.A., 1981. 325.

Guillén, Pedro. "Cultura en México." *Revista Mexicana de Cultura* 882 23 Feb. 1964. 2.

Johnson, Harvey L. "Elena Garro's Attitudes Toward Mexican Society." *South Central Bulletin* 40.4 (1980): 150-52.

———. "Elena Garro y el teatro de lo absurdo." *El teatro de Iberoamérica*. Mexico City: Instituto Internacional de Literatura Iberoamericana, 1966. 123-25.

———. "Papel de la mujer en la obra teatral de seis escritoras mexicanas." *Actas del Sexto Congreso Internacional de Hispanistas* (22-26 Aug, 1977) Eds. Alan M. Gordon and Evelyn Rugg. Toronto: Department of Spanish & Portuguese, Univ of Toronto, 1980. 443-45.

Landeros, Carlos. "Con Elena Garro." *Diograma de la Cultura* [Literary Supplement to *Excelsior*] 24 Oct. 1965. 3.

Langford, Walter. *The Mexican Novel Comes of Age*. Notre Dame, IN: University of Notre Dame Press, 1971. 187-88.

Larson, Catherine. "*Recollections of Things to Come*: Time in the Theater of Elena Garro." *Latin American Theater Review* 22.2 (1989): 5-17.

Larson, Ross. *Fantasy and Imagination in the Mexican Narrative*. Tempe, AZ: Arizona State University, Center for Latin American Studies, 1977. 98-100.

Lerín, Manuel. "Relatos desquiciantes." *Revista Mexicana de Cultura* 926 27 Dec. 1964. 15.

Llarena, E. "Elena Garro: *La semana de colores*." *El rehilete* 13 (1965): 61.

———. "*Recuerdos del porvenir*." *El rehilete* 10 (1964): 49.

Loustaunau, Martha Ocemke. "Mexico's Contemporary Women Novelists." Diss. The University of New Mexico, 1973.

———. *Teatro mexicano del siglo XX*. Mexico City: Fondo de Cultura Económica, 1970. 57.

Maíz, Magdalena. "Una aproximación al paisaje cotidiano: Narrativa femenina mexicana." *Cuadernos de Aldeeu* 1.2-3 (1983): 347-54.

Marx, Joan Frances. "Aztec Imagery in the Narrative Works of Elena Garro: A Thematic Approach." *DAI* 47.1 (1986): 193A.

McMahon, Dorothy. "Changing Trends in Spanish American Literature." *Books Abroad* 39.1 (1965): 15-20.

Méndez Ródenas, Adriana. "Tiempo femenino, tiempo ficticio: *Los recuerdos del porvenir*, de Elena Garro." *Revista Iberoamericana* 51.132-133 (1985): 843-51.

Mendoza, María Luisa. "Naranja dulce y limón partido en el Teatro, de Elena Garro." *El Día* 11.386 21 July. 1963. 4.

———. "El porvenir de los recuerdos." *El Día* 13 Jan. 1964. 8.

Menton, Seymour. "Sin embargo: La nueva cuentista femenina en Mexico." *Tinta* 1.5 (1987): 35-37.

Mercado, Enrique. "Elena Garro: Los fantasmas de la realidad, de la imaginación alegórica a la cotidianidad de la prosa." *La Cultura en México* 100 24 June 1981: 2-7.

Meyer, Doris. "Alienation and Escape in Elena Garro's *La semana de colores*." *Hispanic Review* 55.2 (1987): 153-64.

Miller, Beth and Alfonso González, ed. "Elena Garro." *26 autoras del México actual*. Mexico City: Costa-Amic, 1978. 199-219.

Montenegro, Patricia G. "Structures of Power and Their Representations in Three Fictional Works by Elena Garro." *DAI* 47.9 (1987): 3441A.

Mora, Gabriela. "*La dama boba* de Elena Garro: verdad y ficción, teatro y metateatro." *Latin American Theater Review* 16.12 (1983): 15-22.

———. "*Los perros* y *La mudanza* de Elena Garro: diseño social y virtualidad feminista." *Latin American Theater Review* 8.2 (1975): 5-14.

———. "Rebeldes fracasadas: Una lectura feminista de *Andarse por las ramas* y *La señora en su balcón*." *Plaza: Literatura y Crítica* 5-6 (1981-1982): 115-31.

———. "A Thematic Exploration of the Works of Elena Garro." *Latin American Women Writers Yesterday and Today*. Ed. Yvette E. Miller and Charles M. Tatum. Pittsburgh: Carnegie-Mellon, 1975. 91-97.

Mora, Juan Miguel. *Panorama del teatro en México*. Mexico City: Latinoamericana, 1970.

Muncy, Michele. "Encuentro con Elena Garro." *Hispanic Journal* 7.2 (1986): 65-71.

Neglia, Erminio G. "La escenificación del fluir psíquico en el teatro hispano-americano." *Hispania* 58 (1978): 884-89.

Ocampo de Gómez, Aurora M. and Ernesto Prado Velázquez. *Diccionario de escritores mexicanos*. Mexico City: Universidad Nacional Autónoma de México, 1967. 135-37.

Orenstein, Gloria. "Surrealism and Women: The Occultation of the Goddess: Elena Garro, Joyce Mansour, Leonora Carrington." *The Theater of the Marvelous Surrealism and the Contemporary Stage*. New York: New York University Press, 1975. 99-147.

Ostergaard, Ane-Grethe. "El realismo de los signos escénicos en el teatro de Elena Garro." *Latin American Theater Review* 16.1 (1982): 53-65.

Oviedo, José Miguel. "Notas a una (deprimente) lectura del teatro hispanoamericano." *Revista Iberoamericana* 37.76-77 (1971): 753-62.

Piazza, Luis Guillermo. "México y el tiempo en tres novelas muy recientes." *Cuadernos del Congreso por la Libertad de la Cultura* 84 (1966): 108.

Portal, Marta. "Elena Garro." *Proceso narrativo de la revolución mexicana*. Madrid: Cultura Hispánica, 1977. 223-32.

"*Los recuerdos del porvenir*." *Boletin del Centro Mexicano de Escritores* 11.2 (1964): 3.

Resnick, Margery, and Isabelle de Courtivron. *Women Writers in Translation: An Annotated Bibliography*. New York & London: Garland Publications, 1984. 235.

Reyes, Mara. "Diograma teatral." *Diograma de la Cultura* [Literary Supplement to *Excelsior*] 28 Apr. 1963. 7.

Reyes Nevares, Salvador. "'*Un hogar' sólido*." *México en la Cultura* 517 8 Feb. 1959. 2.

———. "'El hogar' sólido." de Elena Garro." *México en la Cultura* 521 8 Mar. 1959. 2.

———. "El saldo de la novela: 1963." *La Cultura en México* 99 8 Jan. 1964. iii.

Rivera, Margarita Tavera. "Strategies for Dismantling Power Relations: The Dramatic Texts of Elena Garro." *DAI* 47.6 (1986): 2175A.

Robles, Martha. "Tres mujeres en la literatura mexicana: Rosario Castellanos, Elena Garro, Inés Arredondo." *Cuadernos Americanos* 246.1 (1983): 223-35.

Rosas, Patricia. "Destiempo y nostalgia, Elena Garro y *Los recuerdos del porvenir*." *Semana de Bellas Artes* [Mexico] 152 29 Oct. 1980: 10-12.

Roses, Lorraine. "La expresión dramática de la inconformidad social en cuatro dramaturgas hispanoamericanas." *Plaza: Literatura y Crítica* 5-6 (1981-1982): 97-114.

Rosser, Harry L. "Form and Content in Elena Garro's *Los recuerdos del porvenir*." *Revista Canadiense de Estudios Hispánicos* 2 (1978): 181-95.

———. "Regional Reactions to Incursions From the Center: Yáñez, Garro, Mojarro." *Conflict and Transition in Rural Mexico*. Boston: Crossroads Press, 1980. 23-46.

Rubio de Lertora, Patricia. "Funciones del nivel descriptivo en *Los recuerdos del porvenir*." *Cahiers du Monde Hispanique et Luso-Bresilien* 49 (1987): 129-38.

Salazar, Carmen. "In Illo Tempore: Elena Garro's *La semana de colores*." *In Retrospect: Essays on Latin American Literature*. Eds. Elizabeth S. Rogers and Timothy J.Rogers. York, SC: Spanish Literature Publishing Co., 1987. 121-27.

San Pedro, Teresa Anta. "La heroe de mil caras: Una caracterización de los personajes femeninos en la narrativa de Elena Garro." *DAI* 48.3 (1987): 664A-665A.

Seligson, Esther. "In Illo Tempore (Aproximación a la obra de Elena Garro)." *Revista de la Universidad de México* 29.12 (1975): 9-10.

"*La semana de colores*." *Boletín Bibliográfico de la Secretaría de Hacienda y Crédito Público* 311 15 Jan 1965. 20-21.

Solórzano, Carlos. "El teatro de Elena Garro: una nueva frescura literaria." *La Cultura en México* 167 28 Apr. 1965. XVIII-XIX.

Sommers, Joseph. "*Los recuerdos del porvenir*." *Books Abroad* 39.1 (1965): 68-69.

Stoll, Anita. *A Different Reality: Essays on the Works of Elena Garro*. Lewisburg, PA: Bucknell University Press, 1990.

"Un hogar sólido" by Elena Garro. *Latin American Theater Review* 2.1 (1968): 77.

Vázquez Amaral, José. "La novela de Luisa Josefina Hernández, Carlos Fuentes y Elena Garro." *El Gallo Illustrado* [Mexico] 191 (1966): 2-3.

Verwey, Antonieta Eva. *Mito y palabra poética en Elena Garro*. Mexico City: Universidad Autónoma de Querétaro, 1982.

Villaseñor, Raúl. "Libros." *Vida Universitaria* 26 Jan. 1964. 7.

Woodyard, George. "The Theater of the Absurd in Spanish America." *Comparative Drama* 3.3 (1969): 183-92.

Zendejas, Francisco. "El premio Villaurrutia de Literatura." *Diograma de la Cultura* [Lit. Supp. to *Excelsior*] 1 Mar. 1964. 7.

ANGÉLICA GORODISCHER
Argentina

A ngélica Gorodischer was born in 1928, in Buenos Aires, where she spent her early childhood immersed in books. This proved to be fundamental to her artistic development and her perception of the world. She married, had three children and has lived in Rosario for many years, although she travels abroad frequently to deliver lectures. Gorodischer's first literary endeavor was a detective story entitled "En verano, a la siesta y con Martina" (In Summer, During Siesta and With Martina). It appeared in the magazine *Vea y lea* (See and Read) in 1964 and won her an award in the III Contest of Detective Short Stories.

Although she had a late start, her literary career has been steady and fruitful. She has cultivated a variety of narrative expressions including several fabulous science fiction stories about the intergalactic adventures of a businessman named Trafalgar Medrano.

In 1973 Gorodischer's publication of the volume *Bajo las jubeas en flor* marked a high point in her career. Its story entitled "Los embriones del violeta" (The Purple Embryos) is considered the best Argentinian science fiction story of all time. This collection shows Gorodischer's brilliant mastery of stylistic complexities, as well as her extraordinary imagination, in presenting the reader a strange world in a familiar, everyday manner.

Gorodischer revealed herself as a militant feminist with the publication of her work *Mala noche y parir hembra* (Such a Bad Night . . . And to Birth a Female, 1983), a collection of twelve short stories in which the author blends reality and fantasy to create a series of complex, original and humorous texts.

UNDER THE YUBAYAS
IN BLOOM

I entered Sweet Memory of the Yubayas in Bloom Penitentiary an hour after having reached land. As I was the captain of the ship, they reserved for me the most rigorous punishment: they took my men to another prison, whose regimen was more benign, according to what I was given to understand, and I never saw them again. It was not that we had committed some terrible crime in disembarking there; it was not that they considered all foreigners dangerous outlaws. It was much simpler and, to use the appropriate word, more infernal.

Sweet Memory of the Yubayas in Bloom was an enormous, irregular building which rose up in the middle of a saltpeter plain. When the sun was high you couldn't look out because the reflection burned your eyes. I never got to know the entire establishment, and I can't say it was for lack of time. But it was a completely stupid building, of wood and stone: construction seemed to have been started in the central patio, which was paved with stones and surrounded with cells. Sitting in a corner, looking at it, I supposed that later they had built the other pavilions, one above the other, or touching at the vertices, or interconnecting, and that the old cells had been converted into offices and storage rooms. The result was a confusion of constructions of different shapes and sizes, put up in any way, in any place, and all highly disheartening. There were windows that opened onto other windows, stairways in the middle of a bathroom, passageways that led to a blind wall, galleries that at one time, perhaps, had dominated a space which later was outfitted with bannisters and guardrails, doors that didn't open or that opened onto a wall, cupolas that had been converted into rooms one had to enter doubled over, contiguous rooms that adjoined in only a roundabout way.

But I am getting ahead of events. I had scarcely set foot on land when they arrested me, read me a long memorandum in which the charges were expounded, and took me to Sweet Memory of the Yubayas in Bloom. No one wanted to answer my questions as to the rest of the crew, as to whether there would be a trial, as to whether there could be a defense. No one wanted to listen to my explanations. I was simply taken prisoner. The iron gate at the entrance was lifted to let us pass, and my guardians handed me over to the Director of the prison, after a reading of the same memorandum. The Director said, "Aha!" and looked at me, I think, with scorn; no, no I don't think, I am certain. He pushed a button and two uniformed guards entered, with whips in their hands and pistols in their belts. The Director said, take him away, and they took me away. It was that simple. They put me in a little room and told me to undress. I thought they were going to strike me, but I undressed anyway. What choice did I have? They did not strike me, however. After searching my clothes and taking my papers, pencil, handkerchief, watch, money, and everything, absolutely everything they found, they examined my mouth, ears, hair, navel, armpits, crotch, smiling, gesturing approvingly and commenting favorably on the size, shape and possibilities of my genitals. They laid me out on the floor, none too gently, spread my buttocks and toes, and again made me open my mouth. Finally they left off and held out pants and a shirt and nothing else and said, get dressed. "What about my clothes?" I asked. They threw everything in a corner, the money as well as the documents, and shrugged their shoulders. Let's go, they said. That was the first time I lost my bearings in the building. Not they: they made their way surefooted like elephants, slamming doors and navigating passageways in all tranquility. We ended up on the patio and there they left me.

Barefoot on the uneven paving stones, hurting everywhere but especially in the depths of my dignity, with a weight in my gut and another in my spirit, I looked at what there was to look at. There was an oval patio, enormous like an amphitheater and populated by groups of men dressed as I was. They too were looking at me. And now what do I do, I thought, and remembered beatings, tar and feathers, and worse things reserved for the initiate, and there I was barehanded. Against so many, I wouldn't have a chance. They left me alone only for a while. I tried to look like a hardened criminal, but I was riddled with fear. Finally one moved away from the others and came toward me: very young, with curly hair and his face swollen on the left side.

"One of my most ardent desires at this time," he said, "along with freedom and the forgiveness of my elders, is for your god to grant you many happy and peaceful hours, sire."

I should have answered, but I could not. At first I was dumbfounded, then I thought that this was the prologue to a cruel collective joke, and then that he was a homosexual with a curious way of insinuating himself. And then, no. The young man smiled and extended a welcoming arm.

"The Ancient Master sent me to ask if you would like to join us."

"Delighted," I said and started to walk.

But the young man remained planted there and clapped his hands.

"Did you hear?" he shouted at the top of his lungs to the prisoners in the enormous patio, "Did you hear? The foreign gentleman is delighted to join us!"

Here, I thought, is where the trouble starts. Again I was wrong; before long that would be the norm. After nodding their heads approvingly, the others paid us no further attention, and the young man took my arm and led me to the farthest corner of the patio.

We approached an ancient old man surrounded by ten or twelve men.

"They sent me," said the young man, speaking with difficulty, "because I am the youngest and can be expected to be indiscreet enough to ask anything of anyone, no matter how illustrious he may be."

Here's something, I concluded. At least I know that one mustn't go around asking about things.

"Welcome, worthy sire." The ancient old man had lifted his wrinkled face and toothless mouth, and spoke to me in a contralto. "Your god, from what I see, has accompanied you to this remote place."

I confess that I looked around, searching for my god.

Those who were squatting rose and made room for me. When they again crouched down, the kid waited until I followed suit and only then took his place.

Apparently I hadn't interrupted anything for they were all silent and remained so for a while. I wondered if they were waiting for me to say something, but what could I say if all that came to mind were questions and I was already aware that that wasn't done.

The ancient old man promptly said that the kind stranger must surely be hungry, and since I was the kind stranger I realized that the weight in my stomach was, in effect, hunger. The weight in my spirit, no, that didn't go away until I left Sweet Memory of the Yubayas in Bloom and not even then, completely. I said yes, that I was hungry but that I didn't want to bother anyone and only wished to know at what time meals were served. I hoped that I had spoken in accordance with their style and that that last hadn't sounded like a question. The ancient old man assented and said to no one in particular: "Bring something to restore the strength of the kind gentleman and companion, if already we may so refer to him."

Imitating as much as possible the headshaking of the others, I assented with a half-smile. My calves were hurting, but I remained squatting.

One of the group rose and left.

The ancient old man said, "Carry on."

And one of the squatting men began to speak, as though he were continuing a recently interrupted conversation.

"In my opinion, there are two types of numbers: those that serve to measure reality and those that serve to interpret the universe. These last need no connection to reality because they are not composed of units but of meanings."

Two others spoke at the same time:

"Superficially it may appear that there are only two classes of numbers. But I believe that there is an infinity of classes," said one.

"The number as such does not exist, but may be represented. But we must take into account that the representation of a thing is not the thing but that thing's void," said the other.

The ancient old man raised a hand and said that they couldn't keep talking if such confusion was to be the result. And while I tried to guess what was expected of me, if I should say something or not, and what that something might be, the one who had gone to get my food returned and I ate.

In a wooden bowl there was a bright red dumpling floating in a thick broth. With a spoon, also made of wood, I brought to my mouth something with a light seafood flavor, like well-done shellfish in a mild sauce that leaves a sour aftertaste. By the second mouthful it seemed tempting, and by the third, exquisite. By the time I realized that they were solomantide embryos cooked in their juice, I had already been eating them a good while and liked them and didn't care. The first day I scraped the bowl clean, and afterwards they brought me water. I was satisfied, very satisfied and wondered whether or not I should belch. The tension between physical pressure and timidity resolved itself and since everyone smiled at me, I stayed calm. Already my feet had fallen asleep and were numb and my elbows were digging into my muscles, but still I held out. And they kept on talking about numbers. When someone said that numbers not only did not exist but did not exist as representations either, and moreover that they didn't exist in the absolute, another joined in to cast doubt on the existence of all representation, and from there the existence of all things, all beings, and the universe itself. I was sure that I at least existed. And then it began to get dark and turn cold. However no one moved until the ancient old man said the day had ended, just as though he were God the Father, which made me remember my personal god, and I began to wonder where he had taken himself off to.

The ancient old man rose and so did the others and so did I. The other groups began to do the same. It was cold and my body ached. We walked slowly towards a door and went through. For the second time I lost my bearings. We went quite a way inside the building, passing through more complicated places, until we reached a large room with windows on one side, windows that at least looked out on an open space from which you could see the sky if you looked up, because on the other shorter wall—I don't know if I said that it was a vaguely hexagonal room—there were windows that looked out on a stone wall. There were mattresses on the floor, a large stove on one side, and doors, including one in a corner. The ancient old man pointed out a place and informed me that I would bed down there after washing. We washed in basins affixed to the floor and evacuated into holes beneath which you could hear water running. And upon returning, as when I discovered I was hungry, I discovered I was sleepy and decided to put off the problem of my future—which is to say my legal situation and my chances for escape—until the following day. But attentive as I was to the prisoners' customs, I waited to see what the others were doing, and the others were waiting for the ancient old man to lie down. Which unexpectedly he did on the floorboards and not on a larger or softer mattress that I had tried in vain to identify. Others also lay down and I did the same.

But it wasn't so easy to sleep. I was just about to drop off when again I had to resign myself to waiting, because all the others seemed to be talking at once. It occurred to me that they would be talking about me, understandably enough, and I surreptitiously opened my eyes for a look at their faces and again I was wrong. Like me, two others were stretched out and appeared to be sleeping. But the others were debating a difficult question, with the ancient old man as arbiter. After a while, one of the men asked the ancient old man to pick three because that night there were many. Many what, I thought, three what? I closed my eyes. When I opened them the ancient old man had picked three prisoners who silently undressed. I watched, careless of whether or not they saw me. One of the three was the kid with the swollen face. The others looked at the three nude men, touched them and seemed to decide on one whom they set apart, in an orderly way, with neither haste nor anxiety, and I saw how they lay him down, how they took their pleasure and then moved back to give the next one a turn. The three allowed themselves to be done to with their eyes closed, with neither protest nor ecstasy, and the ancient old man remained stretched out on the wooden floor. When all were satisfied, each one lay down on his mattress, and the kid and the other two went into the bath; through the door I could hear water running. I fell asleep.

The next day I was awakened by shouting. Not the prisoners, of course, but the guards. They stood in the corner door, whips in their hands, pistols in their belts, screaming insults, *up you filthy garbage mongers you sons of bitches, disgusting shits*, but they neither entered nor approached. The men got up, slapping on their clothes, it was hot there because the heat from the stove was trapped in the wood and stone, and many slept nude. I also got up. The guards left and we went off for ablutions and the ceremonies of the bath. I would have given anything for a cup of coffee, but led by the ancient old man we went to the patio, to the same spot we had been the day before. Everyone squatted around the ancient old man, and I decided to see what would happen if I sat cross-legged. Nothing happened, and so I remained, dreaming of a warm breakfast.

Before the ancient old man could say "carry on"—I would have bet anything he was about to say it—a man from another group approached and all the faces of our group, including my own, were lifted to look at him.

"May the new day be full of happy hours, meditation and rest," said the newcomer.

The ancient old man smiled and said to someone: "Invite the kind companion to join us."

One of ours said: "We would be extremely pleased if you would agree to join us, kind companion."

The other answered, "I only come as I am sent by my Master, who requests permission of the Ancient Master that one of us, anxious to expand his vision of the world's wisdom, might spend several hours with all of you, understood of course that we will provide for his dietary and hygienic needs."

"Tell your kind companion," said the Ancient Master, "that we will be pleased for him to do so."

The man from our group who had spoken before repeated the message and the other man left, and in a little while the guest arrived and again an incomprehensible conversation about numbers began. I tried to understand a little, but it all seemed either very stupid or very profound, and besides, I was hungry.

I started to think about my problem—not hunger, which could wait—but how to get out of there. It was very clear that I would have to ask how to get an interview with the Director, but I didn't feel encouraged to ask questions because of what the kid with the swollen face had said. And thinking of him, two things occurred to me: first, what had happened in the dormitory the night before; and secondly, how to make him my ally and have him help me when the chance arose. I glanced around but didn't see him. I turned halfway around and found him squatting to my right, a little behind me, nearly grazing me. Splendid, I said to myself, and waited for one of the frequent silences in the talk about numbers. When the others fell quiet, I turned, trying not to think of him crushed nude beneath the other men in the dormitory, and said to him:

"Something should be done about that tooth of yours."

He smiled at me as he had the day before, as though nothing had happened, and replied that his god would determine when the pain should end. I decided to pursue it. I answered that I could see that his god had determined that his pain should end, because I was the instrument designated to end it. He looked at me uncomprehendingly and I was afraid I had made a mistake. But within seconds his eyes were shining and it was plain that he had started out of happiness.

"All you have to do," I said, "is get me some tongs."

He nodded and went to kneel before the Ancient Master. There was a long conversation in which the kid asked permission and gave his reasons, and the ancient old man agreed and gave permission. The kid left, the guest looked at me in astonishment, as though I were a three-headed monster, and the disquisition on numbers or whatever came to a complete stop. I was still hungry and the Ancient Master began a parable.

"In faraway times," he started to recount, "there was a poor man who carved figures in order to subsist. But few bought them and with each one the carver grew poorer, so that each time the figures were less beautiful and less like the model. When the carver had gone some days without eating, the figures that came from his hands were frightful and no longer resembled anything. Then his god took pity on him and determined to make him such a prodigy that people would come from everywhere to behold him. And so he made the carved figures come to life. The carver was very frightened to see this, but then he thought: *The curious and the learned and people from faraway lands will come to see such a prodigy and I will be rich and powerful.* The beautiful figures carved in the days of poverty, but before the days of hunger, smiled and greeted him. But the monstrous figures threatened and grimaced at him meanly. The last one he had carved crawled toward him on its shapeless limbs, to devour him. Terrified, the carver begged for mercy in such a voice that again his god took pity on him and reduced the monstrous figures to ashes, keeping only the beautiful ones alive. And among these the carver discovered a most beautiful woman, whom he married and with whom he was happy for a time. He also grew rich from exhibiting his animated figures to the curious and the wise. But the woman, although made flesh by the carver's god, had kept her soul of wood, and so pitilessly tormented him for the rest of his life. He often begged, sobbing, that his figures be returned to inanimate life—even though he would lose his riches if he were freed of his wife. But this time his god did not want to listen to him."

I kept thinking about what it meant and what it might have to do with the kid's tooth. Obviously, everyone else had understood because they were smiling and nodding and looking at the Ancient Master and at me, but I couldn't make anything out of it and so I smiled without looking at anyone, and this time I hit it right. Everyone, except my stomach, seemed very happy.

Then the kid returned with the tongs. Wooden ones. Which he offered me. I was going to have to make do with them and I felt sorry for the kid. I took hold of the tongs and told him as gently as I could that in order for the tongs to work as an instrument of his god, I had to know his name. It had been weighing on me that I didn't know the kid's name.

"Which of my names," he said.

Apparently there were questions that could indeed be asked. But the bad thing was that I didn't know how to answer him.

"The name I must use," came to me.

Again I had figured it right.

"Sadropersi," he said.

For me, he was always Percy.

"All right, Sadropersi, lie down on the floor and open your mouth."

I seemed to have stopped making mistakes, and felt sure of myself.

He lay down and opened his mouth, not without first looking toward the Ancient Master, and I gestured to some of the others to hold down his arms, legs and head. I had a terrible time of it but I pulled the molar. I had to go very slowly, wiggling it from side to side before pulling so as not to break the tongs. It must have hurt him like the tortures of hell. But not once did he move or cry out. Tears ran down his face and blood filled his mouth; I was afraid he'd suffocate on me, and from time to time I raised his head and made him spit. Finally I showed him the molar in the tongs, and they all sighed as though I had pulled a molar from each one of them.

The Ancient Master smiled and told another parable.

"A woman was cooking cakes in hot oil while waiting for her husband. But the oil ran out before all the dough was cooked. She went to one of her neighbors to get some oil, and was refused. She then went to another of her neighbors who also refused her the oil to finish cooking the dough. Angered, the woman began shouting imprecations in her doorway, arousing the curiosity of passers-by, until one of them shouted, 'Make your own oil and stop making a racket!' So the woman went out behind her house and cut the seeds of the zyminia plant, ground and pressed them in a piece of linen, in this way extracting the oil she needed. When her husband arrived, she presented him with two platters of cakes and said, 'These are made with oil bought from the store, and these others with oil I extracted from the zyminia plant.' The husband ate both platters and the cake cooked in the oil extracted by his wife tasted better in his mouth than the others."

Percy smiled more openly than the others, and so did I, nodding. After letting a little time go by, I would be able to ask him how to get to the Director. And while I was thinking of this and of my empty stomach, suddenly it was mealtime. There was no announcement—no bell, no call, no guards with whips, nothing.

But the Ancient Master stood up, and after him all the others, and we went toward one of the doors to the warm interior of the prison. After following the ancient old man through labyrinthine passageways, we reached the large dining room on the first floor. We went up and down so many stairways so many times that if someone had told me I was on the sixth floor, I would have believed it. But from the windows, you could see the ground floor, the eaves and balconies on the other floors and the white plain beneath the sun. There were a lot of men cooking on stoves set up on the floor, and those of us arriving split up into groups and went toward one or another of the cookstoves. We all squatted around one, and the man cooking gave each of us a wooden bowl with the red broth, and we ate.

I saw that the others were doing what I wanted to do—asking for more—and when I finished my ration I asked for another. I drank a lot of water, and like the day before, was satisfied.

That day slipped by without further incident and the night was calm. Percy seemed happy and looked at me thankfully. There was no other meal during the day, but I wasn't hungry. With the problems of food and Percy's molar taken care of, I had to think about how I would get to the Director and what I would say when I saw him. But I was so tired by the time I lay down that I fell asleep without planning anything.

The next morning there were the jailers' insults and yelling, which the prisoners took with the same indifference. Afterward there was conversation on the patio, the meal, more conversation—always about numbers—and another night. I decided that the next day I would talk with Percy. But at that moment I needed something more urgent: I wanted to take a bath. Before we lay down I said to Percy:

"Sadropersi, dear friend." I was trying to learn, or at least imitate, the way the prisoners spoke. "I would like to bathe."

Percy became extremely upset.

"Bathe, sire?" He looked all around. "The gentlemen guards bathe us. "

"You don't mean those brutes scrub our backs with hair gloves?"

"The esteemed gentlemen guards" (it seemed I shouldn't have called them brutes) "fumigate, disinfect and bathe the prisoners periodically, dear sire and companion."

"All right," I said. "When is the next fumigation, disinfection and bath?"

But Percy didn't know. He figured it could be soon because the last session had taken place quite a while ago, but for now I had to make do with ablutions in the wash basins.

That night also was calm and before falling asleep I pitied myself a little. Here I was, a discoverer of worlds, imprisoned in a ridiculous jail with a ridiculous name, among people who spoke in a ridiculous way, humiliated and not victorious, degraded and not exalted. And what could have happened to my ship and my men? And most important: How was I going to get out of there? And on reaching the end of these black thoughts, I fell asleep.

In the bathroom the next day I again took Percy aside and told him I had to see the Director.

"No one gets to see the Director, sire."

I refrained from cursing the Director's mother and Percy's mother at the top of my lungs.

"Tell me, kind Sadropersi, if someone started a riot, wouldn't they take him to see the Director?"

I was asking questions, too many questions, but that wasn't what Percy had picked up on.

"A riot, my fine foreign gentleman and kind companion! No one starts riots."

"I know, of course, that's clear. But in the theoretical and highly improbable case that I started a fight on the patio, wouldn't they take me to the Director to be punished?"

He seemed to be thinking it over.

Finally he said, "No one would fight with you, kind companion."

Damn you, Percy, I thought, and gave him a big smile. "Fine, fine, let's forget the question, it was academic."

He too smiled. "There is much to say in favor of the academies, illustrious sire."

He had called me illustrious—which was an honor—perhaps thinking back to his molar. With his face no longer swollen he was a handsome kid and one could see why they chose him for love. I felt truly upset. As for the enigmatic observation on academies, I let it pass, lest it occur to him to have changed, in my honor, the subject of numbers—to which I was already accustomed—to that of academies, about which I knew nothing. Of course I didn't know anything about numbers either, at least not the way they discussed them.

We sat on the patio until it was time to eat. We ate and returned to the patio, and the Ancient Master told another parable.

"In olden times, men were very poor for they kept losing their possessions, even the smallest and most insignificant, each time they moved from place to place. They brought only their wives and children and relatives, at least those who were able to walk. The very old stayed behind. And all because transport had not yet been invented. Men traveled empty-handed, lamenting the utensils and clothing left in the place they were leaving. But one man who had to move to a distant city had a wife he loved dearly. The woman was ill, unable to walk, and the man wept at the thought that he had to leave her. He went to the bed in which she lay and embraced her so forcefully he lifted her up. Surprised, he took a few steps with the woman in his arms, and then a few more steps, and then walked out of the house carrying the woman, and took to the road. People came out from everywhere to see him go by, and soon everyone understood that it was possible to take from one place to another as many things as one could carry. And then many were seen going from place to place carrying furniture, utensils, clothing, texts, jewelry and ornaments. This went on a long time, with people traveling in all directions and the roads and byways packed with people showing one another what they were carrying, until everyone got used to it and a man carrying a sack in his arms no longer attracted attention."

Each time the ancient old man told a parable, I honestly tried to understand the meaning. But I never managed to get it. Neither did I get the one about the invention of transport, which seemed stupid to me, even though from time to time I remember it and again wonder if there might not be something important behind it.

That accursed night there was another assembly of men who wanted to fornicate, and I didn't lie down, I stayed with the others and apparently it attracted no one's attention. The Ancient Master again chose Percy and two others, not the same as the last time. The two immediately stripped, but Percy threw himself crying at the Ancient Master's feet begging that he let him be in the other group. Me, I don't know what came over me. I felt sorry for the kid, and it seemed shitty to sacrifice him twice in a row if he didn't want to, but at the same time I was glad because I desired him, and both things made me ashamed, my desire and my gladness.

The Ancient Master told him in his soft contralto that he was pardoning him because he was too young to distinguish between what was proper and improper, but that he, Percy, already knew that one wasn't allowed to appeal commands and that one had to bend to and obey orders. Percy then stopped crying and said yes, and the ancient old man said that he himself, as a special favor, would ask the others to allow Percy to be the object of their pleasure. At that I hated the old man, but the others seemed to think that what he said was just fine, even Percy, who smiled and said:

"Oh ancient, venerable and eminent master, I beg you, as a special and undeserved favor, to allow my kind companions their enjoyment of my contemptible person."

The ancient old man allowed the filthy comedy to continue, as if it weren't decided, and Percy had to insist. I backed away, furious, and decided that I wouldn't take part in that business. But when Percy stripped and smiled at us, I drew close to him and carefully stayed behind him so he wouldn't see my face. When it was all over, I fell asleep, serene and sad.

I was already used to the wake-up routine, but that morning it seemed that the guards' insults were directed straight and personally at me. I almost wanted them to come at me with their whips and beat me. Not for having screwed Percy, but for feeling as happy about it as I did. Percy, on the other hand, treated me as he did every day, and I had to force myself to answer him naturally, and to look at him.

I had to distract myself, at any cost, I had to think of something else and feel something else. On the patio, while they were talking about numbers (I heard a good question that morning: Is it possible to construct another universe with different numbers, or to change the universe by changing the numbers?), I again thought about how to get out of there. Escape seemed the only possibility left, if Percy was to be believed, and why not believe him about no one getting to see the Director. But I was still going to try to open my heart to the Ancient Master. However much I despised him for what he had done to Percy, he still seemed to be the most important of the prisoners. I wondered why the ancient old man was there. For having corrupted young boys, surely. But Percy? These, of course, were the questions one wasn't supposed to ask.

After the meal, another man from another group approached to ask if he might greet the illustrious foreigner. I was already twice illustrious. After the customary formalities, the ancient old man gave permission and we exchanged greetings and good wishes. What he wanted, he didn't tell me. When I realized that he had a toothache, I had to tell him that I would look in his mouth. I found a big ugly hole in an upper molar. I told him I would pull it and he pronounced a string of good wishes and inevitably the Ancient Master told a parable.

"Long ago there was a man who had a multicorn with which he plowed his land. Later, when the time was right, he sowed and sat back to watch the tender plants grow, and when the time came he gathered a plentiful harvest. But one fatal day the animal fell ill, and when it wasn't getting better the man decided to kill it and sell its meat and wool, and did so. Then, not having a work animal, he himself pulled the plow to turn the earth, but the work went very slowly and delayed seeding and the harvest, which wasn't as plentiful as before. A neighbor, seeing him during those troubles, said, 'You should have been prudent and waited. The animal probably would have gotten well, and now you wouldn't be exhausted by work and impoverished by the lack of a good harvest.' Realizing that his neighbor was right, the man sat down at the edge of his field, and for a long time he wept and lamented."

What could be clearer, I said to myself. If the man hadn't killed the animal, two things could have happened. Either it would have gotten better, in which case it could have continued working the land with him, or it would have died, in which case he would have had to sell the meat and wool anyway. But apart from a superficial condemnation of hastiness, I didn't see what was so important there to arouse everyone's veneration. I let the question drop because the imminent tooth-pulling had made me the subject of discussion, and the ancient old man was explaining to my patient the crime I had committed.

"The honorable foreign gentleman disembarked on our land without first signaling with his ship lights and without turning three times in place," he said.

I felt obligated to defend myself on seeing the painful way the man with the decayed tooth was looking at me.

"In the first place," I said, "I didn't know that this land was inhabited. And in the second place, even if I had known, how could I have been acquainted with the protocol requiring lights and turns in place? What is more, no one brought me before a judge, nor allowed me to defend myself, which in my country would be considered a sure sign of barbarism."

Everyone was very serious and the Ancient Master told me that nature is everywhere the same—something with which I could agree or not, but which didn't enter into the case—and that pleading ignorance of a law didn't excuse one from not complying with it. I didn't punch him in the nose because Percy arrived with the wooden tongs, which permitted me to think a little and remember that I needed the old man's benevolence. Again I talked about names, which of my names, the one I would have to use, and the man with the decayed tooth told me he was named Sematrodio.

I made him lie down and again went to work. It was harder than with Percy because the man's rotten molar was more firmly rooted, but in compensation there was less blood. Once more I had a rousing success and once more I was illustrious.

Luckily, that day there were no more parables, but at night the Ancient Master called me to him and after showering me with praise told me that perhaps my sentence would be short in view of my being a foreigner from a distant land—at the most, twenty years. I think I almost fainted. Twenty years! I'm sure I closed my eyes and slumped toward the floor.

"I understand your feelings," the ancient old man told me. "I will probably die here, since I have been accused, in all fairness, of improperly using two qualifying adjectives: two, you realize, during an official banquet." He sighed. "So, honorable foreigner and friend, I want to give you a souvenir to take back to your distant lands when you return to them."

From under his shirt he brought forth a pile of papers tied with string. I could think of only one thing: twenty years, twenty years, twenty years!

"This," the ancient old man was telling me, and I forced myself to listen, "is a copy of the *Code Of What Is And Canon Of Appearances*. Keep it, illustrious foreign gentleman, read it and meditate on it; I know it will provide you consolation, enlightenment and support."

I took the papers. Twenty years, how was it possible? Twenty years! The ancient old man turned and closed his eyes, and I left and lay down, but slept little that night.

At dawn, in an effort to forget about the twenty years—a thought which kept me from planning an escape, or finding a way to see the

Director, or doing anything that would get me out of there, let me search for my crew, get to my ship—I took out the Code and started leafing through it in the brilliant light that was streaming through the window. I understood it about as much as I did the ancient old man's numbers and parables. The Code was like a catalogue with explanations, but with no meaning whatsoever. I read it so many times, I remember it by heart: "The System organizes the world into three categories: In Front Of, Proximate, and Beneath. In the first are energy, insects, numbers, music, water and white minerals. In the second are men, fruit, drawings, liquors, temples, birds, red metal, prophecy and vegetables that grow in sunlight. In the third are food, animals with fur or scales, the word, sacrifices, weapons, mirrors, black metals, rope, vegetables that grow in shade and keys." And so it went, full of enumerations, each more absurd than the next. At the end, precepts and poems, and at the very end a phrase about the string tying the papers given me by the ancient old man, in which case the papers would be the ideas. But all this wasn't important; my prospective sentence was. And thinking of my sentence, with the string-tied papers hidden under my shirt, I got up, left the patio, ate and got through the rest of the day.

At night there was another council of men demanding to fornicate with someone. I feared for Percy and, instinctively, for myself. Yet I had to admit that I also experienced a certain happiness in seeing him chosen again. As it turned out, it occurred to the ancient old man to designate me, *me*, to play the woman for all the others . . . *me*! I was insulted, and told him that it mattered little to me what could and could not be done, that I was very macho and no one was going to take advantage of me. The ancient old man smiled and said a couple of stupid and pompous things: apparently to be chosen for this was a sign of deference, affection and respect. I told him they could start respecting others because I wasn't about to let them respect me.

"Ah, honorable foreign friend and gentleman," said the ancient old man, "who then will feed you, give you shelter, take you into his group! Who will make life tolerable for you at Sweet Memory of the Yubayas in Bloom?"

Drop dead, I thought, and was about to answer: Percy. But I didn't of course, thinking of what would happen to the kid if I did. The ancient old man was waiting; I suppose he was waiting for me to drop my pants, which I didn't do. Instead, I took two steps and gave him the punch in the nose I'd wanted to give ever since the night he had forced Percy to submit himself to the others' pleasure. Blood ran down his face, and a heavy silence hung over the whole dormitory. The ancient old man told a parable, just like that, his lip split and his nose bleeding, and I listened, waiting for it to end so I could give him another punch in the nose.

"Long, long ago," he said, "there was a boy on the brink of becoming a man. When he reached the age where he needed a wife, he fell in love with a third cousin and wished to marry her. But his father had chosen his neighbor's daughter for him, in order to unite the two estates, and ordered the young man to obey him. The son turned a deaf ear to his father's words, and one night he stole his cousin away and escaped with her to the mountains. They lived happily, eating fruits and small birds and drinking water from streams, until his father's servants found them and brought them back to the house. There, with pomp and ceremony, was celebrated the wedding of the young man and the daughter of the father's neighbor. The third cousin was locked in a cage in the plaza, where she was exposed to public mockery."

That parable I certainly understood. And because I understood it, instead of again punching the ancient old man, I grabbed his neck and squeezed until it was broken. I let him lie there on the floor, in the same spot where he always slept, his face bloody and his head forming a right angle to his body. I yelled to the others: "Go to sleep!"

And they all obeyed me and went to their mats. I fell asleep instantaneously, and the next day was awakened not by the guards' insults, but by a deafening uproar. Everyone was running from one side to the other yelling, "Disinfection! Disinfection!" I saw a big group of guards come in, whips in hand. This time they used them: they hit out blindly, and men fled naked through the dormitory. As senselessly as the rest, I also ran. The guards immediately backed towards the door in the corner, and others came in carrying hoses. They overtook us with jets of ice-cold water—here was the bath I had been wishing for, exploding against our bodies and nailing us to the walls and floor. Then I saw that the only one not moving was the Ancient Master, and I remembered that I had murdered him, and why; the guards must have seen him at the same moment, because an order was given and the hoses stopped vomiting freezing water. One of the guards approached the old man's body, touched it so that the now black head wobbled from side to side, and shouted, "Who did this!"

I stepped forward. "I did."

I thought, *if for not having signaled they sentence me to twenty years, now they'll shoot me instantly.* I wasn't even afraid.

"Get dressed and follow us."

I put on my shirt and pants, grabbed the papers given me by the ancient old man, looked at Percy and went with the guards.

At least I had gotten what I wanted; they took me to see the Director.

"I have been informed," he said to me, "that you killed a Master."

"Yes," I answered.

"Take him away," he told the guards.

Again they took me to the room where they had stripped, examined, and dressed me as a convict, and gave me back all of my things. At least I was going to die as a Captain and not a convict, as though that mattered. But it comforted me. I put the *Code Of What Is And Canon Of Appearances* in the right pocket of the jacket. We returned to the office of the Director.

"Foreign sire," he said to me, "you will be taken to your ship, and we pray you, return to your lands as quickly as possible. The action you committed has no precedent in our long history, and you will have to be so good as to pardon us and to understand when we tell you that it is impossible for us to keep any longer in one of our public establishments a person such as yourself. Goodbye."

"What about my men?" I asked.

"Goodbye," the Director repeated, and the guards took me away from there.

They took me to the ship. Motionless on a green plain, so different from the saltpeter surface on which Sweet Memory of the Yubayas in Bloom rises up, it seemed to be waiting for me. I gave her a military salute, which astonished the guards to no end, approached her and opened the hatch.

"Goodbye," I also said, but they didn't answer. I didn't care, for I wasn't saying goodbye to them.

I looked around to see if my personal god was coming with me, and took off in the direction of Earth, with the sunlight of Colatino—as I myself had named the world I discovered—beating down on the fuselage and the countryside and the distant mountains. Goodbye, I said again, and began reading the *Code Of What Is And Canon Of Appearances* with particular attention to amuse myself on my solitary voyage home.

Translated by Marguerite Feitlowitz

Bibliography: Angélica Gorodischer

Fiction

Gorodischer, Angélica. *Cuentos con soldados*. Santa Fe, Argentina: Club de Orden, 1965.

———. *Opus Dos*. Buenos Aires: Minotauro, 1967.

———. *Las Pelucas*. Buenos Aires: Editorial Sudamericana, 1968.

———. *Bajo las jubeas en flor*. Buenos Aires: Ediciones de la Flor, 1973.

———. *Casta luna electrónica*. Buenos Aires: Andrómeda, 1978.

———. "Los embriones del violeta." *Los universos vislumbrados*. Buenos Aires: Andrómeda, 1978. Rpt. in *Lo mejor de la ciencia ficción latinoamericana*. Ed. Bernard Goorden and A. E. Van Vogt. Buenos Aires: Martínez de la Roca, 1982. 122-56.

———. *Trafalgar*. Buenos Aires: El Cid, 1979. Rpt. in Rosario: Ediciones de Peregrino, 1984.

———. "La cámara oscura." *Doce Mujeres Cuentan*. Buenos Aires: La Campana, 1983. 157-74.

———. *La casa del poder*. Buenos Aires: Minotauro, 1983.

———. *Kalpa Imperial*. Buenos Aires: Minotauro, 1983.

———. *Mala noche y parir hembra*. Buenos Aires: La Campana, 1983.

———. "Las mujeres y las palabras." *Hispamérica* 13.39 (1984): 45-48.

———. *Al Champaquí*. Buenos Aires: Ediciones de la Flor, 1985.

———. *Floreros de alabastro, alfombras de Bokhara*. Buenos Aires: Emecé, 1985.

———. "Bajo las jubeas en flor." *Puerta abierta: la nueva escritora latinoamericana*. Ed. Caridad L. Silva-Velázquez and Nora Erro-Orthmann. Mexico City: Joaquín Mortiz, 1986. 141-159.

———. "Man's Dwelling Place." Trans. Alberto Manguel. *Other Fires*. Ed. Alberto Manguel. Toronto: Lester & Orpen Dennys, 1986. 88-94.

———. *Jugo de mango*. Buenos Aires: Emecé Editores, 1988.

Essays

Gorodischer, Angélica. "Contra el silencio por la desobediencia." *Revista Iberoamericana* 51.132-133 (1985): 479-81.

Criticism on the Works of Angélica Gorodischer

Dellepiane, Angela B. "Contar mester de fantasía o la narrativa de Angélica Gorodischer." *Revista Iberoamericana* 51.132-133 (1985): 627-40.

Feitlowitz, Marguerite. "Home Sweet Home: The Fantastical Writings of Angélica Gorodischer." *The American Voice* No. 19 (Summer 1990): 63-67.

Lagmanovich, David. "Gandolfo, Gorodischer, Martini: Tres narradores jóvenes de Rosario (Argentina)." *Chasqui* 4.2 (1975): 18-28.

Mosier, M. Patricia. "Communicating Transcendence in Angélica Gorodischer's *Trafalgar*." *Chasqui* 12.2-3 (1983): 63-71.

Mosier, Mary Patricia. "Comunicando la transcendencia en *Trafalgar* por Angélica Gorodischer." *Foro Literario* 9.15-16 (1986): 50-56.

Orgambide, Pedro and Roberto Yahni. *Enciclopedia de la literatura argentina*. Buenos Aires: Editorial Sudamericana, 1970. 293.

Souto, Marcial, comp. "Angélica Gorodischer." *La ciencia ficción en la Argentina: antología crítica*. Buenos Aires: Eudeba, 1985. 94-98.

Vásquez, María Esther. "Angélica Gorodischer: Una escritora latinoamericana de ciencia ficción." *Revista Iberoamericana* 49.123-124 (1983): 571-76.

SYLVIA LAGO
Uruguay

S ylvia Lago was born in Montevideo, Uruguay, in 1932. She is a
professor of literature at the University of the Republic in Montevideo, and a literary critic for the newspaper *Brecha*. She has written
several novels and collections of short stories, as well as numerous
articles and essays that have appeared in several literary magazines and
journals.

Her first novel, *Trajano* (Trajano, 1962), which deals with the theme
of incest, won her awards from *Revista Número*. In her first two novels
she used a simple style, but by the mid-sixties began to experiment with
complex narrative techniques and a more dynamic use of language.

The short story "Días dorados de la señora Pieldediamante" ("Golden
Days of Mrs. Diamondskin"), published in the collection *La mitad del
amor* (Half of Love, 1966), passionately denounces the use of women
as sex objects. It won her both considerable praise and bitter criticism.

Lago's work clearly reflects her major concerns, which over the years
have encompassed the social, the feminist, and the political. Her characters' personal lives are often eroded by unfair social and political circumstances. Many of her stories focus on the disadvantaged status of
women in Uruguay, and on the hypocrisy of gender roles in a patriarchal
society.

HOMELIFE

And outside, night kept falling.
    Juan Rulfo, *Luvina*

*How are we to keep going, without understanding, picking
our way blindly in this dark age.*
    Joaquin Giannuzzi

I think that it all began when we decided to buy the small sofas for
the bedroom; the two lovely settees covered in brown brocade, with
honey-colored flowers, which are still attractive there, next to the window, near the commode where—still—the crystal ashtray is lying, the
one which your first patient gave you as a present. We had moved the
baby to her own room from the room which she shared with Daniel.
You saw that she was already getting too big to sleep in the same room
with her older brother. And since you had finally made a nice fee—a
sum which, as you said, a young doctor just starting out and concerned
more about his profession than his income, practicing in a provincial
city in the interior, could only expect to receive from very rich patients—
we also decided to buy bedroom sets for the children.

The operation which you performed on don Olegario de la Sierra—the
rancher suffering from a congenital intestinal disorder—brought you
fame and fortune. When don Olegario had fully recovered, he wanted
to pay his bill in person, and turned up one night at the house in his
latest-model Cadillac. Apart from the check, as a token of his gratitude,
he brought us a roast suckling pig and a bottle of the best wine from
his cellar.

That night we had a family supper. Daniel and the baby ate so much
that they ended up with indigestion. You got up at the break of dawn
to take care of them. Anyway, it had been a wonderful meal, lots of
fun. You were so happy, so jolly—I remember that for dessert, on a
fancy china tray, I served your favorite dessert, ambrosia. Yes, Miguel,
I had made it myself, taking extra special care to get it just right: twelve
beaten egg yolks, syrup, vanilla extract—I'd never use liquid extract,
since it gives a bitter and vulgar taste—and three small cups of cognac.

"Doesn't Mom make wonderful desserts?" you said to the children,
and immediately you reached out to me and put your arms around my
waist. I felt your warmth on my skin, and the pressure of your right
hand (the lancet and scalpel hand), so soft when you stroked me. I
stood next to you while you stayed seated, sheltering your face against
my breasts; you spoke again of money.

"O.K., Rocío, finally you will be able to have a handsome sum to spend as you wish; get those sofas you like and the bedroom sets for the children."

Daniel, who was nine then, seized upon the climate of happiness, tinged with the rare aroma of wine, and the atmosphere of unusual luxury, and asked for the meccano set he had been longing for. To Susanna, I promised a doll; that cute MaryLou which said mamá and which was on display, wearing an organza dress, in the window of the toy shop. With Susanna, I got the better of you that time. I said that we would buy her the doll before you would give her one of those mind games which you were crazy about. I always wanted our daughter to become a good housewife, attached to the home.

however, they came to get her at two in the morning and she didn't open her lips when they took her away, and I shouted, tell them no, that you have nothing to do with it, that your whole life is spent studying and doing household chores, that you know how to cook and knit and that you make your own clothes; but she endured the shoving and the manhandling with her lips pressed tight together and they took her away like that.

After supper, I put the children to bed. As usual, you took refuge in your study. When they had gone to sleep, I went to look for you, afraid that your habit of reading at night was taking too much of a hold over you. I wanted so much to be with you that night; I felt weightless, enveloped in a kind of ethereal happiness which made me feel tremendously light, ready to give myself completely, without any holding back.

"Rocío, the sea-nymph, the solitary and taciturn mermaid," you used to call me at the beginning of our relationship, when we began to build our island: that drop of sunshine which I always dreamed was burning on the edge of our world.

I went into your study and pierced the gloomy depths of your reverie, without you particularly noticing it; above you there seemed to float an uneasy pall, which made me shiver.

his face suddenly aged, as if mourning had taken hold of it, the first time they allowed me to see him, when they brought him to the iron bars and around his eyes there was that frightening dark ring, and inside his eyesockets, there were two burning stones which were his eyes. Somebody pushed him forward and when his trembling hands grabbed the bars, the iron bars screeched. Then, everything fell silent.

Even so, I spoke. I told you that I felt happy and that "the island was on fire." It was our language of lovers, Miguel, our private code. A metaphor like that should have made you break out of your private thoughts and give me a smile. But it didn't. I noticed that on the desk in front of you lay your newspaper, and that you had never even heard a word I said. Your voice sounded alien to me when, with your eyes fixed on the open page, you said, "It sounds like they have given them a real beating up north."

I was completely unaware of your train of thought, and I asked "Who?"

You gave me a disconcerting smile, and a look of astonishment, maybe of sorrow, came over your face. "It's incredible that there are so many people like you, sensitive, educated, who still refuse to face up to the realities of the world in which they are destined to live."

Or something like that you said. Later on I learned that Felipe was up north at the time. Of course, you feared for his safety. You didn't see fit, however, to share any of this with me.

That was the first cold underwater current which slid around the "island," like an icy shiver in the intimate water which we had filled with magnificent man-of-wars, rose-shelled snails, sea urchins you could touch, and multicolored coral reefs. We went to bed in silence, and made love with little enthusiasm. But I couldn't get to sleep that night. Sitting on the bed in the dark, I felt for the first time in my heart the full weight of that new sadness which was never again to leave me.

It was after receiving the payment from don Olegario de la Sierra that our family started to live a comfortable life. We didn't buy only the sofas and the furniture for the children, but also an elegant dining room suite and a garden hammock, and for Christmas you gave me the aquarium. That aquarium is what I am looking at now, where a single fish with yellow fins is swimming in the murky, slimy waters—in this room which we used to share, now that you're no longer here, there's nothing to be heard but an extended silence.

We went to the capital and picked out four varieties of fish. The goldfish—remember the goldfish with glowing eyes whom we baptized Nero, making him the king of the fishbowl? So much, so much time has passed since then, Miguel—ten years have slid by since that summer—they are not so long, or at least they shouldn't be.

time, endless, white, and smooth, on his adolescent face. What color, what color were his eyes? Grey with green reflections and gold specks? And wild alloy of lights, his pupils, where life was exploding. However, on the day they brought him home he was sleeping. I laid him down in his bed and his skin got pale, paler every minute. Only that flower, that purple petal where his teeth stuck out, was intense, each time more intense against the strange paleness, against his ashen face.

That February was the anniversary of our first meeting in the water, ten years before. So often we used to say that we belonged to the sea, Miguel. We met one summer, under the sign of Pisces; we met in the sea. A mermaid sleeping on a rock is discovered and seduced by Poseidon, the King of the Ocean. Since that meeting, so many years have passed—I had finished my exams and wanted to spend my holidays on a lonely beach. I chose one where in the sand, rough and burnt, wild plants were growing, drowning, near the shoreline. There were some bushes too, their branches submerged in the water which was dark brown near the shore, but clear further out. Near the cliff, there was a floating raft. I would sunbathe there in the morning, and one day, swimming along, you found me. You emerged from the waves and your body was ablaze with the glare of the noonday sun. Silver-coated fish, your attendants, followed in your wake, and my eyes filled the air with other fish, winged and shining. I dove into the middle of this mirage; if you had dazzled a siren, I, in return, had attracted a god. I swam toward the reef and, as never before, I felt the power of the sea and of life in my body. When I stepped out, strings of algae were curling around my legs. You were waiting for me. Suddenly, we were surrounded by a sort of violent blue haze; in the distance, the beach was a yeilow tongue, writhing in the heat of the sun.

"At last, you reached the white sand," you said, as you offered your hand to me. "Come up. Now that we've discovered this hill, we'll give it a name and it will belong to us."

I smiled into the mirage and triumphantly said, "It will be our island."

"Mermaid island," you said between the flashes of light which framed our dialogue and made it weightless. We were filled with a sort of innocent romanticism which signaled our discovery of each other, and which we would joke about together in the future. Your hand, wet and cold, stroked the skin of my arm.

"From now on, you agree to be the mermaid, right?" you asked.

I was hallucinating, Miguel; nobody can ever blame me for my innocence then. The world, life, was a surging wave breaking and building and breaking again against the reef. And the two of us rushed forward into its vortex.

Yes, ten years had passed since the perfect existence of the "island" and you wanted to commemorate the fact in the way which would please me most. After your celebrated cure of don Olegario, other relatives and friends of the la Sierra family started coming to you; almost immediately you operated on the gall bladder of his older sister, Doña Adelaida, widow of a well-to-do businessman of the region, who owned one of the largest properties in the whole *departamento*. We received an extraordinary sum of money and I suggested that we spend it right away. But at that time something strange was beginning to eat into you. Now I imagine that you were already keeping company with Felipe.

One evening, I went to the clinic and I found you there, gloomy and restless. You had finished your appointments and were smoking one cigarette after another. You told me that you had just seen a rancher from the border—you made it clear that he was "a smuggler"— who was suffering from a duodenal ulcer.

"He left me a check for four times what I asked." My surprised smile offended you. "Take it, then, take it" you blurted out. "Keep on with your shopping and stuffing our house with junk!"

You were not being fair and I told you how I felt. You stood up, upset, looking out into the distance with flashing eyes, and you added, "I had better give it back, Rocío. I don't want people to start thinking that I'm a well-paid servant of the big landowners and swindlers of the region."

We had a quarrel. I argued that we had just begun to settle down, that we had hardly started to decorate our house and now you were sowing seeds of discord, based on absurd conflicts with your conscience.

You reproached me by saying, "Settling down, decorating; you just can't get beyond your world of petty personal ambitions, can you?"

That really hurt me; what harm could there be in wanting us to be comfortable, in wanting to decorate my home and in caring for my family's comfort? Would you rather I had spent my time outside, going to parties or gossiping with the neighbors? You begged me to understand your concerns, but you didn't try very hard to explain to me what they were. The truth was that we were still living in the time when we were following our bodies' appetites, Miguel, and our bed was still a place where we would patch things up. You used to love so much to look at me, naked, not moving, stretched out on the sheets which I myself had embroidered with flower patterns.

naked, yes. She said that they had interrogated her naked, with her eyes covered, and I was horrified. I couldn't understand how she had stood all that, although she tried to explain to me that she had shielded herself with contempt. "You don't know, you don't realize, mamá, what strong weapons hatred and contempt can be." She was naked, smaller than me, and much thinner, her large beautiful eyes covered with bandages and cotton. Naked and defenseless, distant from us.

I couldn't come up with a better idea to celebrate our tenth wedding anniversary than to organize a holiday to the beach that summer. I chose a fashionable seaside resort. Doña Adelaida's money—"her precious gall stones," as you wisecracked—made it possible to rent a California-style beach house surrounded by gardens, with weeping willows and poplars and pines and grassy cliffs, and a beautiful swimming pool. Really, Miguel, today I'd say it was straight out of a fairy tale and its heroes were not really us. I remember the first morning of our holiday as a shining fantasy; you sprang from the diving board and I felt that you had changed yourself once more into a pagan god, and inside me the images of my readings of Homer flashed before me: "Swift-flying Miguel-Apollo descending from Olympus, Miguel-Hermes bestowing upon Earth his messages of eternal delight? Divine Poseidon floating on the surface of the water searching for his beloved Nereids? Rocío the nymph?"

"Rocío the mermaid" I called myself and I threw myself into the pool to surrender myself once more to you, my one and only god. I swam over to you and pressed my body to yours. We began to move gently, like a single creature, while a dazzling light falling from the sky splashed millions of stars upon us.

Stars. They say that when he came to, after the injection they gave him to force him to confess, he too must have seen more and more lights, then later a smell of smoke which transformed the colors: sulphur-solid, green-mallow, or perhaps purple or violet . . . and black spots, then, which got larger and took shape next to him and gained their own voice. *Tell us your nickname. Speak, say your nickname.* And the hair they tore from Daniel's head, my Daniel; the autopsy determined that they first tore off his hair and they burned his skin and then they beat him until they broke him.

Toward the end of our stay, Felipe turned up at our beach house. He was younger than us, at least so it seemed; he looked like an unruly teenager, although he was quiet. His paleness struck me as odd.

"Haven't you been out in the sun during this marvelous summer?" I asked him before inviting him into the pool.

He smiled and answered ambiguously that he had been terribly busy, that he had recently arrived from abroad, things like that. I didn't take to him, Miguel, you know that. Even though he was always very polite with me, and so affectionate to the children. Susanna used to always climb onto his lap and kiss him. Daniel would follow him into the house, wanting him to go fishing or hunting. They went to the nearby

mountains, carrying shotguns, and they brought down some pigeons
. . . My God, how much time it took me to begin to figure them out.

You wanted Felipe to stay at the house until the evening before we
returned home to the village. That night, we threw him a special dinner.
We bought an excellent wine, I cooked a seafood stew and, of course,
ambrosia.

"Food of the pagan gods," commented Felipe. "What a treat."

Later, he assured us that the dessert was delicious. I didn't display
any joy. I had become fond of the pampered life at the resort and it
pained me to leave it—our shining pool, our garden, our bedroom with
its windows open to the sea. All that would go up in smoke the next
morning and it wasn't likely that, the next summer, someone else's
precious gallstones, like Doña Adelaida's, would pay for our holidays.
After Felipe came, I felt that perhaps we would never again have such
a summer as that one. But that whole place, that fleeting moment in
the sun, was nothing but a mask concealing other purposes unknown
to me.

I felt listless as I dressed for the "last supper." I chose a backless
lamé dress (I had bought it in a shop on the main street of the resort
town and hadn't yet worn it), gold earrings and bracelets. I put on my
essence-of-violet perfume. It was my way of saying goodbye to that
dream world, and I wanted to look like a queen, a queen of the night,
magically wrapped in a silver web. However, my other table companions,
Felipe and you (the children were tired and had already gone to bed),
kept quiet and distant. I remember Felipe's smile when I showed up
before the two of you; afterward, I often spoke of it to you with bitterness.
His was a sad, enigmatic smile which made me suddenly feel stripped
of all my fictitious finery. Ridiculous, mute, alone . . . Ah! it was
almost the same smile with which he appeared in the photo, in the
newspapers years after when they announced that, after a confrontation
with a squad of soldiers, they had beaten him in the street, right in the
center of the city.

Forgive me, Miguel, but that night I think I hated Felipe. I don't
know if it was because of his smile or because I had a feeling that he
would be a sharp and relentless wedge which would split apart our
"island," the bright, secluded island of my dreams, on the edge of the
world. His smile had something magical in it, I see that now; it had
the power to change the lamé of my dress into the wretched skin of a
fish. I felt like a fish out of water, suffocating. He left that night in his
red Volkswagen, and before he embraced you and me, he told me to
kiss Susanna and Daniel for him; I felt that I was about to faint. You
walked him to the gate of the beach house. It was dawn. I stayed on
the porch, looking at you. My fingers trembled on my glass of cognac.
You came back changed—transfigured even. Your features seemed to

radiate an intense joy. I knew that your joy didn't belong to me, that he was the one who had caused it and that I couldn't share in it.

Maybe that's what made me provoke you in such an absurd way.

We were alone, relaxing on the deck near the pool. In silence, in front of you I undressed, with the intention of challenging you. The skin of the mermaid fell to my feet. Then your look ran over my body inch by inch, slowly, and it seemed to me that your eyes had become his. Felipe's eyes. And there was already nothing in your look but indifference—or perhaps sadness. Yes, maybe only sadness. I began to shake. You turned your eyes away from me and gazed out into the night, at the stars which glimmered in the dark; there was a shooting star, a point which flashed far away in the depths of the sky, whose bright gleam just barely gave me time to make a wish: that Felipe would never return.

You'll have to understand, you'll have to guess that the sentences between quotation marks in the letter are Susanna's. Also, I have tried to imitate her handwriting in those passages, so you'll recognize both the text and its meaning. I trust in your sagacity, Miguel, in your intelligence, which will remain lucid, I suppose, despite everything you have suffered. And what is happening with me, meanwhile? I shouldn't say it. However, often I think I'll go crazy if I don't tell you what is happening to me. My hours are dragging out nervously with all this lonely waiting. For now, day and night, I just stay seated in front of the aquarium, where there's only one fish left. I'm observing its movements as it glides along, and thinking about you, always thinking, trying to go deeper into areas which still remain incomprehensible.

Sometimes, she phones me; not her exactly, but a girlfriend who mentions the name of the Spanish dressmaker whom I was thinking of asking to make her wedding dress—the white dress of chiffon and lace which I dreamed of using for our daughter's wedding. Miguel. You see how deluded I was! Once I told her, "It's time for you to choose from among your suitors, Susanna, and think about getting married. I have even chosen the design of your dress, and I have planned out the ceremony." She smiled and I think that I detected a sparkle in her eyes, the same one as was in your eyes the night Felipe left, a mixture of tenderness and pity and a strange vitality . . . "I don't know if I'll ever get married, mamá, but I know that if I do, I won't have to buy a wedding dress."

Undressed, yes, stripped. She will never wear a wedding dress. They interrogated her naked, they put her head into a tank of cold water, and on one occasion when they hooded her and they pulled her out, she had almost drowned, and her desperation to breathe made her inhale the dirty water which remained inside the hood.

Of course: who could have imagined that a girl who resisted so much, a woman who was as fearless as a man, more than many, many men, would want to get married in a church wedding, in an elegant white gown.

Susanna's comrade, who has the same name as the Spanish dressmaker, tells me that everything is going along perfectly well, and that I shouldn't worry. And I continue to wait for her. Wondering why she doesn't come home if they didn't sentence her, Miguel. Waiting for her . . . stupid me! I don't want to think that, again, again, she chose the same adventure? On one occasion, I had stopped in front of a shop window in one of the downtown malls, looking at some beautifully embroidered tapestries, when she turned up in front of me, smiling; as if by magic she appeared and I blushed and immediately turned white; however, I couldn't bring myself to talk to her. She squeezed my arm and whispered in my ear, "Cheer up, mamá; you can see I'm doing fine." And into my hand she slipped the letter for you and quickly explained to me that I should insert her sentences between mine when I wrote to you, assuring me that you would understand. Afterwards, she disappeared into the crowd.

And yes, I think that you will understand, since you and she always understood each other. And also, you both got on with Daniel and, since they were children, she and Daniel with Felipe. At times, I imagine a disconcerting complicity to which you are not a stranger. At one time, I thought that I would never manage to understand you. I, the mermaid of your arms and of your desires, raised in the home, hidden away, shy; wanting only the flowers of my garden, our meals and our peaceful evenings. Suddenly, I was confronting another face of the world. Was Daniel the one who first showed me the wrong side of life? Or perhaps Felipe?

Felipe's face on the front page of the newspapers and the headlines which called him the head of the *faciosos*; his broad forehead, his deep, searching eyes, full of conviction and power and harshness and tenderness and values which I didn't even know existed.

However, perhaps it wasn't Felipe, but Daniel, my own son. That time he had blazing eyes and you said that he hadn't been crying and I assured you that he had, that he'd cried the whole night over Felipe's death. Time passed and one day Daniel went away from us. That evening, I felt that my feet no longer were touching the ground, that under my feet there was a vacuum and that an evil force was drawing me toward hell. Suddenly, I stopped seeing reality. I was blind and in my desperation I cried out for him not to leave, but he didn't reply. He turned to you, Miguel, "try to calm her," he said to you, "afterwards she'll understand." He left me, and I fell, lost, into your protective arms. The door closed quietly behind his large figure, behind his canvas satchel in which he had gathered—the following day I checked his closet—a few clothes. When they brought him to me, you were no longer at home. Only we two women were left. It was dawn. They said that he had died of a heart attack during an interrogation. Daniel, my Daniel, the healthiest and most lovely and well cared-for of children . . . dead at nineteen of a heart attack. Who could believe them?

Do you remember when you supplied him with vitamin pills, vaccines and tonics—because I had asked you so often, because I always wanted our children to be beautiful and strong—and you made fun of me, saying that you couldn't explain how a mermaid had given birth to a little bull? I don't know how you felt when they told you. When you became aware that the autopsy had determined that it was death from a ruptured liver and immediate hemorrhaging? They had beaten him so much, Miguel, so much. Perhaps it's better if we never talk about this. Sometimes, I think that it would be better if, when you come home—because I know that they won't be able to keep you in prison, although they want to, because I know that if you helped the rebels by giving them medical assistance it is because you are, and always have been, an unselfish humanitarian doctor, ready to exercise your profession in the service of mankind. I think that it might be better if I am not here when you come home. Anyway, Miguel, I'm sure that you love me, that I was and always will be your mermaid, although the island has lost its fire and has sunk once and for all into a quagmire of bitterness.

At home, you will meet Susanna. You two can sit down and relax on the settee and chat. You were always such good company for each other. With her, also, you defeated me, although for a long time I thought I had won, at least in that battle. Since she was so obedient, she never objected to the fact that I taught her how to do household chores. I dreamed that she would choose the path I wanted for her—the life at home. Meanwhile, however, without my noticing it, she too was learning the other path, your path. That's why, on the many occasions I asked her to spend more time with me, sharing feminine chores, she smiled, and the shining spark would appear in her eyes: love-tenderness-pity-understanding which, I see now, was Felipe's legacy to you and her.

You two will talk and go over the times you had with Daniel and Felipe.

But maybe, after all, it would be better if I were at home when you two come back to chat and smoke and recall what happened, what is happening; or that I don't disappear at the moment in which at last we will be together. The three of us will remain here, and we'll remember them. We'll have lunch, and I'll serve you coffee and sometime I'll approach you and I'll ask you to explain things to me. Probably someday I'll understand the truth in your eyes and your hands and in the eyes and hands of our children and in the eyes and hands of Felipe.

Translated by Ian Martin

Bibliography: Sylvia Lago

Fiction

Lago, Sylvia. *Tan solos en el balneario*. Montevideo: Editorial Feria del Libro, 1962.

————. *Trajano*. Montevideo: Editorial Alfa, 1962.

————. "Días dorados de la señora Pieldediamante." *La mitad del amor*. Montevideo: Arca, 1966. Rpt. in *Narradores uruguayos*. Ed. Rubén Cotelo. Caracas, Venezuela: Monte Avila Editores, 1969. 257-289.

————. *Detrás del rojo*. Montevideo: Alfa, 1967.

————. "Las horizontales." *La nueva narrativa*. Ed. Mercedes Ramírez de Rossiello. Montevideo: Centro Editor de América Latina, 1968. 57-65.

————. "Los peces rojos." *Antología del cuento uruguayo VI. Los Nuevos*. Montevideo: Ediciones de la Banda Oriental, 1968. 73-82.

————. *La última razón*. Montevideo: Arca, 1968.

————. *Las flores conjuradas*. Montevideo: Girón, 1972.

————. "Tema de amor." *Cuentos de la revolución*. Ed. Mario Benedetti. Montevideo: Girón, 1972. 43-60.

————. "Vida de hogar." *Los últimos cuentos*. Montevideo: Girón, 1972. 21-32.

————. "Recibir al campeón." *Catorce cuentistas*. La Habana: Casa de las Américas, 1969. 133. Rpt. in *El cuento uruguayo contemporáneo*. Buenos Aires: Centro Editor de América Latina, 1978.

————. "Ninfas: Pasión y muerte." *Hispamérica* 7.22 (1979): 49-64.

————. "Vida de hogar." *Puerta abierta: la nueva escritora latinoamericana*. Ed. Caridad L. Silva-Velázquez and Nora Erro-Orthmann. Mexico City: Joaquín Mortiz, 1986. 161-71.

————. *El corazón de la noche*. Montevideo: Ediciones de la Banda Oriental, 1987.

Essays

Lago, Sylvia. *Eduardo Acevedo Díaz: El combate de la tapera*. Montevideo: Editorial Técnica, 1976.

Criticism on the Works of Sylvia Lago

Foster, David William. *Dictionary of Contemporary Latin American Authors*. Tempe: Center for Latin American Studies, Arizona State University, 1975. 57-58.

Rama, Angel. *La generación crítica 1939-1969*. Montevideo: Arca, 1972. 198.

Rela, Walter. *Diccionario de escritores uruguayos*. Montevideo: Ediciones de la Plaza, 1986. 197-99.

Shimrose, Pedro. *Diccionario de autores iberoamericanos*. Madrid: Ministerio de Relaciones Exteriores, 1982. 236.

Visca, Arturo S., ed. *Antología del cuento uruguayo VI: los nuevos*. Montevideo: Ediciones de la Banda Oriental, 1968. 73-82.

ELENA PONIATOWSKA
Mexico

E lena Poniatowska was born in Paris in 1933. She is the daughter
of a Mexican mother and a Polish father who emigrated to Mexico
when she was nine years old. She completed primary school in Mexico,
and was later sent to the convent of the Sacred Heart in Philadelphia
for her secondary education.

In 1954 she started working as a journalist for the newspaper *Excelsior*,
and later worked for the magazine *Novedades*, where she still publishes
weekly. She has published in other newspapers and magazines such as
El día, *Siempre!*, *Mañana*, *Artes de México*, and *FEM*.

Poniatowska's testimonial novel *Hasta no verte, Jesús mío* (Until I
See You Again, 1969) is based on the author's interviews with Jesusa
Palancares, a traditionally neglected witness to Mexico's history from
the time of the revolution to the present. It explores the role of working
class women in the Mexican Revolution, as well as in contemporary
society.

Following in the tradition of testimonial narrative, in 1973
Poniatowska wrote *La noche del Tlatelolco* (*Massacre in Mexico*, 1975).
This book is a literary report of the 1968 massacre of three hundred
people who gathered in the square of Tlatelolco to hear political protest
speeches by students. Through the use of collage and the dramatic
montage of the first-person account, Poniatowska vividly brings the
reader into the horrifying event. Other works such as *Gaby Brimmer*,
1979 and *Dear Diego, te abraza Quiela*, 1978 (*Dear Diego*, 1986)
display her art of editing and modifying exchanges with real historical
characters to create their own literary testimony.

Elena Poniatowska's work exhibits a continuous effort to give original
expression to the silent voices of society: women, politically oppressed
people, the physically handicapped, and emotionally abused individuals.

SLIDE IN, MY DARK ONE, BETWEEN THE CROSSTIE AND THE WHISTLE

The tube of light perforates the night and the engine makes its way among the walls of trees, walls choked with inextricable vegetation: "Am I the one moving forward or is it the trees that are walking toward me?" the engineer asks himself, surrounded by the nocturnal density and the sugary smell of the tropics. Birds fly into the light, aim at the headlight and are dashed to pieces. A moment before they die, their eyes are red. All night the engineer watches the birds die. The headlight also blinds the plants; it turns them white, and they only recover their opulence after it has passed and, up above, the dark masses of the mountains are once again sketched on the horizon. Pancho likes to stick his head out of the locomotive and see how, in the train's wake, everything comes back to life: the bushes of thick vegetation revive, transfigured, ghostly; they cross themselves, dazed by the light. Afterward, the night swallows them up, immense and harsh like that army of trees that unfolds over hundreds of kilometers around them, with who-knows-what secret military strategy.

Meanwhile the intersecting flights of a thousand luminous insects cross the darkness of the sky; Pancho can even hear the death rattle of some animal caught in a trap and the occasional cry of a wounded bird. Fascinated, he thinks about the thousands of birds that fall on the tracks. Probably not even their little bones are left, their little bird bones, sticks, twigs; nothing is more fragile. The electric reflector weighs half a ton and illuminates half a kilometer in front of it; inside that white light the insects dance until dawn. (Camilo calls them "inseps.")

As it begins to turn light, the sounds of the night die down: the cicadas; the strangely human cries of the birds; the dark movements of the heavy, plant-covered ground; the secret, sinuous water, which is finally drowned in the swamp. Then Pancho, his senses overloaded, closes his eyes, sighs, leans back on the iron bench, brushes his strong hand over his face as if to wipe it off. All he manages to do is knock off his cap. He smooths his hair; it's time to go to sleep. Any minute now he will get off the locomotive to fall into any cot, the first one he can find, until night returns. Then, rested, he will once again climb onto his engine, his waking love, the river of steel that runs through his veins, his steam, his air, his reason for being on earth, his only bridge with reality.

The nicest thing about Teresa, besides her ample flesh, was her prudence, or rather, her absolute incapacity for intrigue or malevolence. He would come home swearing a blue streak against the yard chief, saying that they were going to all get together to get rid of the sonofabitch, that the union was there for a reason, that . . . and Teresa, with her steady cow eyes, would respond calmly:

"Well, we'll see."

Never a judgment, never an unnecessary word. She would slowly shift her great passivity from the kitchen, to the bedroom, to the patio, and seem to embrace everything. Nothing got to her, nothing altered her even temper.

Still, Pancho liked it when Teresa sat on top of him while they made love, he on his back in bed and she crouched over him, mounted on his chest, her legs encircling him, so enormous that Pancho couldn't see her face, smothered as he was by her stomach, her powerful thighs, but what sweet, what comforting asphyxiation. Pancho felt as satisfied then as he did before his engine's control panel. A dense happiness slid through him; the liquid metal that comes out of the foundry bubbled inside him, with the pure, white color of sunlight. Pancho went from the nocturnal plenitude on the tracks of the Southwestern route, standing erect before the window of the locomotive, to the plenitude of his three-o'clock nap, when he reached out his hand to feel Teresa's thick, hot arm, and to draw her to him, to embrace that tender, soft *mole*, and to dive into her time and again, like the birds flinging themselves against the headlight time and again, their eyes red. They always made love around noon, with a diadem of sweat on Teresa's brow.

From the kitchen came the crackling of pork frying, covered with a lid so it wouldn't dry out, and Pancho's appetite would double. He would fuck sluggishly and go from one table to the other, barely taking time to put on his pajama bottoms. He would sit before the marrow broth that Teresa served him, a strap from her slip straying down her arm. She would eat too, gazing at his face while she flipped the tortillas on the *comal*, her arm outstretched. They would sop up their food, taking their time, sipping it, accumulating new sensations on their hot, agitated tongues, as if they were continuing and perpetuating the act of love. Many times, when he finished wiping his mouth with his hand, Pancho would again pull Teresa toward the disheveled, greasy bed. Afterward they would remain in each other's arms, the nape of Teresa's sweaty neck against Pancho's shoulder, Pancho's wet organ fallen against Teresa's leg, so she could feel how the semen still trickled out. They would sink into sleep like that. But sometimes Teresa clung to Pancho's neck as if she were going to drown, as if she were on the verge of falling into the deepest part of the ocean, of her ocean, her own water. Then Pancho would desire her furiously for the dependency in her embrace and for that distracted expression in her round eyes.

At exactly six-forty he would say good-bye to her from the door, as Teresa would finally set about washing the dishes, cleaning up the kitchen. When Pancho would return from his run at six in the morning two days later, he would find her asleep. As he slipped under the sheets next to her, she would receive him with a murmur of acquiescence. In the course of the morning Teresa would abandon the bed; she would sweep, or "dustmot," as she called it, and do the ironing. Around two in the afternoon she would lie down next to him again, still dressed, to be within reach of his desire when he woke up.

"No, Pancho, this shouldn't be greased."

"You mean I shouldn't grease the bearings?"

"No, in a diesel engine all this work is automatic."

"And what about the joint pins, I don't grease them either?"

"No, everything's already done, see."

"But who does the engine maintenance?"

"She does her own maintenance, all by herself. A hydrostatic lubricator, run by steam, pressure, water and oil, greases the cylinders. This diesel was built to make things easier for the people who operate it. All you have to do is drive."

Pancho looks uneasily at the engine; he doesn't recognize it, doesn't know how to get a hold on it. For the first time he feels out of place in a locomotive. Everything is hidden; the controls are contained inside a steel surface so shiny that it repels him. The yard up above also shines; the picture windows make the station look like a glass store.

"Nothing is like it used to be," he thinks, "nothing."

In the old days the dark *mole* of the locomotive would sprout up on the horizon, followed by its plume of smoke and, in less time than it takes a cock to crow, there it was, parked, blocking out the clarity of the morning with its blackness. It would enter, snorting its weariness, out of breath, and would settle in on the rails defiantly, with a screech of springs. Its triumphant panting would still echo through the station. The railroadmen would climb off her and say good-bye or shout their hellos, overjoyed at coming home. As they got off, they would pat their engine, slapping her back as if she were a good old animal, caressing her with an open hand, ample caresses, trying to take in everything. Pancho would stay with La Prieta in the loading yard, cooling her down; he liked to hear the hammering that came from the workshop, cars, axles and wheels, one, two, one, two, on top of the anvils, and the echoing in his ears, the purring of the lathes, as the whistle of the locomotive had once echoed. As the workmen straightened the old, arthritic track with bars, they would groan and yell as they tried to lift it: "Ahhhhhhh! Ooooooooooh! Ahhhhhhh!" It was as if they felt the rails' discomfort in their own bodies and were showing solidarity with them. And all of this amidst the even breathing of the boilers and the constant chugging of the air pistons.

As he would head off, feeling contented, king of the road, Pancho would tell the mechanic: "I'm leaving her in your hands; I'll be back in a while to take her for a spin." The trainmen would pass by cans of tar, piles of burlap; they would jump over the ballast with the heady joy of a traveler who recognizes his house; they would skirt around the empty containers, worn-out boxes, twisted iron, junk. It's true, everything wasn't clean; the ballast was covered with trash, with living things that were now charred, with loose chunks of carrion, with discarded tools, all the garbage that, ten thousand years from now, will be indistinguishable from organic and inorganic waste that time, or perhaps the sea, will pulverize into sand. An upside-down lantern dug into the earth, an abandoned cart displayed its guts, the trash was forming a mountain, but now the brightness of the tracks was driving Pancho crazy.

"So, this doesn't need to be greased?"

"No, Pancho, I told you it doesn't."

"O.K., and what about La Prieta?"

"We're sending her to Apizaco. They'll run her on some short stretches."

"But why the hell didn't you tell me you were going to take her away?"

"No one was told, Pancho. The three-thousand-horse-power diesels arrived and we wanted to put them into service immediately."

"I was off yesterday, and you took advantage."

Just like Teresa. Treacherous, sneaky. One morning she wasn't there anymore. Afterward a railroad worker told him that he had seen her get into a car, hoisted by a man's hand; he hadn't been able to get a look at the man, but he sure noticed how Teresa walked fast, without looking around her. At home the old, pot-bellied suitcase that the engineer always took with him was missing. For many days Pancho kept reaching out to take Teresa's thick arm and pull her toward him, until he finally decided to go to the station and escape into the dark chamber of his other woman, to take refuge in her womb which, even when stationary, seemed to be rocking, and to sleep curled up against the steel plate, telling her what he never told Teresa, "Prieta, my pretty little dark one, my darling, pretty Momma, Prieta, little railroad girl, you're my love, Prieta, you flirt," until his lips kept forming an *a*, the *a* of Prieta, that name pronounced like a charm against pain and abandonment. And now they come out with this business that La Prieta isn't there anymore either.

"When did they take her away?"

"Last night."

Pancho was at a section meeting at the very moment that La Prieta, slowly, sneakily, slid away along the rails, driven by another engineer.

"Who took her out?"

The superintendent is getting impatient. "Go ask in the office."

"I don't have anything to do with ink-shitters. They're not even railroad-men."

"Man, it isn't like that; things are changing for the better. It's the new rules and regulations; the power of the railroad has to grow. It'll be good for us all. Anyway, thank your lucky stars that your locomotive isn't being sold as scrap iron to the United States. We're going to sell them almost three thousand cars that are in really bad shape."

"Fuck you."

Pancho turns around before the superintendent can respond. He walks away—he has always been a fast walker—and thinks, "If he catches up with me, we'll have it out right here." He almost wishes it would happen, but the other man doesn't come after him, no one follows him. He walks among the burning of the rails that flash in his eyes, waxing them, slicing them; he steps onto the ballast so he won't get tar on his shoes, and he remembers with what pleasure Teresa used to sweep the ground, even though she did it with a worn-out broom. He tries to retain the image, which begins to smear before him, but the heat seems to melt everything—signs, crossties, loading platforms, rivets—into a thick, gray gelatin. The iron disintegrates; now it is just clumps of earth; yes, it is common dirt.

"If a train comes, fuck them; I'm not moving."

On a newly tarred wall a sign glitters: "Long live Demetrio Vallejo!" Pancho walks without stopping, the sun on his neck boring into his shoulders. It was a while back that he left Balbuena and passed under the bridge at Nonoalco; it was a while back that he entered the plains. Now there aren't even any crossing gates, not a single man sitting on the platforms, no one bent over kicking the gravel, no one playing with the sand, with the rocks that fall down onto the coal wagons; just a stray worn-out shoe, defeated like him, and over there, a caboose rotting in the sun. Now there aren't any guard towers or cranes. He thinks he hears the wailing of a brake shoe—"Goddamn, now I'm hearing voices."— There isn't a single convoy of cars loaded with sulphur from the Isthmus of Tehuantepec, not a single convoy of salt. He has to go on, put one foot in front of the other, for who knows how many hours, until dusk, his throat dry. Anyway, he's used to it by now; he can put up with that and a lot more; he can put up with a helluva lot.

"I have to reach some station so I won't be stranded here in no-man's-land."

But since no house shimmers in the distance, Pancho leaves the rails and stretches out alongside the tracks, and there he sleeps like an angel, like a rock at the bottom of a well, like a dead man.

"You know, prices are getting to be sky-high."

When Teresa spoke it was to complain about the high cost of living. Otherwise she kept silent as she went from one chore to another. Only when she made love did she articulate words of love that started with *m*, "*more*," "*mmm*," slowly, softly, in a hoarse cooing, yes, that was it, a dove cooing, which Pancho always found gratifying. Precisely because of that moan, suddenly, in the middle of a meal, Pancho felt a piercing, an infinite desire to possess her. It was he who provoked that woman's moan, and on top of her, embracing her womb, he awaited the moment when it would begin, just as he waited for the instant La Prieta would begin backstitching the plains with the clacking of her wheels on the tracks. When she ran quietly, sheathed in silence, he felt the same desire as when he mounted Teresa. He was the master of time, of all that darkness, of the blackness that his headlight penetrated; those shadows that he crossed over were conquered territory, lands owned by him, his booty; he had extracted them from the night. They warbled like Teresa, they flooded over him with their incredibly white, luminous masses; white like milk, thighs, breasts of night, almondlike fruits; skin that softly, tenderly enveloped him.

At first, Teresa had been more communicative. She had talked about her sister Berta, about how Berta used to hit her; about how once, when she couldn't delouse Teresa, she had shaved her head. Every so often she would complain to Pancho, "Hey, how come you never have anything to say?" And Pancho would mumble, "We railroadmen are married to silence." That's why Teresa became quiet. Since she was only answered in monosyllables, little by little she stopped opening her mouth, spoke only when it was absolutely necessary, said only what came out in spite of her, beyond her control: that cooing, and the harping on sky-high prices.

"Pancho, get up, you sucker."

"Pancho!"

The shadows of two faces fall over him. Pancho rubs his eyes.

"We've been following you for hours. Come on, let's go."

El Chufas and El Gringo pull on him; El Chufas has already put his hands under his arms and lifted him up. "The hell you're going to stay here; let's get going."

El Gringo gets mad: "I'm on duty tomorrow, you sonofabitch. Come on, stop farting around."

"Hey, who asked you? You're the one that's farting around." Now it's Pancho who gets good and mad, so mad that he gets up. "I suppose I went looking for you guys? You're the ones who're fucking with me; I was just fine here."

El Chufas hasn't taken his hands out from under his arms, as if he's afraid Pancho will run away.

Pancho breaks loose violently, although all his anger is directed at El Gringo. "You go to hell!"

"Thatta way, Pancho, don't let anyone order you around."

"Who told you guys to come after me, huh? I didn't ask you."

"El Chufas started looking for you."

"So what the hell's with El Chufas? He doesn't give a damn."

"El Chufas saw you walking off along the track, mad as hell, and he hollered at you but you didn't turn around. That's why he got worried. Just forget it. We were in the loading yard . . . Come on, let's get out of here.

Without realizing it, Pancho has started walking alongside his buddies. It's been a long time since he has hung out with them. He didn't even go looking for them when Teresa left, didn't show his face at the cantina. Anyway, he had La Prieta, and that's where he went to sleep, cradled in the tremulous viscera that held him warmly, in the internal combustion of his own blood which demanded his recognition as the night advanced, to foresee her reactions, to guess the secret of her most hidden sounds, her tinklings, signals and sighs. He wrapped his legs around her ardor, as Teresa used to imprison his, so that when they woke up they only had to turn over to be in each other's arms. He could predict her least convulsion: "Now she's going to shudder because the guys from the shop will come, and the hammer blows on the anvil will echo all through the steel plate. I'm going to feel the blows myself, here inside her. In a minute the boilermakers will come, along with the superintendent, and she'll soften up, happy." Before, Pancho had the habit of going to the cantina with his buddies, and when they shouted, "Wine for the men and water for the asses," he would belly up to the bar to guzzle his beer, then go the house with the red light to dance with the broads who smell like rotten corn. But when Teresa came into his life, he no longer needed anything, not hell-raising, not clinging women from the cathouse. So long, Canicas, Camilo, Babalú, Gringo, Chufas, Luciano! Luciano had given his engine a name, too: "The Flirt," and he had her all dolled up, with her hanging trinkets and mirrors, her Virgin of Guadalupe, and even a picture of himself leaning out the window of the locomotive. Now that Pancho has had time to think about it, he feels kind of warm inside, walking with his friends, his buddies, his pals, who have come all this way to look for him, forgetting that he dumped them a long time ago.

"Climb into the caboose. Let's go have a cold one."

These fellows are good guys, really good guys.

"Pancho, a coupla beers'll do you good."

Pancho doesn't say yes or no.

"They're probably closed up already," says El Gringo.

"Well, let's go to Martita's."

Martita is a real hellcat. When the railroadmen are out to party and everyone at the bar orders them out—"O.K., you crazies, get going, it's time to call it a night, go sleep it off!"—and a good cup of coffee is nowhere to be found, not even an eggnog or one last round, the front door of her house is always open. She doesn't mind climbing out of her hammock and waiting on them with her big, beautiful smile, a slow wave of light moving through her eyes, like a mother looking at her children, showing no favorites. No matter how wasted they might be, really out of it, hanging onto each other like they have been hanging onto the lamp posts, like masts, feeling as if their ships are sinking, just seeing her raises their spirits. She immediately brings out the *mezcal* or makes a steaming pot of spiked coffee sweetened with condensed milk that comes gushing out of the can, and if they can pay her, fine, and if not, they'll drop by with the dough when they can. She brought the hammock from Juchitán, since she never could get used to sleeping in a bed: "It's the rocking I miss."

"It's the rocking that keeps her in a good mood," the railroadmen say. They always feel good as hell at Martita's house; their raw stomachs settle down and, even if they're sloppy drunk, she takes the edge off with her spiked coffee, so good for warming the belly. And none of this nagging or scolding them, none of that; Martitita is beautiful, her eyes with those slow waves of light are beautiful. What more could you hope for in this goddamn life than to feel welcome, sheltered by the eyes of a woman who's happy to see you, what the hell more could you ask for, anyway? Pancho also stopped hanging out at Martita's when Teresa arrived.

"The superintendent wants to see you tomorrow," El Gringo says to him as they nurse their second cup of java.

"I already told him to fuck off."

"He said he wants to see you."

For the superintendent, Alejandro Díaz, Pancho is a real character. He even gets a kick out of watching him walk by with his gray hair and his slumped shoulders, on his way to the section local, saying gravely, "Tomorrow at noon the strike begins, the two-hour work stoppage, because the deadline we gave management is past . . ." Alejandro Díaz is a company man. When he sees Pancho, he wishes he weren't, so he could hear him arguing in the assembly, see his strong, challenging gaze, the gaze of a free man, when all day long he's followed around by so many hangdog expressions. And he's only the superintendent. Imagine how many despicable expressions the President of the Republic must see! They say—but no one knows it for a fact—that Pancho once spoke at Section 19 in Monterrey, before an assembly of one thousand railroadmen who believed in the Charro, Díaz de León. The first three speakers supported the Charro, and when Pancho Valverde got up to speak, everyone thought he would join them; but they were all taken aback when he said the Charro was a corrupt leader, out for the company, the government, and especially himself, his own petty self-interest. All those people knew that Pancho was a straight-shooter, but still the assembly ended up divided. That was one of the biggest blows in Pancho's union career, but he never mentioned it. Sometimes in the cantina he remembers the assembly and murmurs, "It's no good, it's no good."

That's why the older guys respect Pancho and the younger ones want to be noticed by him, to make an impression on him. The superintendent feels the same way. Alejandro Díaz knows he doesn't count in Pancho's book, that the engineer would lay down his life for Timoteo, for Venancio, for Chon, for Baldomero, for El Gringo, for Camilo, for El Babalú, but not for him. For them he would. Alejandro Díaz has seen how Pancho demands compensation, fights for the retirees, stays up into the wee hours going over contracts, memorizing clauses, almost all of them in the company's favor, so he can shoot them down at the meeting. His "Shut up, you motherfuckers" is more effective in the assemblies than any reasoned argument; his fist hitting the debate table covered with cigarette burns is definitive; and the first thing you see in the presidium is his face, because of the intensity of his expression. It isn't even that he wants power; it's that Pancho is a friend of Timoteo the switch-engine worker, who is looking at him now, his stub resting on the table because he left his forearm trapped between two cars during one of so many maneuvers. And he is also a buddy of Venancio, a retiree who is starving to death inside the railroad car where he lives, even though his wife has hung geraniums in the windows. And he cares about Lenche the fireman, who these days shovels rancor instead of coal, and he likes Concepción, and Chonito, who practically lives in the Temple of Noon, under the Nonoalco Bridge, on Luna Street, waiting for Roque Rojas— never mind Jesus Christ!—to take possession of his human form and free him from arthritis, old age, his breath smelling like slimy water, which tells him that his insides are rotting.

Pancho Valverde has never let himself get discouraged: "I speak up because I want to and because I can and because I've been giving 'em hell here for a lot of years." He peppers his allegations with sayings: "The fewer the burros, the more corn cobs there are," "The shrimp that falls asleep gets carried away by the tide," "He who is an ox even licks the yoke." And Alejandro Díaz finds it amusing to associate Pancho's sayings with expressions like "gross national product" (We're the ones who are gross), "holidays" (He who is born to be an old pot can't even hope to become a sooty grill), "contractual" (There are no more railroadmen with pocketwatches and caps), and other wonderful sayings that Pancho has learned by heart in his many shifts as a warehouseman. "Come on, come on, don't start running around like a chicken with its head cut off." It was Pancho who started the initiative against the company men, whatta we need with so many of them, what is that bunch of dolled-up accountants good for, those secretaries who totter around on their high heels like hens. Pancho said that, out of Pacific Railway's five hundred classified employees, the company men didn't even amount to fifty, and he called for at least twenty-three of them to be laid off, because he was here to tell you that they didn't do a damned thing. He identified the culprits, and two of them turned out to be sons of Benjamín Méndez, the manager. He said the eight thousand rail workers—now *they* were underfed and underpaid—were up to here with the bureaucracy, with so much dull paperwork. And naturally, the company didn't give in; they fired a lot of people.

But what a great fight Pancho put up, great even in the eyes of Alejandro Díaz, who intervened on Pancho's behalf so they wouldn't dismiss him, and he never even knew it. It's a helluva good fight, because Pancho pushes strikes but has always come out against acts of sabotage. He loves the trains too much to put up with a runaway engine, a crash; the least dent on his locomotive makes him flinch as if the blow were to his body. An attack on the track hurts him personally, like that time some bastard blocked the safety pedal on Train 6093, placing a plate of steel over the accelerator. He pulled the lever and the engine shot away at more than eighty kilometers an hour, heading straight for Train 9854, the Flirt, Luciano's engine, which was being moved around the yard. Luciano just about got it, but he took off the brakes and immediately jumped off his locomotive. He saved his own skin but not the Flirt's; she was transformed into a spine-chilling mountain of twisted metal. Months later, Luciano died of sadness.

At Luciano's side, Pancho had lived through strikes and other adventures. One time Luciano held tight to the driving shaft, trying to stop five runaway trains, and he only jumped off at the last minute, when he saw the wreck was imminent. Pancho used to sing, sitting on a crosstie, "Wherever I come / and wherever I go / the hen I don't take with me / I leave cackling." And the two of them would laugh, because when they were young they were both on the sign committee, and along with "Down with the company" and "Railroad workers with Vallejo," they used to write on the sides of the cars, in black tar, holding their sides and dropping the buckets, "What a rail I've got!" "I want to go clacketyclacketyclack with you," "Don't worry that the tunnel's dark, we'll slide in on the rail," "Just give me a good engine and I'll pull out all the stops," "Fuck you, Díaz de León," "Between the rails and between your legs, we make it from town to town," "Slide in, my dark one, between the crosstie and the whistle," "Onto a good caboose you can hook anything you want," and other delectable sayings that they drew with care, licking their lips, because they had just discovered women and the rails. Goddamn Luciano, one helluva guy, what a pal, he's like a brother to me, my man!

For Alejandro Díaz, the superintendent, it is painful to look at Pancho. The expression on his face is absolutely desolate; he looks like a dog without a master. Deep down inside, Alejandro Díaz would like to tell Pancho that, if his steam locomotive means so much to him, he will arrange for his transfer to one of the less-traveled routes, so he can keep driving it. But Pancho is one of the best engineers in the system, and now that his temples are turning gray and his face, which has always looked like a railyard, is wrinkled, the company is taking away his engine to give him a diesel, one they just bought from the United States. Instead of feeling proud, Pancho Valverde is suspicious. He wooed La Prieta, o my Prieta!, because she was always finicky and you had to figure out how to treat her. He dressed her up; he bought her a bronze whistle, picking the deep tone himself: "Give me a whistle that sounds downright pretty for my Prieta, because I've got a three-star Prieta." On the days when it was his turn to take her out, he would arrive with the oil can, the cushion to protect him from the heat when the seat was on the sunny side, the heavy sweater for nighttime, the little suitcase, the hand mirror, the lantern. The other railroadmen would laugh:

"Here comes Pancho with his trousseau for the honeymoon."

Actually, every run is the first night, the wedding night. Pancho installs himself in the seat, grabs the lever and, while he transmits an order to her, caresses her. When the engine emits steam with the sound of a pressure-cooker, Pancho also relaxes, and he tenses up like a cable when he puts on the brakes, when he checks on hills to see that the rail stops respond and brake, all of his concentration focused on keeping the cars in check. It's nice to hear the engines being hooked up; it's as familiar to him as the sound of a door closing!

Once they are out of the station, Pancho opens up the regulator all the way and speaks to his mount, to his iron mare, to his wide and powerful animal of fire; he strokes her with his hand, he acknowledges her: "O.K., O.K., Prieta, hold it, Prieta, take it easy, take it easy, slow down, girl!" Camilo or Sixto or Supertino or Juan, whichever engineer's helper is on duty, is so used to Pancho's voice that he doesn't even listen. In fact, it puts him to sleep; it's a real drag, because Pancho doesn't like to share La Prieta with anybody. He leads her over the tracks almost as if he were dancing with her; his hand on her waist, the tips of his fingers on her side, they both sweep to the right, to the left, a two-step, dum dum, like someone running through the fields, over the ochre land, the brown dirt, the deep black soil that emerges from a swampy bed and approaches the track without respecting the fifteen meters on either side: the track's right-of-way. The land rolls down from the mountain to cuddle up against the track and penetrate the crossties. It pushes up the stones of the ballast, it nudges in everywhere, wheedling its way in, laughing at the train that runs along the wide track tooting and tooting and scurrying along.

Before noon, the sun begins to heat up; it flings itself against the metal, attacks the chimneys, crashes into the glass, turning it iridescent, heat against heat, fuel against fuel. Pancho shifts the cushion under his behind. Even the oil can is boiling. Threads of greasy sweat slide down from Camilo's railroad cap; Pancho's helper is sleeping while he cooks in his own juice, his mouth open like the chimney of the train, an oven of steam that also vanishes in thin air. From noon on, the towns around Veracruz are no longer towns, but rather corners of Hell. When he stops at the stations, Pancho sees the burros hitched up, the tables that have been brought outside, the sausage blackened by flies, the lard under the table melting, and the little old woman who shades herself from the heat, covering her head and fanning herself with the fringe of her shawl, as if that could do any good. Those who approach the train observe it silently; the only ones who shout are the women vendors who go to the last cars, hawking their sandwiches of head cheese, their candies, their fruit-flavored water that is now lukewarm from the sun. In a little while they will take off again: "Come on, Prieta, pull hard, don't give out on me, because it's the last stretch." Near the engine, a passenger in a threadbare suit says to another man who has just woken up:

"You can't even feel this thing moving."

"That's because it doesn't move, it just inches along."

Pancho nearly talks back to that dandy; for a minute he considers sounding the alarm whistle just to give him a good scare, but self-discipline wins out. Pancho's a good engineer for two reasons: first, because he's a good driver, and second because he knows how to run his engine to get the most out of the steam and water. He could care less what the passengers say; they aren't aware that La Prieta is over twenty years old but is in better condition than almost any train. It is no accident that don Panchito, as the younger railroadmen call him, goes with her to the shop to supervise her maintenance. The mechanics know her and take special care in examining all La Prieta's parts. Pancho himself paints her; he goes over her from head to tail so she won't get run down, she won't get mildewed, so not a single hinge will be forgotten, so each part will be oiled. When a young boy started working as his helper and

saw the piles of black grease, he exclaimed, "What a filthy job!" Pancho
replied, "Get out of here, you bum, you son-of-a-bitch!" and he kept
calling him a queer. The other railroadmen followed suit, making fun
of him, laughing and cursing; they themselves have grease up to their
hineys, heavy, black, visceral grease, because it is what they use to
cover the insides of the engine, rubbing it in, coaxing it into the smallest
seams, ready to sing out gruffly, rounding off the angles with a thick,
padded coat, lining the intestines of the locomotive with this new amnio-
tic fluid that softens her and renders her docile. In the shop, grease has
never been considered dirty; on the contrary, it's a blessing, and yet now
the superintendent, Alejandro Díaz, begins lecturing him as if he had
never been a railroadman:

"With the diesel engine the work is cleaner, more technical; you won't
get dirty anymore. Anyway, you're going to save God knows how many
days that you spend lubricating the engine to death."

Pancho looks at him without comprehending. For him, manually
lubricating the piston rods, taking them out of their axles, rubbing them
over and over again, and putting them back, is a pleasure, a physical
necessity.

"You'll see how fast you take to it, Pancho; it's just a matter of getting
used to it."

Pancho shakes his head. "There are some of us who just don't get
used to certain things."

"You'll see how much you're going to like it. Tomorrow we'll run the
engine to Veracruz. You're going to take her out . . . hauling cement."

"To Veracruz?"

With this new, orange, stiff engine, Pancho doesn't speak. In the
stations nothing has changed; there are the same rickety, flea-ridden
benches; the same stalls selling toasted, dried beef; the same wobbly
tables; the same swarms of flies; the same burros with their scar-lined
backs. Still, it is as if Pancho, in his engineer's cab, is riding higher,
more distant. He can't hear what the passengers say to him, their suits
wrinkled from an overnight trip; nor can he hear the cries of the food
vendors who lift their baskets up from window to window. During the
night the cab didn't get hot; he didn't need his cushion or the oil can,
and the second machinist slept soundly, used to Pancho's ways, and
without threads of black sweat running down his face. Still, Pancho
woke him up several times, feeling uneasy. "Come on, cuz I don't know
how to do it in this one." With this one he's going to have to throw
away the bridal trousseau; none of that is necessary, not even the little
suitcase, because there in the corner is a locker where you can hang
your jacket; you can adjust the air conditioning, so you don't even need
a sweater, or a mirror, because the cab is full of rear-view mirrors.

Pancho keeps a suspicious silence and yet the diesel is so powerful, so noble in the upgrades, so good-natured, that the next day he is pleased with the notion of going with her to the shop for her check-up after the trip. "That's how I'll get acquainted with her," like with a new, three thousand-horsepower love that one grows to admire, then care for; then it becomes that thing which makes one forget old flames, the Prietas, the Teresas. Who knows if it will happen, but it might.

The next morning, before Pancho goes into the shop, the yard boss tells him, "The engine has already been called in."

"Fine, I'll go in with her."

"No, a machinist is coming to get her in a few minutes."

"What do you mean?"

"That you leave her here and another driver will take her away."

"But it's just that I want to see how they get her ready for the next trip."

"On the next run you're going to take another 5409 out, not this one."

"What do you mean, another one?"

"That's right, any of the eight diesel engines that were bought in the United States. Those are the new rules. You leave her here and the shop takes care of her. Someone else will take this engine out. That's how it is now, like in the auto industry; engines are put through a process involving a lot of people. It's so we can speed up service."

Pancho pulls his cap down over his eyes. They're even taking that away from him! Watching, feeling how the engine molds to you, how she runs along memorizing the route, how she talks, after her own fashion, to ask for what she needs. Even that! Seeing how his hands begin to leave prints on the lever, on the regulator, hearing how the sound of his breathing infiltrates the steel plates day by day, until his warmth is transmitted to them. Even that, dammit!

"They're modern techniques; that's how the engineers have planned it, to save time."

Teresa also liked it when he caressed her little by little, softening her, carving her, coaxing his hand into her smallest seams to pull out her oil, her delicate juices. Then Teresa would open up, her thick legs far apart, forgetful of everything, and she would sway under his arm, her large, erect breasts pointing toward him, her sex twisted, liquid, a fruit of the sea, undone in his hands, whipped into foam, about to come. He liked waiting until the last minute so he could see her, listen to her changing rhythms, look at her open caldron-mouth full of saliva, her eyelids half-closed, her hands spread out over the sheets, the palms turned up, the fingers spread as wide as her oiled thighs which rose up in search of his hand. That's how he lubricated her, with her own flow, her own humors, until he had rendered her docile, until his hand was soaked and his arm was also soaked under her neck, while her head bobbed to the right, to the left, and her ample, sweaty buttocks also came and went in a wave that filled the bed with water. Only when her broad womb was shaken by spasms, only when the dove's cooing began, only then did Pancho penetrate Teresa, "Now, honey, now," and he wasn't inside of her five minutes before she had come in an avalanche of moans, of sobs, arching her back over and over again until she was fulfilled. Pancho sought the expression of satisfaction, never seen on her features except during lovemaking; that's why he couldn't stop looking pointedly at her until he saw her face relax, her mouth sucking gently like that of a newborn, the sucking, then the letting go, spilling over all her features. How glorious it was for him to see this big, panting woman, her eyes blank, unblushing, loose, the wide, bulky mountain now quiet, blind, then slowly coming back to life, drained, having given away all her fruits, one by one! Within the hour, Teresa would get out of bed, and just like that, without even going to the bathroom, she would go into the kitchen to light the fire. They would eat, then go back to bed filled with liquid murmurs, and he would mount her hurriedly because he had to go to work, and she would offer herself again, tender, whole, dry, good, what a good woman Teresa was, what goodness; she mended quickly, and he would start again, his hand groping, moving over her with familiarity, until his caresses drew out her water. Here? Lower? Lower? Tell me where, honey, here?

"I want to transfer to Apizaco."

"Don't be stupid, how could you possibly leave? Pancho, you'll lose your seniority, just for the hell of it."

El Gringo is getting mad. They call him El Gringo because of his blue eyes, but he's from the mountains in the state of Puebla.

"I'm going to talk to the superintendent in charge of Locomotive Power."

El Gringo is a seasoned man; he started working for the railroad as a laborer; then they promoted him from cleaner to fireman. "All we need now is for flies to be conductors!" But El Gringo had also been a stoker and a brakeman. He went all the way through the ranks: yard brakeman, foreman, yard boss, assistant to the general yard boss, and that was the end of the line, because the next position, that of general yard boss, the one who gives the orders in the terminal, is classified and he, like Luciano Cedillo Vásquez, would rather stay on this side of the curtain . . . of pesos. He knew the place inside and out. Just four months ago he had asked them to give him the rules and regulations for the diesels because these locomotives, which were much more powerful than the steam engines, went out with up to forty or fifty cars but used the same number of personnel, so a lot of railroad workers were laid off. El Gringo put up a fight because the engineer's helpers also had contracts, but he lost. What he never lost, not even in the slammer, was hope.

"You can get thirty thousand pesos out of the company when you retire."

"Don't bullshit me, what's the matter with you? How many retirees do you know who aren't starving to death?"

El Gringo slams his glass down on the table. "You can get up to forty thousand out of them."

If he weren't El Gringo, Pancho would tell him to get lost, but this old guy is prepared. El Chufas, a bit tipsy, laughs softly. El Gringo slams his glass down again and hollers at the bartender: "Where are the rest? We're going to accuse you of tortoise-ism." The bartender, peeved at seeing the glass in the air, is about to reply, "If you break it you buy it," but he thinks better of it.

"They took my little dark one away from me," says Venancio as he comes up to the tables. "But that doesn't mean I've looked down my nose at the new ones."

"Get out of here."

Pancho likes the taste of the first beer when it slides down his throat, sort of bitter and scratchy. With the back of his hand, El Chufas wipes the foam off his mustache. Only El Gringo downs it in one gulp, and then it's too late; he orders the others, and he's paying, so before his buddies have had time to finish theirs, they have new bottles in front of them.

"In those mountains, the track is just an opening in the forest."

"Around those parts," insists El Chufas, "the runs last for days, not just hours."

"And what about me?"

"That isn't an engine," Venancio retorts, "it's a chicken basket."

"Get out of here!" Pancho shouts again.

And this time Venancio gets up; anyway, he's finished his beer. "You and your engine get out of here."

Caritino sits down in the place that Venancio vacated; he orders a beer, leans back in the chair, and pulls his cap down over his face. He always does this. "I come here to relax," he explains. He only wakes up when the swinging starts, because he does like to join in a good fight.

In the warmth of the cantina, Pancho gives free rein to his memories, even more so now that he's feeling down in the mouth. He tells stories about the Brotherhood of Boiler Makers; about the Fraternity of Train Workers; about the struggle of 1945, which turned bloody; about Reza the foreman, who was fatally wounded by a bullet in the neck, right in the main railroad station; about his fellow yardmen. He speaks about past strikes that were invariably lost, about the Vigilance Committee that he once headed, and finally, at the very end, about how wonderful it is to stick your head out the window of La Prieta to feel the gusts of wind. And in a soft voice, he informs them:

"Tomorrow I'm leaving for Apizaco."

El Gringo interjects, "As if we'd let you."

Caritino uncovers his face, his railroad cap tilted back, and he takes a long, slow drink of his beer. "If I were him, I'd leave too."

"You guys are against progress."

"Progress, my ass."

The next day Pancho didn't come in to work. The railroad workers thought he had gone off to Apizaco, that in a few days they would have news about him. The superintendent, Alejandro Díaz, personally asked the telegraph operator to let him know as soon as Pancho was seen, although in the mountains the telegraph operators have the irritating habit, especially in the out-of-the-way stations, of turning off their machines and not transmitting orders. That's why there are so many train accidents.

A few days later, Alejandro Díaz learned that La Prieta wasn't parked at the platform of the Apizaco railway station, either. Since she was an old engine, he didn't report it immediately; that way the company wouldn't make a stink and they would have a few days to cover for Pancho, find him, send him word that he should stop acting like a fool.

"He's not going to be able to stay out long in that old coffeepot, and if he does, he'd better not have any illusions that we won't arrest him."

"What do you mean, arrest him? That rickety old heap of junk is going to die on him at the first stop. Haven't you seen her joints?"

At the cantina conjectures were flying: "Poor Pancho. That's what usually happens to old railroadmen, they get a screw loose." "If Pancho hangs on to that lever, he's going to kill himself!"

The railroad company began sending messages that, at the first stop, Pancho should be informed that he was under arrest, that he was endangering the lives of the other people who used the minor routes. But not a single telegraph operator ever reported the arrival of La Prieta. At Buenavista, only El Gringo tried to organize teams to search the line from Apizaco to Huachinango. He even went along in the caboose, but he didn't see any engines; no locomotive that fit the description had taken in fuel; no white-haired engineer had gotten off to load up on supplies. Either they were protecting him or he had met his maker.

The railroad company deduced: "He must have gone over into a ravine on his first run, vanishing without a trace." "He must be down at the bottom of the gorge." "But an engine with a man in it can't disappear just like that!" "A lot more than that disappeared in Rome, and who even remembers now!"

The strange thing is that, on many stretches of track, there were carbonized bats on the rails and ballast, as if a train had actually passed by and they, with their big eyes, had crashed into its headlight. Still, no station reported any engine; nothing, not a sound on the rails. After a few months had gone by, the dispatchers no longer received La Prieta's code among their orders, her distinctive markings, size and dents, so they could recognize her. And if anyone did lay eyes on her, those who recognized her played dumb, because no one reported it to Buenavista.

From Apizaco to Huachinango, and among the villages high in the mountains, in the vicinity of Teziutlán, a rumor is spreading of a runaway engine that makes ghost runs, and at night you can hear how the engineer opens the steam valve and then the mountain echoes with a long lament, like the cry of a wounded animal, a deep, pained cry that cuts the mountains of Puebla in two. No one has seen her. But once a dispatcher who was starting out in a remote station in the Huasteca region, one of those stations where you never see a living soul and where they usually send rookies to be trained, amidst the dark abysses, sent a telegram that was read at Buenavista: "Slide in, my dark one, between the crosstie and the whistle." El Gringo, who was in the cantina at the time, heard about it, and was the only one who smiled. But since he didn't like to shoot the breeze anymore, he didn't offer any explanations. Nor did Alejandro Díaz, the company man.

Translated by Cynthia Steele

Bibliography: Elena Poniatowska

Fiction

Poniatowska, Elena. *Lilus Kikus*. Mexico City: Los Presentes, 1954.

———. *Los cuentos de Lilus Kikus*. Xalapa: Universidad Veracruzana, 1967. Rpt. in Mexico City: Grijalbo, 1982.

———. *Hasta no verte Jesús mío*. Mexico City: Era, 1969. Rpt. in Mexico City: Era, 1984.

———. "Love Story." *14 mujeres escriben cuentos: antología*. Mexico City: Federación Editorial Mexicana, 1975. 158-70. Rpt. in *Latin American Literary Review* 3.26 (1985): 63-73. Rpt. in and trans. by Anne Twitty. *Longman Anthology of World Literature by Women 1875-1975*. Eds. Marian Arkin and Barbara Shollar. New York: Longman, 1989. 856-62.

———. "La borrega." *Cuentistas mexicanas siglo XX*. Ed. Aurora M. Ocampo. Mexico City: Universidad Nacional Autónoma de México, 1976. 283-84.

————. "La procesión." *Cuentistas mexicanas siglo XX*. Ed. Aurora M. Ocampo. Mexico City: Universidad Nacional Autónoma de México, 1976. 281-82.

————. "El recado." *Cuentistas mexicanas siglo XX*. Ed. Aurora M. Ocampo. Mexico City: Universidad Nacional Autónoma de México, 1976. 285-86.

————. *Querido Diego, te abraza Quiela*. Mexico City: Era, 1978. Rpt. in Mexico City: Era, 1984.

————. *De noche vienes*. Mexico City: Editorial Grijalbo, 1979. Rpt. in Mexico City: Grijalbo, 1983.

————. *Dear Diego*. Trans. Katherine Silver. New York: Pantheon Books, 1986.

————. "La hija del filósofo." *Puerta abierta: la nueva escritora latinoamericana*. Eds. Caridad L. Silva-Velázquez and Nora Erro-Orthmann. Mexico City: Joaquín Mortiz, 1986. 199-203.

————. "The Night Visitor." Trans. Catherine S. White-House. *Other Fires: Short Fiction by Latin American Women*. Ed. Alberto Manguel. Toronto: Lester & Orpen Dennis, 1986. 125-45.

————. "And Here's to You, Jesusa." Trans. Greogory Kolovakos and Ronald Christ. *Lives on the Line: The Testimony of Contemporary Latin American Authors*. Ed. Doris Meyer. Berkeley: University of California Press, 1988. 137-55.

————. *La flor de lis*. Mexico City: Era, 1988.

Essays

Poniatowska, Elena. *Palabras cruzadas*. Mexico City: Era, 1961.

————. *Todo empezó el domingo*. Mexico City: Fondo de Cultura Económica, 1963.

————. "Alusiones críticas al libro *Hasta no verte Jesús mío*." *Vida Literaria* [Mexico] 3 (1970): 22-24.

————. "Un libro que me fue dado." *Vida Literaria* [Mexico] 3 (1970): 3-4.

————. *La noche de Tlatelolco*. Mexico City: Era, 1973. Rpt. in Mexico City: Era, 1983.

————. "Las escritoras mexicanas calzan zapatos que les aprietan." *Los Universitarios* 5-31 October (1975): 4.

————. *Massacre in Mexico*. Trans. Helen R. Lane. [Prologue by Octavio Paz]. New York: Viking Press, 1975.

————. *El primer primero de mayo*. Mexico City: Centro de Estudios Históricos del Movimiento Obrero Mexicano, 1976.

————. *Gaby Grimmer*. Mexico City: Grijalbo, 1979.

————. *Fuerte es el silencio*. Mexico City: Era, 1980. Rpt. in Mexico City: Era, 1983.

————. "La literatura de las mujeres en América Latina." *Revista de la Educación Superior Asociación Nacional de Universidades e Institutos de Enseñanza Superior* [Mexico] 10 (1981): 23-25.

————. *Domingo 7*. Mexico City: Ediciones Océano, 1982. Rpt. in Mexico City: Ediciones Océano, 1983.

———. *El último guajolote*. Mexico City: Cultura, 1982.

———. *Pablo O'Higgins*. Mexico City: Fondo de Cultura Económica, 1985.

———. *¡Ay vida no me mereces!* Mexico City: Joaquín Mortiz, 1985.

———. *Nada, Nadie*. Mexico City: Joaquín Mortiz, 1988.

Theater

Poniatowska, Elena. *Melés y Teléo*. *Panoramas* 2 (1956): 135-299.

Criticism on the Works of Elena Poniatowska

Aguilera Malta, Demetrio. "Elena y Alberto." *El Gallo Ilustrado* [Literary Supplement to *El Día*] 56 21 Jul. 1963. 4.

Alegría, Fernando, ed. *Nueva historia de la novela hispanoamericana*. Hanover, NH: Ediciones del Norte, 1986. 426-28.

Alvarez, Federico. "*Todo empezó el domingo*." *La Cultura en México* 72 3 July. 1963. xx.

Beer, Gabriela de. "La revolución en la narrativa de Campobello, Castellanos y Poniatowska." *Semana de Bellas Artes* [Mexico] 165 28 Jan. 1981: 2-5.

Bruce-Novoa, Juan. "Elena Poniatowska: The Feminist Origins of Commitment." *Women's Studies International Forum* 6, 5 (1983): 509-16.

Capistrán, Miguel. "La transmutación literaria." *Vida Literaria* [Mexico] 3 (1970): 12-14.

Carballo, Emmanuel. "Elena Poniatowska una de las escritoras más auténticas de México." *La Cultura en México* 148 16 Dec. 1964. xviii.

———. "*Lilus Kikus*." *México en la Cultura*. 294 7 Nov. 1954. 2.

———. "*Melés y Teléo*." *México en la Cultura* 382 15 July. 1956. 2.

Cardoza, Lya de. "Un libro con duende." *La Cultura en México* 75 24 July 1963. xviii.

Cardoza y Aragón, Luis. "*Todo empezó el domingo*." *El Día* 378 13 July 1963. 9.

Carmona, Krista Ratowski. "Entrevista a Elena Poniatowska." *Mester* 15.2 (1986): 37-42.

Chevigny, Bell Gale. "The Transformation of Privilege in the Works of Elena Poniatowska." *Latin American Literary Review* 13.26 (1985): 49-62.

Christ, Ronald. "The Author as Editor." *Review* 15 (1975): 78-79.

Chumacero, Alí. "*Todo empezó el domingo*." *La Cultura en México* 69 12 June 1963. xv.

Crespo de la Serna, Jorge J. "La hierba que crece. La ecuación Poniatowska-Beltrán." *El Día* 3 Dec. 1963. 5.

"*Los cuentos de Lilus Kikus*." *Recent Books in Mexico* 14.5 (1967): 5.

Davis, Lisa. "An Invitation to Understanding among Poor Women of the Americas: *The Color Purple* and *Hasta no verte Jesús mío*." *Reinventing the Americas: Comparative Studies of Literature of the United States and Spanish America*. Eds. Bell Gale Chevigny and Gari Laguardia. New York: Cambridge University Press, 1986. 224-41.

Donoso Pareja, Miguel. "La caducidad del realismo." *Vida Literaria* [Mexico] 3 (1970): 10-11.

Fernández Olmos, Margarite. "El género testimonial: Aproximaciones feministas." *Revista/Review Interamericana* 11.1 (1981): 69-75.

Flori, Monica. "Visions of Women: Symbolic Physical Portrayal as Social Commentary in the Short Fiction of Elena Poniatowska." *Third Woman* 2.2 (1984): 77-83.

Foster, David William. "Latin American Documentary Narrative." *PMLA* 99.1 (1984): 41-55.

Fox Lockert, Lucía. *Women Novelists in Spain and Spanish America*. Metuchen, NJ: The Scarecrow Press Inc., 1979. 260-77.

Franco, Jean. *Plotting Women: Gender and Representation in Mexico*. New York: Columbia University Press, 1989. 177-87.

Friedman, Edward. "The Marginated Narrator: *Hasta no verte, Jesús mío* and the Eloquence of Repression." *The Antiheroine's Voice: Narrative Discourse and Transformations of the Picaresque*. Columbia: University of Missouri Press, 1987. 170-87.

Fuentes, Carlos. "*Lilus Kikus*." *Universidad de México* 4.1-2 Sept.-Oct. 1954. 30.

———. "Vivir del milagro." *Vida Literaria* [Mexico] 3 (1970): 8-9.

García Flores, Margarita. "Entrevista a Elena Poniatowska." *Revista de la Universidad de México* 30.7 (1976): 25-30.

García Pinto, Magdalena. *Historias íntimas: conversaciones con 10 escritoras latinoamericanas*. Hanover, NH: Ediciones del Norte, 1989. 173-98.

Gazarian Gautier, Marie-Lise. "Elena Poniatowska." *Interviews with Latin American Writers*. Elmwood Park, Ill.: Dalkey Archive Press, 1989. 199-216.

Gertel, Zunilda. "La mujer y su discurso: conciencia y máscara." *Cambio social en México visto por autores contemporáneos*. Ed. José Anadón. Notre Dame, Ind.: University of Notre Dame, 1984. 45-60.

Hancock, Joel. "Elena Poniatowska's *Hasta no verte, Jesús mío*: The Remaking of the Image of Woman." *Hispania* 66.3 (1983): 353-59.

Jean, Didier T. "La neopicaresca en México: Elena Poniatowska y Luis Zapata." *Tinta* 1.5 (1987): 23-29.

Jorgensen, Beth Ellen. "La intertextualidad en *La noche de Tlatelolco* de Elena Poniatowska." *Hispanic Journal* 10, 2 (1989): 81-93.

———. "Texto e ideología en la obra de Elena Poniatowska." *DAI* 47.4 (1986): 1344A.

Kushigian, Julia A. "Transgresión de la autobiografía y el Bildungsroman en *Hasta no verte Jesús mío*." *Revista Iberoamericana* 53.140 (1987): 667-77.

Landeros, Carlos. "Con Elena Poniatowska." *Diograma de la Cultura* [Literary Supplement to *Excelsior*] 23 Jan. 1966. 3.

Lara, Josefina. *Diccionario bio-bibliográfico de escritores contemporáneos de México*. Mexico City: Instituto Nacional de Bellas Artes, 1988. 175-76.

Lemaitre, Monique J. "Jesusa Palancares y la dialéctica de la emancipación femenina." *Hispamérica* 10.30 (1981): 131-35. Rpt. in *Texturas*. Mexico City: Oasis, 1986. 77-82.

López Negrete, Cecilia. "Con Elena Poniatowska." *Vida Literaria* [Mexico] 3 (1970): 16-20.

Loustaunau, Martha Oehmke. "Mexico's Contemporary Women Novelists." Diss. The University of New Mexico, 1973.

Melo, Juan Vicente. *"Palabras cruzadas." Universidad de México* 16.8 (1962): 31.

Méndez-Faith, Teresa. "Entrevista con Elena Poniatowska." *Inti* 15 (1982): 54-60.

————. "Translation of an Interview with Elena Poniatowska." *Atlantis: A Women's Studies Journal/Journal d'Etudes sur la Femme* 9.2 (1984): 70-75.

Menton, Seymour. "Sin embargo: La nueva cuentista femenina en México." *Tinta* 1.5 (1987): 35-37.

Miller, Beth. "Elena Poniatowska." *Mujeres en la literatura*. Mexico City: Fleischer Editora, 1978. 89-91.

————. "Interview with Elena Poniatowska." *Latin American Literary Review* 4.7 (1975): 73-78.

————. "Personajes y personas: Castellanos, Fuentes, Poniatowska y Sáinz." *Mujeres en la literatura*. Mexico City: Fleischer, 1978. 65-75.

Miller, Beth, and Alfonso González. "Elena Poniatowska." *26 autoras del México actual*. Mexico City: Costa-Amic, 1978. 299-321.

Monsiváis, Carlos. "Las palabras cruzadas de Elena Poniatowska."; "Mira, para que no comas olvido . . ."; "Las Precisiones de Elena Poniatowska." *La Cultura en México*. [Mexico] 100 15 July 1985: 2-5.

Monterde, Francisco. "Cuadro vivo del pueblo." *Vida Literaria* [Mexico] 3 (1970): 3-4.

Morente, Javier. "Sala de lectura." *Diorama de la Cultura* [Literary Supplement to *Excelsior*] 28 July 1963. 4.

"Mujeres de México." *Nivel* 21 25 Sept. 1960. 1,3.

Noriega, Raúl. "El domingo nuestro de cada día." *México en la Cultura* 742 9 June 1963. 8.

Palma, Martín. "Los silencios de Elena Poniatowska." *Universidad de México* 13.5 (1959): 16-17.

Pérez-Robles, Xiúhnel. *"La noche de Tlatelolco." Cuadernos Americanos* 177 (1971): 79-82.

Portal, Marta. *Proceso narrativo de la revolución mexicana*. Madrid: Espasa-Calpe, 1980. 285-92.

Resnick, Margery and Isabelle de Courtivron. *Women Writers in Translation: An Annotated Bibliography 1945-1982*. New York: Garland Publishing, 1984. 243.

Río, Marcela del. *"Todo empezó el domingo." Diorama de la Cultura* [Literary Supplement to *Excelsior*] 14 July 1963. 3.

Rodríguez, Antonio. *"Todo empezó el domingo." El Día* 16 Aug. 1963. 9.

Roses, Lorraine. "Entrevista con Elena Poniatowska." *Plaza: Literatura y Crítica* 5-6 (1981-1982): 51-64.

Selva, Mauricio de la. *"Todo empezó el domingo."* *Cuadernos Americanos* 4 (1963): 283-84.

Shimrose, Pedro. *Diccionario de autores iberoamericanos*. Madrid: Ministerio de Relaciones Exteriores, 1982. 340.

Starcevic, Elizabeth O. "Breaking the Silence: Elena Poniatowska, A Writer in Transition." *Literatures in Transition: The Many Voices of the Caribbean Area: A Symposium*. Ed. Rose S. Minc. Gaithersburg, MD: Hispamérica, 1982. 63-68.

————. "Elena Poniatowska: Witness for the People." *Contemporary Women Authors of Latin America: Introductory Essays*. Eds. Doris Meyer and Margarite Fernández Olmos. Brooklyn: Brooklyn College Press, 1983. 72-77.

————. "Neglected by the Boom: So What Else is New?" *Festschrift* AN80-2-134 (1980): 103-09.

Steele, Cynthia. "La creatividad y el deseo en *Querido Diego, te abraza Quiela*, de Elena Poniatowska." *Hispamérica* 14.41 (1985): 17-28.

Tatum, Charles M. "Elena Poniatowska's *Hasta no verte, Jesús mío*." *Latin American Women Writers: Yesterday and Today*. Eds. Yvette Miller and Charles M. Tatum. Pittsburgh, PA: Latin American Literary Review, 1975. 49-58.

"Todo empezó el domingo." *Cultura de Buenos Aires* IV.7 (1963): 92.

Torres, Juan Manuel. "Hasta el fin de la esperanza." *Vida Literaria* [Mexico] 3 (1970): 15.

Young, Dolly J. and William D. Young. "The New Journalism in Mexico: Two Women Writers." *Chasqui* 12.2-3 (1983): 72-80.

Young, Linda Rebeca Stowell. "Six Representative Women Novelists of Mexico 1960-1969." *DAI* 36 (1976): 6092A-6093A.

ARMONÍA SOMERS
Uruguay

Armonía Somers, pseudonym of the distinguished writer Armonía Etchepare de Henestrosa, was born in Uruguay around 1900. Before publishing her first novel in 1950, Somers had a long and outstanding career in education. She taught in Montevideo and was director of the National Museum of Education. She has published widely in the field of education and was editor of several journals in Montevideo.

Somers' first novella, *La mujer desnuda* (The Naked Woman, 1950), caused a sensation in literary circles when it was published by the magazine *Clima*. Its overt sexual overtones were considered scandalous in the provincial Uruguayan society of the time.

Following *La mujer desnuda*, Somers continued to address the topics of sexuality, eroticism and death. From 1953 to 1988 she published five volumes of short stories and four novels. In her narratives, the Uruguayan author presents despairing people, both men and women, seeking redemption from a useless, hopeless existence. These stories all treat common themes: violence, lack of communication, despair, death, desperation, and loneliness.

In recent years, Armonía Somers' production has increased in quantity and quality. Her later works contain diverse experiments in fictional technique and a more complex use of language.

Somers is a rebellious writer whose originality clearly rests in her unusual presentation of themes—a blend of realism, fantasy and absurdity—written in lyrical, symbolic and poetic language. Her work is polemical, her style vigorous, with touches of humor and keen sarcasm.

THE IMMIGRANT

The letters which compose the first part of this series, and to which I added others, entitling them all THE IMMIGRANT, *mostly appeared without heading and none of them had signatures.*

The hastiness and the lack of style of the beginning letters can be explained by the place where they were written, the store that my mother managed for many years.

She was the protagonist of what follows, and that fact, according to certain theories of a man who looked very much like me physically (my estranged father), and whose portrait is connected to this case, should have forced me to destroy the documents . . . I know, Father, it is not the morality of the island, but rather the social morality that matters. But it is also true that it has always rained like that night upon the naked flowers of this world, and it must be because of this that we still have a bit of courage left to continue living, to see how grace has not yet been covered by old dust in such a worn-out land like ours.

Juan Abel Grim
Collector and annotator of the letters

I

I am sending you this message with the elevator boy, the only person whom you can trust with minor tasks, in the event that you are fit for the job. I have been here for twenty years and the fact that I am the general manager has allowed me to catalogue the young people who make up the staff as if they were merchandise (you, too, and don't be offended). My intent is not to speak to you of matters which ought to be discovered on their own, but rather of others which place me under certain obligations to the person who has recommended you. And, as I do not want you to fail in this test and I am your supervisor, I ask you, please, to indicate to the elevator boy where I can meet you at the end of the day. And I hope that my openness in pointing out your weaknesses on the job may be as helpful to you as I have promised your sponsor.

Distinguished by temperaments, these strange, always hasty notes were exchanged from then on, all of them seemingly robbed from the hell that was the store within which my mother must have played a tremendous role for so many years. I remember her with awe as provoked by myth. She was feared and almost cruel to her poor trained ants. But, from the depths of that slavery, there rose a mist of admiration which sustained her tenuously above the vulgarity of the lower world, so much so that later, without her, everything disintegrated. That place grew to be what it is today, a place about which one would say, "I don't know if it was here or next door that I bought this . . ."

II

Forgive me, but I am going to use your system to confide in you that, after your comments yesterday, I tried to find the image of the person who bore my name, my face, my other personal attributes, in every mirror in the store. And to what end? Because it was certain that each of the clumsy gestures that you pointed out to me at our meeting at the bar—my way of assaulting customers, intending to force a sale, my uncontrollable rage when they withdrew without playing the game, and later, my tendency to search out the display windows looking for freedom outside as if it had been lost in some bad exchange—all this seemed to peel away from me like the skin of an onion.

After the first transaction I began to follow you with ease. This—yes, that one—no, careful . . . And best of all: that no one suspects I am creating my own model, that the others know nothing of my process of self-discovery. Tell me, even with a look: Am I doing well, do you approve?

The manager then pushed to another aspect of the problem. With her chin held high she was, without a doubt, the proud woman I knew, and later this would explain many things to me.

III

No, my dear, nor is it necessary to exaggerate the way you did a moment ago. Better to let women of that special kind leave the way they came in, with their sparkling jewels, their chauffeur at the door, their four surnames. I couldn't wait, not even until later, to tell you that, in spite of everything, our dignity must continue to serve us. To retain a measure of pride, that is the secret. The very least of rights I granted myself from the start. Besides, it will always be your slim young waist that wins out over their midriff bulges, which seem to have taken revenge on an overload of gold. They are the wives of some of the present government officials, of certain industrialists and bankers who started out in the basement with brooms in their hands. Don't cater to them so much, all right? Even if it is to develop what you have called your "own process of self-discovery."

IV

Nevertheless I must tell you that I have failed today. I feel bad and don't think that I am cut out for this. It is true that you, the real you, could justify my misfortune of stepping into this place. But even with you here, I think I ought to leave. Yes, LEAVE, in capital letters. Just think, that lady who came in, asking so sweetly for the children's department, and whom I waited on, using all my imagination—almost able to see the light blue room, the plush bears on the shelves—took advantage, while waiting for the elevator, to show me the photo. She opened her purse, went through a mountain of things from which there rose a certain strange odor, and as I stood open-mouthed, took out a picture of a dog dressed in infant clothing. Then she turned into the real mother of that child and even seemed to sniff my side. I went to the ladies' room and vomited. After that I was not good for anything.

One day I may buy that perfume you use, in order to remember you; it was the only thing that managed to put me back together again. I walked by you, breathed in, and continued living. It is certain that you will come out of the bottle as soon as I take the cap off the one I buy. What is it called? I can't go on any more, I can't . . .

V

My little one*, don't distract me with your perfumes today, I beg you. We have a directors' meeting to decide on certain purchases which must be made in Europe for the next season. In my experience, the important thing at this kind of meeting is to appear completely neutral to them, like a mechanical Store-Woman, so that no one can perceive anything other than this mechanism. I remain centered by using the technique of looking at myself in the mirror of the meeting room from time to time in front of their very noses. But what a pain, the bell is ringing now. Besides, a certain handsome young boy is coming your way. One who ought to smell of gasoline or of a leather jacket. Now you see that not everything in this world will smell of dog's breath. Ah . . . and at the moment when the young man takes out his wallet to pay, try to look more discreetly at the photos that shine under the plastic.

How different the handwritings were. When I divided the letters to arrange them in their proper order, they began to seem like the same mosaic executed from two styles of craftsmanship.

* In my handwriting "the boss was slowly yielding." J.A.G.

VI

You toyed with me before the meeting, didn't you? Certainly I looked at the photo in your wallet the first day. But that's natural, I think. Many times I realize that, besides your well-hidden good nature, there must be other secrets in your life. And who was that boy in your photograph then? The same one who comes in sometimes, gives you a kiss that leaves all the girls' mouths watering and leaves like he came, without buying anything.

Think for a moment that at the beginning I had considered myself a gem in this place for having arrived here with some knowledge in one subject or another, a membership card to a film club, certain other small things which made me think myself of another class. And that, later, I encountered something which dazzles (you), but which will never be able to illuminate what I want (you as well), your world, not the one of that Store-Woman you speak of, but the other where you probably have an armchair to forget all this, a bathroom with its little vials, a curtain which obeys you when the light bothers you. Here no one seems to know much about you. They respect you, they hate you, they envy even the length of your eyelashes and the quality of your hands. But they stop there. Would I have more rights? And why would I have them, in the end?

VII

Very good, that is how to do it. I watched you let that chance go by so that the customer would not notice the other girl's approach. The customer must be completely unaware of the internal quarrels over a better commission. But systems also exist to prevent someone from always beating us by a hair.

VIII

There is only one system I would like to master today, that of questions and their answers.*

IX

Unmanageable and delicious creature. It is obvious that the former will always be more important than the latter. And I have come to my desk solely to please you. Well then, it would seem that, while not as the manager of a large fashionable department store, but rather as a woman who inspects herself every once in a while in the mirror in the meeting room and sees that she is still attractive enough, I have always

* To challenge Mother, what courage . . . J.A.G.

been vulnerable, in spite of my reputation as a tough woman. On another level of reality: my son, that young man who comes to give me a kiss and seems to stir up your co-workers when he walks near them.

I am forty and he is twenty. By simply comparing our ages, you will gather that he should not be considered only as my son, but also as the result of a fabulous moment in the life of a woman your own age, and, in time, the only thing that will remain when the ghosts retire. I live with him; he studies, smokes, muddies the apartment with dirty foot-prints, and gets telephone calls from various female voices. And, in addition to giving me silver cigarette cases which he buys with the money I give him on his birthday, he knows how to laugh like few people can.

I started here after that great misfortune which is usually reserved for us. Yours, I believe, was of an economic nature; mine was different.

But then everything began to fall into place again. The child smiled with his toothless mouth, the sky seemed to me to be small and pale then, the store always paid regularly, bakers know how to knead what they have in their hands, and foolish men what is between theirs. If life worked like the cord of the drapes that you spoke of, nothing would be necessary except a simple contract: pull softly so that nothing breaks. Are your questions answered now? Oh, I am sending you the perfume so that you do not waste your wages on little whims. Take note of its name: Violeta de Parma. We ought to have names like that, chosen. This one suits you well, therefore it will be yours.

Perhaps at the moment of sending it, the manager crossed out a few final words of this letter. It would have been possible for me to have uncovered them with the techniques known today. But I preferred not to do so. Between that woman and me there has always been a silent, implicit respect for the other's decisions, whatever they may have been. Later I thought it best to put this little sales slip chronologically in tenth place; on the back it read:

X

I would like to see you one more time. But outside the city, far from here, for a fabulous weekend. Where, where?

From now on, my mother will write only to me. Peace be with her delicate spoils. Whosoever looks to question her conduct will have to face me.

XI

. . . Then, my darling, upon surprising a certain farewell kiss you went into a state of shock which I did not know how to remedy; instead, I heightened it with my silence. Perhaps by putting together all these papers as best you can, you will be able to reconstruct it completely.

The girl who was embracing me when you got home came to return those crumpled notes which you are looking at right now, asking that I save or destroy them. She had just married a certain young proprietor of some spinning mills outside the city and decided to get rid of them. I certainly hope that you will repeat your rather melodramatic, "I want to know everything," from that day. In addition to that tone, which we have laughed at so much in others, I am bothered by the kind of strange fervor which has thrown you beyond your discreet respect for my affairs. I have always thought that if I protected you from the outside world, that would give you so much strength that you would not be interested in my affairs. You were my son, were you not? And, according to what we have always believed, you were a little different from the rest of humanity. Nevertheless, still being somewhat connected with the lies of the world, I repeat my question to you. Are you still in need of unlocking the door that swings open for each individual alone, and that, at times, not even that person himself can manage?

XII

Mother. After that first disconcerting episode, it occurs to me suddenly to imagine that nothing ever happened, that the pieces in our world will return to place normally without regard for the art of gluing things together so the seam may not even be noticed.

But, digging deeper, I also feel that I do not want this. The kind of gale wind which has risen to undo us is not contained by new glass, by righting the furniture, or by simply moving away to a new house.

I remember that one time, when I was a child, I asked you to give me nothing less than a beach. You laughed for a long time about my fantasies, and I, with the impotent expressiveness of a child my age, swore that someday I would have the eloquence to tell you my reasons. I am sure the moment has arrived. Certainly that which is strange will always be the unknown circumstance which awaits us. A boy desperate because he lacks the means to express himself. Later a man who is able to do so. And when does he discover it? The day his mother appears in the embrace of a young woman who is kissing her right on the lips and who then leaves in tears, moving away down the halls of the building.

That summer you were lying on the sand (right now I am thinking of how magnificent you have been at every age) when it occurred to me to draw a great circle around you, which would have you for its center. In those days I had just tried out my first bed, I was in school and I was learning what it was like to increase the property of one's own body, to not be caught in a small crib with bars like a cage. The kind of restitution I paid you when I placed you within a vast expanse of sand surely penetrated into other darker abysses. No one had the right to leave those grotesque footprints within our boundaries, like the tracks of those bears in the snow which appeared in my imagination and in your stories. In a word, I had raised boundaries around you, and I was as certain of their importance as all those who had invented them before me. But the same thing happened to me that had happened to them. In one of my comings and goings to the shore, I discovered the zone had been profaned by footprints, and that no one, not even you, knew it. I started to cry with all my might. Those very same bears ran to comfort me. I don't know what strange thing took the blame in the end. As always, the real enemy remained outside the story.

(Everything you write to me you can leave in my handkerchief drawer.)

XIII

Then there is no alternative, isn't that right? I must tell you that, on the day agreed upon, after that very special "where," we left the city one weekend. You were studying with friends and I could tell that all of you were glad to see me go. I left the refrigerator full of enough food for an expedition and you, noticing my nervousness, sat down on that little crooked bench in the kitchen and rocked with laughter. In passing I must remember that your laughter, at that moment, had the same pitch as another's. You simply inherited it, that's a¹¹ ᵀ⁻ ¹   ⁺ was to bump into an echo delayed for many years, and from the kettle-drums of death, no less. But I am unable to go on. I see that my nails need a touch-up or it will never be said that they shine perfectly.

XIV

Mother. The truth is that, because you mentioned something else, nails and other excuses aside, today I wouldn't have been able to follow the story of your departure from the city either. It is imperative that, before anything else, you tell me all of those things which make you stop, like a watch which suddenly would like to start marking time backwards. Because everything which hasn't been explained is also a kind of lie. And I am fed up with all that silence which offers nothing, which begins to seem dirty to me.

Until I was four I lived caught up by the idea of your paternity like the wooden doll belonging to Collodi's old man. At fourteen or fifteen, one prefers a certain rancor mixed with love, which one day appears to break loose from the root of those first hairs different from the rest which sprout from the body, from the first spot of acne, from the little shouts of pleasure drowned under the sheet. But twenty comes and no more miracles can be performed. One day the shadow, which threw itself between us like a dog, gets up and wants to search the house. This is the opportunity to open the locked cabinets, even though the keys have always been in sight. Now or never, then? And, in addition, all or nothing.

XV

Well then. Long and difficult again, like the stories you used to ask me for in the time of your private beach when the summer sun was the one to take the blame. (Now you see that I, too, have fresh memories.)

There are some photos and various press clippings in the bottom drawer of my dresser. There you will find the names and faces which may help you as you reflect on all this. I am not bothered by the slightly artificial response they may arouse in you. Your chain broke when you were conceived inside of me. But I am the one who has been unable to stir up those times without feeling as if my heart were in my hand. That, and we ought to talk one day of what that was, that is always there, completely alert. Sometimes I imagine it as a hidden monster, breathing, nourishing itself with the secret air of the boxes where it is kept. Passively, to be sure, but to the extent that every spring I take it out carefully. I fit it under my skin and I ought to explain it somehow, with reasons that people swallow with the same innocence that you swallowed those innocuous little pills that never did your sore throats any good.

My dearest. I certainly will never be able to forget that man. We loved each other with such splendor that I have often thought that might have been the very reason for our failure, especially when so many unimportant people can be seen, destined to laze nonchalantly in the best loveseats. One night, in the clearing of a pine forest (your origin revealed) it suddenly occurred to us to project ourselves into space. But I don't know how many unknown planets we would have already explored, since in our case there was the constant renewal of situations, and every time we kissed we were suspended in a different sky. Nevertheless, the disaster was to be as great as our passion. In the depths of my soul a small childhood memory exists that I shall exchange for the one you have from the beach, and it may explain everything. A little friend my age, named Georgina, I think, the daughter of a poor woman, had taken a great liking to my sandals. One day, no longer able to resist her envious stares, I took them off and offered them to her. And she was going to take them when, as if stung by a familiar scorpion, she said she was going to ask her mother first and disappeared. I never saw her again. The woman, humiliated or incredulous, chose to keep me away from her daughter. I had to keep my sandals and everything I had not been able to give along with them.

Now you will undoubtedly understand the rest. Georgina may be used as a symbol. Georgina may well represent the blood with which one will have to learn that most people are frightened by everything that is too grand for them. (My treasure, what will your destiny in love be? How good we felt that day long ago within your boundaries on the beach . . .)

I didn't write for a few days. My father's face, imprisoned in the photos I found in that spot, a face which mine had badly duplicated, reflected an ironic smile at me from every mirror in the house. I began to understand maniacs. My dilemma burst forth from those mirrors in which my unknown rival was reflected in my very image. At times, especially when I shaved, I suffered a crazy urge to talk to him, man to man, to offer him a cigarette, to talk about my mother like two suitors who meet again once their lover has died. But mother was alive and beautiful. And besides, I had never met him before. It was then that I remembered the rest. Violeta, that Violeta de Parma. My mother was going to tell me about the famous weekend in an open and sincere letter, written with the warmth and the sound of whispered words.

XVI

And after all that, what about our Violeta de Parma?

For two or three days there was no answer in my handkerchief drawer. Until, opening it one morning with the caution of one carrying a bird cage, I found what I was looking for.

XVII

Ah, that's right, we did begin with that . . . And the name's not bad. Planning to indulge herself in a great feast, her first adolescent adventure, Violeta waited for me at the bus station on the agreed day.

Without her store uniform, and free of all the artifices I myself had transmitted to her, I could recognize in her a daring personality, perhaps the product of certain vicissitudes which had been confided to me second hand, and which were as capable of drawing out her temerity as a green pasture would draw out a young mare. Like a diminutive pioneer she had already chosen a hotel and imposed conditions. Of course, without having any experience whatsoever, she was guided by a natural instinct to subordinate, to enforce the kind of obedience created by overpowering creatures even if they are the size of mere peas. Although such boldness did not allow her to completely control her trembling hands, which she often thought to cover up by going through her overnight bag.

That is how I allowed myself to be swept away, misleading her with a false air of submission. Because everything in her which seemed aimless, even when set off by the most intimate and exact desires, had a name for me, and it could only lead to one end. But here another avalanche overtakes me, yours. What will be the result of telling to you this long woven tale, which must still unravel before you come of age, if you yourself snatch from it Godiva's hair under which it is hidden from the world?

XVIII

Mother. In some notes written in your strange handwriting, which I found in the usual place, you remarked that that man, my father (to think that he is inside me like a tenant who has taken over the house), used to say that morality is a doubtful invention, because events that move us in society would not affect us if we were on a deserted island.

Very well. Whether on that famous deserted island or shouted out at a crowded rally, I am sure that your intuitive poetry will always be a formidable bully. Or do you really believe that before I knew the store's miseries, I had any realistic concept of that illuminated cave? No, you have never been a flesh-and-blood mother directing a crew of slaves that kills itself for a tiny commission, but instead you have been a kind of magical influence suspended over an unsteady sea which I have seen turn blue in your shadow and return to black in your absence. You have nurtured me with a strange milk, I think. And as I may have inherited my liking for integrity from you, I demand that you speak without fear on that island. At this point, you and I both realize that we have prolonged the preface more than necessary.

XIX

And how painful for the handkerchief drawer that you don't want to drop the subject, right?

The truth is that we finally arrived at a place that from the beginning I decided to call "I don't know where." It was deathly cold and they assigned us a room that seemed to have stored the cold, but with one advantage, its isolation along with other small rooms in the main wing of the building.

Forming part of the old section of the hotel, the room opened onto an uncovered patio with plants hung from the eaves and a windmill in the center. I know all this will sound cheap to you, because it bothers me too, as I write about it. But when an atmosphere is created in which we leave our mark, we can expect certain things to come to haunt our thoughts for the rest of our lives, like a postcard you can't throw away. Our blessed and good memory adheres like our skin to those landscapes in blue and green. They become ridiculous, and to merely remove them would end up hurting us as much as being skinned alive.

The place: wooded. Also a detail of no importance, but which suddenly, as I relive it, I come to realize controlled everything else. Because the wind which the trees* let loose upon us began to whip at the windows which faced north and then that initial tumult resolved itself by unleashing the rain which threatened to flatten the broken-down hotel.

There were two beds in the room. But someone to whom they have given the picturesque name of demon, perhaps to avoid having to name oneself when standing to be judged, began to stealthily say, "Join them, join them, God has given ardor to your flesh and no longer has the curiosity to spy on old houses like this one."

Meanwhile, removed from the situation and in a complete state of that last-minute fright which I had predicted, she watched me push the two beds together as she sat on the floor, imprisoned between the storm that raged without and the mystery within.

Frozen to the bone, and taking off only my shoes and my raincoat, I finally got under the covers. They smelled like an old closet, like something second-hand. But not even that could detract from their effectiveness, which was nothing more than old tenderness prostituted by so much human contact.

> We were going to have supper. From my room I listened to Mother rattling things around in the kitchen. For a moment, it seemed that the woman who had gone to bed in that hotel and the one who moved among the household objects were not the same. I needed my father to come in to occupy the void, to install himself with all his physical presence in the ambiguous air of the house.

Suddenly, and more because of my sighs of pleasure at being wrapped up in the covers than anything else, she began to undress decisively, throwing her clothes every which way, and jumped into bed beside me. Lastly she took off the only piece of clothing that she seemed to have left on to protect her life, a bra so small it made one laugh, and everything came into view. It was like finding two birds' eggs like those which are speckled and are always of an unknown species. I told her so and that

---

* At last I would find it said by someone else, that the wind comes from the trees! Only Mama, and the child Chesterton, could think of such a thing. J.A.G.

prompted her to begin searching my body, which was still covered. She poked, I think she broke something, and suddenly I heard her say, choking on her words, "God, why, they must be magnolias. This must be what perfumed the store, not Violeta de Parma . . ."

Her own voice shook her from her ecstasy, returning her to a reality which seemed to have momentarily abandoned her. From then on a kind of peasant terror began to overtake her, as if she had been discovered by all the simple women who had come before her.

"That isn't possible," she said, suddenly with her former vehemence. "It is necessary to die; better yet I would have died before being born, I died without having been born."

An impetus of destruction had possessed her, so strong it shook her from the bed and attempted to pull her onto the flooded patio. I managed to grab her at the door like a cat in a trance of madness, her hair and eyes electrified.

"Come on," I said to her, trying my luck with any banality, "they won't try us without legal counsel in the hotel's kitchen for this, nor do we have to fling ourselves out into the rain for sins that haven't been committed."

She let herself be led back to bed. She then looked at me with a velvety light which she saved for certain moments, and shading her eyes with her hands, she asked me to dim the lamp. I covered the ridiculous thing badly with a fashion magazine, and everything seemed to take on a normality which seemed a little suspicious.

"I am sorry," she said finally in a solemn voice, "I was giving a great deal of importance to doing things properly, the way books in a public library are catalogued. I came here because I wanted someone like you to caress me completely for the first time in my life. If you were a man, I would be here with you all the same. But the men I have known until now, including one, have provoked nothing in me, not even laughter. The day that one of them can at least do that, making me laugh so wholeheartedly that I twist and stretch over something he says or does to me, then I will come here with him to this same spot and I will give him whatever you may have left me."

Perplexed, I listened to this change in position, and for a moment it seemed to me that one lives prudently for many years so that someone else's madness can burst in one's face, like a stone that leaps off the road onto the windshield and shatters it to pieces.

She took advantage of my stupor then and leaped out of bed again, stopping to face me, framed in the bathroom door. She had the graceful and nervous body of a colt, but, not even in the dizziness all of that provoked, was it vulgar. We came from a decayed and shallow world. In exchange for that sordidness, she would only have needed a small basket on her hip for that miserable little room to have blossomed like a field sown with tulips.

"Well," she asked suddenly as if she were mocking me, leaving the doorway, "should we go to that rancid jury in the kitchen or not?"

The worn carpet, like the very earth that rocked us, brought her along slowly. I looked at her long-boned feet, the kind that seem to be searching for the floor as if they were dancing with every step. But those feet were the stem that supported the entire flower. And she radiated up from there, concentrating in her triangular field a heat more memorable than that of the famous world war.

Of course it was necessary to go to supper at a specific hour announced by the bell. We separated the beds again, admiring our great precaution, and left for the dining room, under the same raincoat.

All the details of our entrance to the dining room, and of our being seated at a table for two, seemed to be recorded on the eyes of the girl as if on virgin film. I saw her take the napkin off her plate, spread it over her knees and brush away the inevitable nocturnal fly with the same degree of inaugural importance with which she greeted the first guests who passed by, a mature pair who sat down at a nearby table. Then, with the same prolixity as that of a catalogue, she became interested in some pills which they took from the same bottle, letting the water they swallowed be heard in their stomachs.

"They must be the pills of boredom, see the effects?" I said, pretending to read the menu which was on the table. Cautious and silent until that moment, she let out a laugh which made everyone turn their heads.

"Delightful," she added in a low voice, "but over there are two who look like honeymooners. Might it occur to them to take pills someday?"

"The pills." I said absent-mindedly to the waitress who came to serve us.

"What pills, madam?"

"Oh," I answered, feigning my carelessness badly, "one always thinks one is at home."

The woman looked at me with an air of secret complicity about my forgetfulness, and began to fill our plates.

It continued to rain in torrents. I thought of what this rain would be like, pounding on the door of room number . . .

"What number?" I asked Violeta. "Do you remember it so we'll at least be able to get back to the room?"

She hadn't noticed it either. At that moment the young man on his honeymoon, who was in a bad mood because of the poorly lit room, threw the newspaper on the table, as if that were the only thing on his mind at that moment. The digestive process was in full gear. Every once in a while, Violeta put her knife and fork on the edge of her plate to listen to the concert of porcelain and metal which filled the air.

"Don't worry about the number," I told her, "you'll see how our door shines behind the curtain of water."

When we returned the twin beds were freshly made up, and it seemed that someone had sprayed more cold into the atmosphere.

Suddenly, while we were putting the beds back together the lock next door squeaked.

-Psst,- I said, -it is an accident which can't figure into anyone's plans, we are going to live alongside them now.-

-I hope that they are not the ones with the pills- added Violeta, getting under the covers, this time without any problems.

The pacers went back and forth as if they were sinking into a floor of decayed boards. Then one was not heard anymore; the other, the woman, collapsed on the bed, sinking into it as if the bed was receiving an elephant.

-Hey, filthy loafer,- one heard her shout suddenly,—do you have to forget to flush the toilet here too?-

-Always your healthy spirit of waste,- the accused replied from a distance.

-Waste, with what we're paying? As if they didn't charge the price of gold even for the air we breathe in this frozen pigsty.-

The water was heard running. The water bound for that dirty destiny and the free water outside had surrounded us in a circle. Impossible, then, to leave one or to fall into the other . . .

-Never, never.- I heard her say meanwhile, lying next to me with as much tension as a cord which was about to break.

-What is that "never," what does it mean?-

-That nothing can ever come of this, never, not ever.-

It was then that I had to help with words like a mother who resorts to the faucet when her child is slow about something else. Sometimes, who knows if today isn't the last time, it has occurred to me to evoke that unfolding of suggestions: "Alone you will be climbing a mountain whose peak you can't see (inventing the pain of scaling), and the more you bruise yourself, the more desperate you are to reach the top (but a scaling which at the same time would have a goal); it could be because of a black diamond which is buried there. The rest of the people shout and shout from below so that you'll lose hope and leave it just to them, but you, deaf, don't understand their evil language, and all of this so that in the end, when you reach the peak, you will understand that there is no such thing; rather there is deception so you will never forget that earth, the real earth, is in heaven."

There on the edge of midnight she found her diamond. I was going to note the exact time. I took the magazine off the lamp and I looked at my watch.

"Damn!" I whispered. "The crystal has fallen off and the hands have flown off, who knows where."

"And now," she asked breathlessly, "what will happen in the regimented store?"

A little laugh filled with sounds that interfered with our waves. It was almost a message substituted for a nose and an eye at the keyhole.

"How do you like that, two women," said the voice of the little man who conserved water, and who seemed plastered to our ears. "If one could still do that nowadays, at least try to do it; if you would let me try it, only . . ."

"Ugh," groaned the elephant woman, "how disgusting. That was all I needed to make everything complete. Give me the sleeping ones, they're in the big bottle."

A kind of amphibian sun finally began to filter through the crevices. Doubtlessly it had stopped raining, but I heard water falling, always more water. I opened the outside door a crack and I saw it. It was running down over the windmill, overflowing like a sort of liquid hair. Violeta, the color of her name, slept face up between the reality of the room inside and my sleepwalking eyes which carried her to the mill.

I wrapped myself in my raincoat and went out to explore the park. I must have been out for an eternity, walking under the trees, sinking into dead leaves covered with mud. At times the sinister pines wanted to drive their needles into my shrouded heart, to return me to the moment that I told you about in the beginning, always those damned trees in my life, with their green signals on the firing line.

When I got back she was already dressed, seated on a suitcase and crying silently. Outside one could hear some travelers preparing for the return trip. She continued to fuss, unaffectedly, but with the weight of solitary ruins.

And it was in that moment that it occurred to me to see her as I still do now, in the guise of a small, dirty and ugly immigrant who has arrived from afar and still doesn't know if back home they think she is here, or if she really is here. She sat on her ordinary suitcase and, perhaps because she knew it was filled with dirt from her poor homeland, or because she feared the wealth of the new land, too attractive to be true, the immigrant looked at me suddenly, between her tears, and as the noise outside continued, said to me:

"And now I want a diamond again, this time without attaining it, so that it will last my entire life. I am going to marry and I am afraid."

"You're going to do what? You're afraid of what?" I asked her, hastily, feeling all of that was too obscure for a final act.

"Of a wealthy man's poverty, speaking in a language that he doesn't understand. Of reaching the peak of the mountain and of still being alone when the black diamond appears . . . and of having to destroy it so that each person may possess his own in a different way."

Essay of Telepsychic Experience Violeta or the Immigrant.-Mills with hair of water.-Mother.-Sand.-Wind and Rain.-Black Diamond.-All or nothing.-Georgina or Idiocy.-The Monster with my face, nourished in a box.

These incoherent words appeared at the end, in my handwriting, that handwriting so lacking in blood stains, so inexperienced at the time.

Today I record the experiment of repeating them again and again, for the possible survivor named Georgina, who probably still walks barefoot. And for my unknown father's soul wandering through the pine forests, in search of the evaporated scent of love.

Juan Abel Grim
Collector and annotator of the letters

Translated by Anne Hohenstein

Bibliography: Armonía Somers

Fiction

Somers, Armonía. *La mujer desnuda*. Montevideo: Revista Clima, 1950. Rpt. in Montevideo: Tauro, 1966. 2nd. ed. Montevideo: Arca, 1990.

———. *El derrumbamiento*. Montevideo: Ediciones Salamanca, 1953.

———. *La calle de viento norte y otros cuentos*. Montevideo: Arca, 1963.

———. *De miedo en miedo. Los manuscritos del río*. Montevideo: Arca, 1965.

———. *Todos los cuentos, 1953-1967*. Montevideo: Arca, 1967.

———. "El entierro." *Antología del cuento uruguayo. Vol. VI. Los Nuevos*. Ed. Arturo S. Visca. Uruguay: Ediciones de la Banda Oriental, 1968. 11-26.

———. "El derrumbamiento." *Narradores uruguayos*. Ed. Rubén Cotelo. Caracas, Venezuela: Monte Avila Editores, 1969. 149-70.

———. *Un relato para Dickens*. Montevideo: Editorial Arca, 1969.

———. "Madness." Trans. Susana Hertelendy. *The Eye of the Heart: Short Stories from Latin America*. Ed. Barbara Howes. Indianapolis and New York: Avon Books, 1973. 419-21.

————. *Muerte por alacrán*. Buenos Aires: Editorial Calicanto, 1979.

————. "The Immigrant." *Diana's Second Almanac*. Trans. Anne Hohenstein. Ed. T. Ahern. Providence, Rhode Island: Diana's Bimonthly Press, 1980. 4-35.

————. *Tríptico Darwiniano*. Montevideo: Ediciones de la Torre, 1982.

————. *Sólo los elefantes encuentran mandrágora*. Buenos Aires: Editorial Legasa, 1983.

————. "The Fall." *Other Fires: Short Fiction by Latin American Women*. Ed. and Trans. Alberto Manguel. Toronto: Lester & Orpen Dennys, 1986. 9-23.

————. "La inmigrante." *Puerta abierta: la nueva escritora latinoamericana*. Ed. Caridad L. Silva-Velázquez and Nora Erro-Orthmann. Mexico City: Joaquín Mortiz, 1986. 205-22.

————. *Viaje al corazón del día. Elegía por un secreto amor*. Montevideo: Arca, 1986.

————. "The Burial." *Women's Fiction from Latin America: Selections from Twelve Contemporary Authors*. Ed. Trans. Evelyn Picón Garfield. Detroit: Wayne State University Press, 1988. 39-50.

————. "Plunder." *Women's Fiction from Latin America: Selections from Twelve Contemporary Authors*. Ed. Trans. Evelyn Picón Garfield. Detroit: Wayne State University Press, 1988. 51-65.

————. *La rebelión de la flor*. Montevideo: Librería Linardi y Risso, 1988.

————. "The Tunnel." *Women's Fiction from Latin America: Selections from Twelve Contemporary Authors*. Ed. Trans. Evelyn Picón Garfield. Detroit: Wayne State University Press, 1988. 31-38.

Essays

Somers, Armonía. *Educación de la adolescencia: el adolescente de novela y su valor de testimonio*. Mexico City: n.p., 1957.

————. Postscript. "Diez relatos a la luz de sus probables vivenciales." *Diez relatos y un epílogo*. Eds. Campodónico et al. Montevideo: Fundación de Cultura Universitaria, 1979. 113-54.

Criticism on the Works of Armonía Somers

Ainsa, Fernando. "Armonía Somers y los lobos esteparios." *Tiempo reconquistado*. Montevideo: Geminis, 1977. 124-25.

Araújo, Helena. "El tema de la violación en Armonía Somers y Griselda Gambaro." *Plural* 15.179 (1986): 21-23.

————. "Escritura femenina: sobre un cuento de Armonía Somers." *Cuéntame tu vida* [Cali, Colombia] 5 (1981): 19-24.

"Armonía Somers: los lobos esteparios." *Capítulo Oriental* [Montevideo] 33 (1968): 563.

Benedetti, Mario. "*El derrumbamiento*." *Número* [Montevideo] 5.22 (1953): 102-03.

————. *Literatura uruguaya siglo XX*. Montevideo: Alfa, 1969. 205-09.

Cosse, Rómulo. ed. *Armonía Somers, papeles críticos*. Montevideo: Librería Linardi y Risso, 1990.

Cousté, Alberto. "Armonía Somers, al este del paraíso." *Primera Plana* (Buenos Aires) 242 (1967): 52-53.

De Espada, Roberto. "Armonía Somers o el dolor de la literatura." *Maldoror* [Montevideo] (1972): 62-66.

Erro-Órthmann, Nora. "Armonía Somers." *Spanish American Women Writers*. Ed. Diane Martin. Westport, CT: Greenwood Press, 1990. 493-500.

Figueira, Gastón. "*La calle del viento norte*." *Books Abroad* Summer (1964): 295.

Foster, David William. *A Dictionary of Contemporary Latin American Authors*. Tempe: Center for Latin American Studies, Arizona State University, 1975. 98.

Gandolfo, Elvio E. "Para conocer a Armonía Somers." *Clarín* Jan. 1986: 1-3.

Garfield, Evelyn Picón. "Armonía Somers." *Women's Voices from Latin America: Interviews with Six Contemporary Authors*. Detroit: Wayne State University Press, 1985. 29-51.

———. "La metaforización de la soledad: los cuentos de Armonía Somers." *Revista de la Universidad Nacional* 2.10 (1986-87): 25-30.

———. "Yo soplo desde el páramo (La muerte en los cuentos de Armonía Somers)." *Texto Crítico* 3.6 (1977): 113-25.

García Rey, José M. "Armonía Somers: Sondeo intuitivo y visceral del mundo." *Cuadernos Hispanoamericanos* (1985): 101-04.

Rama, Angel. "La insólita literatura de Somers: la fascinación del horror." *Marcha* [Montevideo] 1.188 (1963): 27-30.

———. "Raros y malditos en la literatura uruguaya." *Marcha* [Montevideo] 1319 (1966): 30-31.

———. *La generación crítica 1939-1969*. Montevideo: Arca, 1972. 29.

Rela, Walter. *Diccionario de escritores uruguayos*. Montevideo: Edición de la Plaza, 1986. 124-27.

Rodríguez-Villamil, Ana María. "Aspectos fantásticos en *La mujer desnuda* de Armonía Somers." *Río de Plata* (1985): 147-63.

———. *Elementos fantásticos en la narrativa de Armonía Somers*. Montevideo: Ediciones de la Banda Oriental, 1990.

Shimrose, Pedro. *Diccionario de autores iberoamericanos*. Madrid: Ministerio de Relaciones Exteriores, 1982. 405.

"Testimonio: una gran escritora uruguaya (A.S.) habla para *Rumbos*." *Rumbos* [Montevideo] 3 Oct. 1969. 8-9.

Visca, Arturo Sergio. *Antología del cuento uruguayo: los nuevos*. Montevideo: Ediciones de la Banda Oriental, 1968. 11-26.

———. "El mundo narrativo de Armonía Somers." *Nueva antología del cuento uruguayo*. Montevideo: Ediciones de la Banda Oriental, 1976. 260-63.

Zum Felde, Alberto. *Indice crítico de la literatura hispanoamericana*. Vol. 2, *La narrativa* 2nd ed. Madrid: Aguilar, 1964. 501.

GLORIA STOLK
Venezuela

G loria Stolk was born in Caracas, Venezuela, in 1918. She studied at the University of Paris and at Smith College, where she specialized in literature. She wrote poetry, short stories, novels, and literary criticism. In 1956 her novel *Amargo el fondo* (Bitter is the Bottom) won her the Arístides Rojas Prize, which is considered the highest literary distinction given in Venezuela to a novelist.

For many years she wrote a column in the newspaper *The Caracas National*, and she was a distinguished writer for several literary journals in Venezuela. While posted as Ambassador of Venezuela to the Dominican Republic, she wrote the stories in her well-known collection *Cuentos del caribe* (Short Stories from the Caribbean, 1975). These stories reveal a profound respect for human dignity and a delicate equilibrium between the forces of good and evil in the world.

Gloria Stolk's literary and cultural efforts brought her considerable recognition and success; however, her personal life was marked by tragedy. She enjoyed several years of a loving marriage with children, but that happy life ended abruptly with the suicide of her husband. In 1979 Gloria Stolk also committed suicide in Venezuela.

CRICKETS AND BUTTERFLIES

B ecause he had the soul of an explorer, Enriquillo turned out to be an inspired doctor. Beyond the suffering raw material he discovered the caged and sick spirit which took vengeance upon the flesh, or escaped by torturing it in order to divert its unbearable anguish. Enriquillo unmasked the hidden evil, using his eager and smiling goodness, and the patient felt his symptoms diminish, his body rejoice and become healthy, while at the same time his suffering spirit, which was fighting against life's implacability, was gradually letting go.

Enriquillo was not really a psychiatrist. It was enough for him to be a man with an insatiable human curiosity, a cheerful and silent discoverer of those islands which are men and women. Of their mountains and their springs, their dark places and their crystalline fountains. He would play at performing good deeds just as others play golf, for pure sport, and with a ferocity incomprehensible to those who watched him.

Thus, leaving the beautiful and hypocritical city, he came one day to that faraway village in the mountains. He arrived by sea. The sea brought him on its back of deep and rippled blue. He came to one of those scientific things—a conference or a lecture—and surprising everyone, even himself, decided to stay on. Up there, on the mountain, where the Yaque and the Jimonea rivers flow, in a cool spot on the hot island, amongst stands of unexpected pine trees, the doctor pitched his solitary tent. He wanted to write, he wanted to reflect, to survey from above the route taken, to better spy what he needed. But soon he was interrupted in his intense contemplation of his interior landscape.

His fame had arrived with him, and timidly the sick began to approach him. The little girl who sang had now gone forever, and her sad mother could not bring her to Enriquillo so that the girl could be cured. The foreign woman who loved love with an insatiable passion could not bring herself to see him fortunately, or unfortunately for both of them, but day after day God's humble creatures came to see him asking for his help to be relieved of their suffering: those sick from hunger who needed affection more than bread; children without fathers, or even worse, with false parents; women of the earth who seemed to be made of clay, kneaded with the sweat of ancestral desperation; men who emptied out their profound impotence in the face of life. with blind rage, drunk with poverty, and drugged with the fear of being alive.

It was a long line of pilgrims, an endless line, that would disappear with the night to form again when the sun came out. He attended to every one and, using few medicines and long talks, helped them slowly to live, which was tantamount to helping to cure them.

The druggists in the nearby towns ground out all the indignation of the world in their pestles. Except for three or four simple remedies, the doctor did not prescribe anything. The physicians from the nearby region also came up to see him without revealing who they were, pretending to be sick, and the diagnosis of their new rival amazed them.

"My friend, you don't have anything wrong with you," he said to one who was describing with a wealth of detail supposed symptoms that were bothering him.

He advised another one, who came with the same predicament to observe the new doctor on the sly, "Your problem is that you find yourself bothered by my presence here and that causes you to feel certain discomforts. Don't worry, for I'm not coming to compete with anyone, but rather to help wherever possible."

"And how do you know I'm a doctor?"

"I saw it in your eyes. You have a clinical eye," replied Enriquillo, laughing.

The witchdoctor, Chilapa, who lived in a small cave in the surrounding area, did not come to see Enriquillo because a witchdoctor does not like any other doctor who is not himself; but he cast all kinds of spells on him, sprinkled incense, and used other kinds of herbs so that he would leave. Small packages carefully tied up and filled with disgusting things would frequently appear at the doctor's door. He opened them carefully and declared in a loud voice:

"Take them to Señor Chilapa's laboratory so he can analyze them."

Thus Chilapa remained calm. Enriquillo lived happily in that remote and beautiful place; by night he read and meditated, and by day he kept on conducting his necessary consultations, incapable as he was of rejecting the sick, even though they left him with little free time for contemplation. Sometimes he thought about going further afield to a place that was really solitary, higher up on the steepest mountain peak.

One sunlit morning he saw a young woman followed by two children coming along the narrow, leafy path to his tent. The older one was a boy of about ten, with a dark and tormented face, and the other a girl, small and chubby with a far-away look in her eyes. Both, when seen at a glance, were far removed from ordinary reality, and had, at the same time, a vacant and anguished look on their faces.

The woman said to him simply:

"I bring them here to you, Doctor. This one, Juan de la Cruz, has crickets in his head, and she, Lucinda, has butterflies. Don't you know it!"

"Crickets? Butterflies? Can you possibly mean that they have manias and strange ideas, that kind of thing?"

"No, Señor. Crickets, crickets. Crickets like those that go chirp, chirp. He has had them since he got back from down there. Her butterflies were already in her mind, it seems to me, but they have bothered her ever since he came to live in the house. Before that she didn't mention them, now she does."

The doctor bit his lips lightly.

"Are they your children?"

She laughed coquettishly.

"Those kids, so big? No, they're the late Lucrecia's children. I took them in and I said to my man, 'Our mother brought us up lovingly, and since Lucrecia my sister drowned during the flood, it's my turn to bring up her little ones.' My late mother, Minán, always said that loving is what counts the most in families. Because you see, Doctor, we are the daughters of good parents even though we're poor. Who has said that we poor people don't have manners or love for our fellow creatures. Oh, no!"

The young woman was talkative, but charming.

"Tell me briefly the story of the children before I go in to examine them."

"At the same time that the late Lucrecia died, the children's father lost the little bit of land he had, decided to go and look for work in the capital, and took the children with him. Around there he took up with another woman, and one day Juan de la Cruz ran away from home. His father searched for him, but didn't find him. I don't imagine he looked very hard for him, I say, because the woman was already pregnant and didn't want to have more than her own kids around. I learned about this and went to get the little girl and brought her here. She was chubby when I found her, yes, but half crazy as well. I think that already she had this thing with the butterflies. I brought her here, Doctor, because that woman had no love for the daughter of my dead sister. I noticed as soon as I saw her. It's a shame that the girl, who isn't ugly, is bewitched by that business of the butterflies. At first they weren't noticeable, Doctor."

"How is that?"

"Well, when he feels the crickets, right away she feels the butterflies that fly around inside her head. I go up to her and hear the noises that their wings make ever so softly."

"Do you believe that?"

"How am I not going to believe it? I hear them, ever so softly flying around in circles inside her head, and when they get stirred up, the child spends days not saying a word, looking at the ceiling; she doesn't sleep, not one wink, and eats without taking any notice of what she's eating. Listen to them, Doctor, ever so softly they go around and around her."

The doctor bent his face over the girl's and noticed that a very soft, almost inaudible whistle was coming out of her half-opened mouth.

"How do you do that?" he asked the girl suddenly, with notable kindness.

"I . . . I don't do anything," she countered defensively. "It's the butterflies. Here, Doctor." And she placed her chubby hands on her temples with a tragic gesture, while she looked at her brother, asking with her blank eyes for an approving glance.

"Now I see," said the doctor seriously. "And you, young man?"

"I, nothing . . . It's the crickets . . . but not today. Today they are quiet," said the boy, blushing as he lowered his stern face.

The young woman continued to explain without pausing:

"I took the girl to Señor Chilapa and he made her eat a live butterfly, a big one, one of those velvety ones, to see if the ones inside her would be frightened. Lucinda was sick for three days; she vomited up all her insides, and we thought she had been cured, but it came to nothing. After a few days, with the new phase of the moon the crickets came back, and the damned butterflies were flying around inside her. What she ate didn't make a bit of difference."

Enriquillo admired Chilapa's practical wisdom, although it was obvious that the boy's infectious influence was stronger. He focused his attention on the boy who was looking behind him because he wanted to leave.

"Tell me about the boy."

She raised her eyebrows to make a point, and speaking very softly, she said:

"That one is certainly a really sad case, Doctor. He has never said anything to me about anything that happened to him since he fled from his father's house. You can't talk to him about that because he gets almost crazy with his crickets. One day when my husband and I insisted on his telling us, he had something like a dead fainting spell and we had to . . ."

"Aay! The crickets! Chirp, chirp . . ." shouted the child suddenly, as if he had been overcome by a sharp pain while he looked with anguish at his aunt who was speaking softly to the doctor. He fell to the floor in a kind of attack, half real, half fake, which the doctor recognized at once as an hysterical trick to distract his attention.

"Didn't I tell you, Doctor? Look at that!"

They shook him, they threw water on his face, and soon he came to his senses.

"Juan de la Cruz, go to the patio and help the gardener water the lettuce. Go on, get out of here now." In a firm but gentle manner the doctor made him go to the vegetable garden, then continued with his questions:

"How did you find him?"

"I didn't find him. I didn't have any idea where to look for him. Some people in a big car brought him. It seems that they had seen him a lot at the door of the three movie theaters in the capital. The lady used to give him some coins, and one day the gentleman began to talk to him, and they decided to bring him back to their home because he was smaller that the others and had an innocent face. The lady felt sorry for him. They intended to send him to school and he would help in the house and so on. He went off happily with them, but then the business of the crickets started, and he became a calamity case. Because the man didn't want to abandon him to roam around on the streets, he decided to bring him here to me. Good people, don't you think? Because they made that trip which was so long to bring him. The boy remembered the name of the town, and my name, and everything. He was about six when his late mother died, and his father took him away to the capital. What a bad time that was! There those crickets put themselves into his head, or was it that they were born inside him, eh, Doctor?"

"Let's see, Señora. To find that out, and other things as well, it would be best for the boy to remain here for the day. Let's ask him if he wants to."

First Juan de la Cruz said no, but ended up accepting the idea. At the same time he both wanted and did not want to be free of the crickets that were making him suffer horribly.

His aunt and little Lucinda went back to the town and Enriquillo spent the rest of the day working in the garden and chatting nonchalantly with Juan de la Cruz.

He didn't clarify anything. The child was amiable, respectful, but laconic.

"I was around there, with some people," he said when Enriquillo questioned him about the time he spent away from his home. His face became contorted, nevertheless, when he mentioned the crickets.

"I can't see them, they're disgusting and I have them inside of me. How revolting!"

The doctor let him be. They planted rosebushes in the garden and ate a seven-meat stew before Juan de la Cruz left.

"Come back whenever you feel like it, " said the doctor over his shoulder.

"Could it be on Sunday, Señor? Your stew is very good and . . . I like talking with you."

A friendship was established between the two in which it was the doctor who would chat and tell stories about his childhood, about his studies, and other countries. The child listened, amazed.

"I would like to study too," he said once, "but with what? I have to work to help my aunt and uncle."

"If you are cured, if you get rid of the awful insects that bother you, maybe someone will want to pay for your studies."

"Do you think so, Doctor?" Mischievously, he let out a laugh. For the first time in years, a clear and childlike laugh. He had understood the veiled promise.

"Yes, I think so," said Enriquillo, looking him in the eyes, seriously, insistently, and the poor child, almost in a hypnotic trance, burst into tears, and sobbed:

"I can't stand these crickets any longer, Doctor, I'm going to tell you everything, now, everything, everything."

But he had an attack. The most intimate part of him rebelled against confiding his secret, and that day, after he had recovered his senses, the doctor sent him home.

"Not yet, Juan de la Cruz. You will tell me another day." And the boy, again taciturn, said:

"No, never, ever. It's too horrible."

"Then don't tell me. Come back another day when you are free."

"I'm not free, Señor. I'm not ever going to be, with these crickets!"

And sighing, he went off down the mountainside. When he returned some days later, the doctor had prepared a tiny cage made out of pieces of reeds.

"It's for the crickets," he told him.

And the boy laughed, before he remembered his anguish. "Yes, you believe they're nothing," he said in a resentful manner.

"I *know* they're not anything. They are a pretext that you give to confuse and punish yourself, and also, so as not to think about anything worse."

When he heard this, the boy began to tremble, shaking like a leaf, out of control in a full-blown fit, and foaming at his twisted mouth.

"He cut off her hands, both of them, first one then the other. Ayyy! And I didn't say anything. I remained silent. I was very scared of him. He hit me hard several times on my head and it was then that the crickets entered my head. Ayy! Chirp, chirp . . ."

He rolled around on the ground and moaned. He was sweating copiously, and it seemed like he was about to die.

It was necessary to sedate him.

When he regained consciousness, Enriquillo said to him, smiling: "Juan de la Cruz, you are cured."

"How is that, Señor, if I feel destroyed inside and with nothing in my head?"

"That's because the crickets are gone. They went away one by one. I saw them leave. They are gone forever. Do you see how it doesn't bother you to hear me talk about them?"

"That's true," said the child, vaguely surprised, and he closed his eyes as if falling into a stupor. After a little while he woke up, calmly.

"Listen to me, Juan de la Cruz. You aren't to blame anyway. Not at all. Do you understand me? The members of the gang that took you away were much stronger than you. You became a beggar for them, not for yourself; a thief perhaps, but for them, not because you wanted to. And the horrible thing that happened with the other child, you wouldn't have been able to avoid it."

"She was a tiny little girl like Lucinda, but smaller still; they found her walking alone in the countryside and they took her to the cave. One of the boys called her the butterfly, making fun of her, because she went around with her dress like this, as if it were wings, when they found her.

"They kept all of us in a dark cave, almost under the sea, on the coast, you know, almost without any food, and in the afternoon they would let us loose in the city so we could beg. They had threatened us that if we talked with the police or with anyone, they would kill all of us. They were very capable of doing it. The fat old man was very evil. He talked strangely. He wasn't from around here. He was the one who hit us, for everything, for nothing. Behind the ears, look."

"Yes, I had already noticed those scars."

"But the worst part was the day they took the little girl into the capital to beg, and afterwards they said that no one would give her money because she was chubby and healthy looking. One of the big men carried her in his arms and collected almost nothing. They waited a few days, looking in the newspapers, and because no one advertised for her, they decided to do that to her . . . what I told you about her hands. They got her drunk first so she wouldn't cry. She screamed a lot anyway. The noise of the sea covered her screams. On the rock . . . with a machete . . . I saw it, I saw it all, and I didn't go and tell the police. I got sick. Then the old man insulted me, threatened me, he was like a crazy man, and he hit me on the ear with a piece of iron. I fell down and fainted, but before that I heard the crickets and I saw inside myself with my eyes how they were getting themselves into my head. Dirty, disgusting things. Probably it was an idea of mine, like you say, but I felt them. Three days later I went out again onto the street. I was dying of hunger, and around there, on Guibia beach, where the shark bit the American's leg off last year, I started to beg.

"I brought lots of coins to the cave that night. And they gave me food too. I had the face of a dead man, believe me. That night when I lay down to sleep on my mattress, I heard the crickets again. At first they horrified me. Finally I became more or less accustomed. And now you say they've gone, Doctor?"

Don't you believe it, Juan de la Cruz? Look how calmly you've spoken about all that."

"Yes, I believe it too. I don't feel them any more. Ah . . . Doctor, look, listen. I have to tell you something else. My crickets were real, but Lucinda's butterflies, those I put into her head so she would have something to tell her aunt as well. Lucinda reminded me of that other poor little girl, so I talked to her about the butterflies without telling her why, of course, and she began to feel them. Now they're going to leave her too, isn't that right, Doctor?"

"Yes, they will leave her easily, because they never existed. Just like your crickets. You don't need them any more to torment you, and for that reason they went away."

"Yes, Señor, I'm not afraid of them any more. Now I've taken that weight off of me. Ah! . . . Doctor, excuse me. I'm very sleepy."

He gave a big yawn, was totally exhausted, and slept peacefully like an innocent child.

Translated by Brenda Segall

Bibliography: Gloria Stolk

Fiction

Stolk, Gloria. *Bela Vegas*. Caracas/Madrid: Ediciones Edime, 1953.

———. *Amargo el fondo*. Caracas: Tipografía Vargas, 1957.

———. *Cuando la luz se quiebra*. Caracas: s.n., 1961.

———. "Amargo el fondo." *Antología venezolana*. Ed. José Ramón Medina. Madrid: Gredos, 1962. 268-73.

———. *Angel de piedra*. Caracas: J. Villegas, 1962.

———. *La casa del viento*. Caracas: Editorial Arte, 1965.

———. *Cuentos del caribe*. Caracas: Monte Avila Editores, 1975.

———. "Grillos y mariposas." *Puerta abierta: la nueva escritora latinoamericana*. Ed. Caridad L. Silva-Velázquez and Nora Erro-Orthmann. Mexico City: Joaquín Mortiz, 1986. 223-30.

Essays

Stolk, Gloria. *Manual de buenos modelos*. Caracas: Instituto Nacional de Cultura y Bellas Artes, 1967; Santo Domingo: Listín Diario, 1973.

———. "Georgina inexistente y Juan Ramón Jiménez." *Repertorio Latinoamericano* 5.37 (1979): 7-8.

Poetry

Stolk, Gloria. *Rescate y otros poemas*. Caracas: Tipografía Americana, 1950.

———. *Cielo insistente*. Caracas: Asociación de Escritores Venezolanos, 1960.

Criticism on the Work of Gloria Stolk

Aldariz, José R., ed. *Enciclopedia popular venezolana: esto es Venezuela, 1987.* Caracas: Torre Phelps, 1988. 440-41.

Araujo, Orlando. ". . . *Bela Vegas.*" *Papel Literario de El Nacional* [Caracas] 28 Jan. 1954: 7.

———. *Narrativa venezolana contemporánea.* Caracas: Editorial Tiempo Nuevo, 1972. 233-37.

Calzadilla, J. "*Amargo el fondo.*" *Revista Nacional de Cultura* 123 (1957): 145-46.

C.D. "Amargo el fondo." *Papel Literario de El Nacional* [Caracas] 10 Jan. 1957: 7.

Cardozo, Lubio. *Diccionario general de la literatura venezolana.* Mérida, Venezuela: Centro de Investigaciones Literaria, Universidad de Los Andes, Facultad de Humanidades y Educación, 1974. 736-37.

Medina, José Ramón. "*Los miedos.*" *Revista Nacional de Cultura* 111 (1955): 180-81.

Paredes, Pedro Pablo. "37 apuntes de crítica literaria." *Revista Nacional de Cultura* 111 (1955): 191-93.

Pía P. y Beltran. "*Amargo el fondo.*" *Cultura Universitaria* [Caracas] 63 197-98.

Ramos Q., Elías A. *El cuento venezolano (1950-1970): estudio temático y estilístico.* Madrid: Playor, 1979. 196.

R.P. "Tres libros de Gloria." *Papel Literario de El Nacional* [Caracas] 26 Aug. 1954: 7.

———. "Versatilidad de Gloria Stolk." *Papel Literario de El Nacional* Caracas 8 Sept. 1955.

Salazar Martínez, F. "Novela." *Papel Literario de El Nacional* 7.1 (1953): 3.

Telémaco. "*Bela Vegas.*" *Papel Literario de El Nacional* 28.1 (1954): 7.

Tello, J. "Cuando la luz se quiebra." *Revista Nacional de Cultura* 148-149 (1961): 248-49.

Ungaro de Fox, L. "*América cuenta.*" *Revista Nacional de Cultura* 173 (1966): 146-47.

LUISA VALENZUELA
Argentina

Luisa Valenzuela was born in Buenos Aires in 1938. Literature was an important part of her upbringing, since her mother, Luisa Mercedes Levinson, was a well-known Argentine author. She began an early literary career working on the staff of the newspaper *La Nación*.

Valenzuela has traveled extensively, and has lived in Paris, New York City, Mexico City and Iowa City. She is one of the few Latin American women writers well-known in the United States. Her work has received several distinctions; among them, Guggenheim Fellow in 1982; and Distinguished Writer-in-Residence at New York University in 1985.

Luisa Valenzuela's fiction can best be characterized as revolutionary. It challenges the validity of social structures and institutions: religion, machismo, marriage and sexual taboos. At another level, it pursues self-development and a re-arrangement of male/female relationships, based on self-knowledge and mutual acceptance. At a metaphysical, creative level, it promotes the idea of a world understood in terms of everlasting, ever-moving, atemporal energy.

She achieves such a diversity through several literary techniques: multiplicity of points of view, fractured time and elusive narrators, but mainly through language. Her use of language is a game of self-invention and demythification which constantly boycotts the seriousness of language's role as a communicator of reality.

UP AMONG THE EAGLES

You'll find what I tell you hard to believe, for who knows anything, nowadays, about life in the country? And life here on the mountains, up among the eagles. You get used to it. Oh yes, I can tell you. I who never knew anything but the city, just look at me now, the color of clay, carrying my pails of water from the public fountain. Water for myself and water for others. I've been doing it to eke out a living ever since the day I made the foolish mistake of climbing the path that borders the cliff. I climbed up and, looking down at the green dot of the valley below, I decided to stay here forever. It wasn't that I was afraid; I was just being prudent, as they say: threatening cliffs, beyond imagination— impossible even to consider returning. Everything I owned I traded for food: my shoes, my wristwatch, my key holder with all the keys (I wouldn't be needing them anymore), a ballpoint pen that was almost out of ink.

The only thing of any value I kept is my Polaroid camera; no one wanted it. Up here they don't believe in preserving images, just the opposite: every day they strive to create new images only for the moment. Often they get together to tell each other about the improbable images they've been envisioning. They sit in a circle in the dark on the dirt floor of their communal hut and concentrate on making the vision appear. One day, out of nothing, they materialized a tapestry of nonexistent colors and ineffable design, but they decided that it was just a pale reflection of their mental image, and so they broke the circle to return the tapestry to the nothingness from which it had come.

They are strange creatures; normally they speak a language whose meaning they themselves have forgotten. They communicate by interpreting pauses, intonations, facial expressions, and sighs. I tried to learn this language of silences, but it seems I don't have the right accent. At any rate, they speak our language when they refer to trivial matters, the daily needs that have nothing to do with their images. Even so, some words are missing from their vocabulary. For example, they have no word for yesterday or for tomorrow, before or after, or for one of these days. Here everything is now, and always. An unsatisfactory imitation of eternity like the tapestry I have already mentioned. Have mentioned? Oh yes, I'm the only one to use that verb tense; I may also be the only one who has any notion of conjugation. A vice left over from the world down there, knowledge I can't barter because no one wants it.

Will you trade me some beans for a notion of time, I went around asking the women in the marketplace, but they shook their heads emphatically. (A notion of time? They looked at me with mistrust. A way of moving on a different plane? That has nothing to do with the knowledge they are after.)

Who dares to speak of the passage of time to the inhabitants of this high place where everything endures? Even their bodies endure. Death neither decays nor obliterates them; it merely stops them in their path. Then the others, with exquisite delicacy—a delicacy I've seen them employ in connection with newly dropped kids or with certain mushrooms—carry the corpse beyond the rushing stream with the precise symmetry arrange it in the exact place it occupied in life. With infinite patience they have succeeded in creating, on the other side, a second town that obliterates time, an unmoving reflection of themselves that gives them a feeling of security because it is mummified, unmodifiable.

They only allow themselves changes in respect to the images. They grow, yes, they grow up and reach adulthood with only a suspicion of old age, remaining more or less the same until they die. In contrast, I discover with horror that I have a sprinkling of gray hairs, and wrinkles are lining my face; premature, of course, but who could keep her youth in this dry air, beneath such intense skies? What will become of me when they discover that time passes in my life, and is leaving its marks?

They are absorbed in other concerns, in trying to retain visions of what appear to be jeweled palaces and splendors unknown on this earth. They roam around latitudes of awe while all I can do—and very infrequently and with extreme stealth at that—is take a photo of myself. I am down to earth despite living in this elevated land floating among clouds. And they say the altitude deranges those of us who come from sea level. But it is my belief, my fear, that they are the ones who are deranged; it's something ancestral, inexplicable, especially when they are squatting on their haunches, as they almost always are, looking inward in contemplation. I'm always looking outward, I search every road, almost nonchalantly nourishing my fear. They watch me go by carrying water, the pole across my shoulders and the two pails dangling from it, and I would like to think they do not suspect my fear. This fear has two faces, not at all like the one that kept me from returning after I had climbed the mountain. No, this is not a simple fear; it reflects others, and becomes voracious.

On the other hand, I am here, now. That now grows and changes and expands with time and, if I am lucky, will continue to evolve. I do not want them to be aware of this evolving, as I have already said, and even less do I want to be like them, exempt from time. For what would become of me if I kept this face forever, as if surprised between two ages? I think about the mummies in the mirror city, oh yes, absolutely, only mummies are unchanged by time. Time does not pass for the dead, I told myself one day, and on a different day (because I, if not they, am very careful to relate question to calendar) I added: nor does it pass for those who have no concept of death. Death is a milestone.

The inhabitants here, with their language of silence, could teach me the secrets of the immobility that so closely resembles immortality, but I am not eager to learn them. Life is a movement toward death; to remain static is to be already dead.

Sit here, little lady, nice and quiet here with us is one of the few things they consent to say to me in my own language, and I shake my head energetically (one more way of insuring movement), and as soon as I am out of their sight, I begin to run like crazy along the neglected paths. More often than not I run up, not down, but either way, I don't want to get too far from the town, I don't want to stumble into the still city and find myself face-to-face with the mummies.

The secret city. I don't know its exact location but I know everything about it—or maybe I only suspect. I know it has to be identical to this humble little clump of huts where we live, a faithful replica with the exact same number of bodies, for when one of them dies the oldest mummy is thrown into the void. It's noisy in the secret city. The noise announces its proximity, but it also serves a more basic purpose: scraps of tin, of every size and shape, hang from the rafters of the huts to scare away the buzzards. They are all that moves in the secret city, those scraps of tin to scare away the vultures, the only thing that moves or makes a sound. On certain limpid nights the wind carries the sound to where the living dwell, and on those nights they gather in the plaza, and dance.

They dance, but oh so slowly, almost without moving their feet, more as if they were undulating, submerged in the dense waters of sound. This happens only rarely, and when it does I feel an almost uncontrollable urge to join in the dance—the need to dance soaks into my bones, sways me—but I resist with all my strength. I am afraid that nothing could be more paralyzing than to yield to this music that comes from death. So that I won't be paralyzed I don't dance. I don't dance and I don't share the visions.

I have not witnessed a birth since I have been here. I know they couple, but they don't reproduce. They do nothing to avoid it, simply the stillness of the air prevents it. As for me, at this point I don't even go near men. It must be admitted that men don't come near me either, and there must be a reason, considering how often and how closely they approach almost anything else. Something in my expression must drive them away, but I've no way of knowing what it is. There are no mirrors here. No reflections. Water is either glaucous or torrential white. I despair. And every so often in the privacy of my cave, sparingly and with extreme caution, I take a new photo of myself.

I do this when I can't stand things any longer, when I have an over-whelming need to know about myself, and then no fear, no caution, can hold me back. One problem is that I am running out of film. In addition, I know perfectly well that if they find my photographs, if they place them in chronological order, two things can happen: they will either abominate or adore me. And neither possibility is to be desired. There are no alternatives. If they put the photos in order and draw the conclusions; if they see that when I arrived, my face was smoother, my hair brighter, my bearing more alert; if they discover the marks of time they will know that I have not controlled time even for a moment. And so if they find I am growing older, they won't want me among them, and they will stone me out of town, and I will have to face the terrifying cliffs.

I don't even want to think about the other possibility: that they will adore me because I have so efficiently, and so concretely, materialized these images of myself. Then I would be like stone to them, like a statue forever captive and contained.

Either of these two lapidary prospects should provide sufficient reason to restrain my suicidal impulse to take yet another photograph, but it doesn't. Each time, I succumb, hoping against hope that they will not be alerted by the glare of the flash. Sometimes I choose stormy nights; perhaps I conjure up the lightning with my pale simulacrum. At other times I seek the protective radiance of dawn, which at this altitude can be incendiary.

I make elaborate preparations for each of my secret snapshots, prep-arations charged with hope and danger, that is, with life. The resulting picture does not always please me but the emotion of seeing myself—no matter how horrible or haggard I appear—is immeasurable. This is I, changing in a static world that imitates death. And I feel safe. Then I am able to stop and speak of simple things with the women in the market and even understand their silences, and answer them. I can live a little longer without love, without anyone's touch.

Until another relapse, a new photo. And this will be the last. On a day with the sound of death, when the minimal activities of the town have come to a halt and they have all congregated to dance in the marketplace. That deliberate dancing that is like praying with their feet, a quiet prayer. They will never admit it, but I suspect that they count to themselves, that their dance is an intricate web of steps like knitting, one up, two backward, one to the right. All to the tinkling of the far-off tin scraps: the wind in the house of the dead. A day like any other; a very special day for them because of the sound that they would call music, were they interested in making such distinctions. But all that interests them is the dance, or believing they are dancing, or thinking of the dance, which is the same thing. To the pulse of the sound that floods over us, whose origins I cannot locate though I know it comes from the city of the dead.

They do not call to me; they don't even see me. It's as if I didn't exist. Maybe they're right, maybe I don't exist, maybe I am my own invention, or a peculiar materialization of an image they have evoked. That sound is joyful, and yet the most mournful ever heard. I seem to be alive, and yet . . .

I hide in my cave trying not to think, trying not to hear the tinkling; I don't know where it comes from, but I fear where it may lead me. With the hope of setting these fears to rest, I begin my preparations for the last photo: a desperate attempt to recover my being. To return to myself, which is all I have.

Anxiously, I wait for the perfect moment, while outside, darkness is weaving its blackest threads. Suddenly, an unexpected radiance causes me to trip the shutter before I am ready. No photograph emerges, only a dark rectangle that gradually reveals the blurred image of a stone wall. And that's all. I have no more film so I may as well throw away the camera. A cause for weeping were it not for the fact the radiance is not fading. A cause for uneasiness, then, because when I peer out I see that the blazing light is originating from the very place I wanted not to know about, from the very heart of the sound, from a peak just below us. And the radiance comes from millions of glittering scraps of tin in the moonlight. The city of the dead.

Spontaneously, I set forth with all my stupid photos, responding to an impulse that responds, perhaps, to a summons from the sonorous radiance. They are calling me from down there, over to the left, and I answer, and at first I run along the treacherous path and when the path ends I continue on. I stumble, I climb and descend, I trip and hurt myself; to avoid hurtling into the ravine I try to imitate the goats, leaping across the rocks; I lose my footing, I slip and slide, I try to check my fall, thorns rake my skin and at the same time hold me back. Rashly I pull ahead and it is imperative I must reach the city of the dead and leave my face to the mummies. I will place my successive faces on the mummies and then at last I'll be free to go down without fearing stone for I'll take my last photo with me and I am myself in that photo and I am stone.

Translated by Margaret Sayers-Peden

Bibliography: Luisa Valenzuela

Fiction

Valenzuela, Luisa. *Hay que sonreír*. Buenos Aires: Editorial Americana, 1966.

———. *Los heréticos*. Buenos Aires: Paidós, 1967.

———. *Hay que sonreír*. Buenos Aires: Editorial Americana, 1969.

———. *El gato eficaz*. Mexico City: Joaquín Mortiz, 1972.

———. "The Door." Trans. N.T. Di Giovanni. *Mundus Artium* 7.2 (1974): 120-23.

———. *Aquí pasan cosas raras*. Buenos Aires: Ediciones de la Flor, 1975.

———. *Clara: Thirteen Short Stories and a Novel*. Trans. Hortense Carpentier and J. Jorge Castello. New York: Harcourt, Brace, Jovanovich, 1976.

———. *Como en la guerra*. Buenos Aires: Editorial Sudamericana, 1977.

———. "Excerpts from *Strange Things Happen Here: Twenty-six Short Stories and a Novel*." Trans. Helen Lane. *American Poetry Review* 8.2 (1978): 8-10.

———. "The Best Shod" and "A Story about Greenery." Trans. Helen Lane. *Ms* 7.12 June 1979: 60-61.

———. *Strange Things Happen Here: Twenty-six Short Stories and a Novel*. Trans. Helen Lane. New York: Harcourt, Brace, Jovanovich, 1979.

———. "Three Stories from *Strange Things Happen Here*." Trans. Helen Lane. *Review, Center for Inter-American Relations* 24 (1979): 44-53.

———. "The Censors." Trans. David Unger. *City 8* 1.8 (1980): 8-10.

———. *Libro que no muerde*. Mexico: Universidad Nacional Autónoma de México, 1980.

———. "Papito's Story." Trans. David Unger. *City 8* 1.8 (1980): 66-68.

———. *Cambio de armas*. Hanover, NH: Ediciones del Norte, 1982; Mexico: M. Casillas, 1983.

———. *Cola de lagartija*. Buenos Aires: Brugera, 1983.

———. *Donde viven las aguilas*. Buenos Aires: Editorial Celtia, 1983.

———. "The First Feline Vision." Trans. Evelyn Picón Garfield. *Anatena* 48 (1983): 75-78.

———. "Generous Impediments Float Down the River." Trans. Clementine Rabassa. *Contemporary Women Authors of Latin America: New Translations*. Eds. Doris Meyer and Margarite Fernández Olmos. Brooklyn, NY: Brooklyn College, 1983. 245-49.

———. *The Lizard's Tail*. Trans. Gregory Rabassa. New York: Farrar, Straus, Giroux, 1983.

———. "The Efficient Cat." Trans. Evelyn Picón Garfield. *River Styx* 14 Jan. 1984: 87-89.

———. *Other Weapons*. Trans. Deborah Bonner. Hanover, NH: Ediciones del Norte, 1985.

———. "From *The Motive*: A Novel in Progress." Trans. Cynthia Ventura. *Review of Contemporary Fiction* 6.3 (1986): 22-24.

———. "Springtime." Trans. Evelyn Picón Garfield. *Formations* 3.1 (Spring 1986): 1-3.

———. "My Extraordinary Ph. D." *Review of Contemporary Fiction* 6.3 (1986): 7-8.

———. *He Who Searches*. Trans. Helen Lane. Elmwood Park, Ill.: Dalkey Archive Press, 1987.

———. "Blue Water-man." *Women's Fiction from Latin America: Selections from Twelve Contemporary Authors*. Ed. Trans. Evelyn Picón Garfield. Detroit: Wayne State University Press, 1988. 281-87.

———. "I am Your Horse in the Night." *Women's Fiction from Latin America: Selections from Twelve Contemporary Authors* Ed. Trans. Evelyn Picón Garfield. Detroit: Wayne State University Press, 1988. 311-14.

———. "On the Way to the Ministry." *You Can't Drown the Fire: Latin American Women Writing in Exile*. Ed. Alicia Partnoy. Pittsburgh: Cleis Press, 1988. 86-90.

———. *Open Door*. Trans. Hortense Carpentier, et al. San Francisco: North Point Press, 1988.

———. "Other Weapons." *Women's Fiction from Latin America: Selections from Twelve Contemporary Authors*. Trans. Deborah Bonner. Ed. Evelyn Picón Garfield. Detroit: Wayne State University Press, 1988. 288-310.

———. "Pantera Ocular." *El muro y la intemperie: el nuevo cuento latino americano*. Ed. Julio Ortega. Hanover, NH: Ediciones del Norte, 1989. 433-38.

———. "Strange Things Happen Here." Trans. Helen R. Lane. *Longman Anthology of World Literature by Women 1875-1975*. Eds. Marian Arkin and Barbara Shollar. New York: Longman, 1989. 939-44.

———. *Novela negra con argentinos*. Hanover, NJ: Ediciones del Norte, 1990.

———. *Realidad nacional desde la cama*. Buenos Aires: Grupo Editor Latinoamericano, 1990.

Essays

Valenzuela, Luisa. "Los porteños y sus literaturas." *Literature and Popular Culture in the Hispanic World: A Symposium*. Ed. Rose S. Minc. Upper Montclair, NJ: Montclair State College, 1981. 25-29.

———. "Mis brujas favoritas." *Theory and Practice of Feminist Literary Criticism*. Ed. Gabriela Mora and Karen S. Van Hooft. Ypsilanti, MI: Bilingual Press, 1982. 88-95.

———. "I Was Always a Bit of a Rebel." *Artists in Exile*. Ed. Jane Katz. New York: 1982. 59-70.

———. "The Word That Milk Cow." *Contemporary Women Authors of Latin America: Introductory Essays*. Eds. Doris Meyer and Margarite Fernández Olmos. Brooklyn: Brooklyn College, 1983. 96-97.

———. "La mala palabra." *Revista Iberoamericana* 51.132-133 (1985): 489-91. Rpt. in *Repertorio Latinoamericano* 12.67 (1986): 8-9.

————. "Dangerous Words," "Dirty Words," "In Search of My Own Back Yard," and "Little Manifesto." *Review of Contemporary Fiction* 6.3 (1986): 9-21.

————. "The First Word." *Américas* 38.6 (1986): 3-4.

————. "Los frutos del verano." *Hispamérica* 15.45 (1986): 83-85.

————. "Peligrosas palabras." *Hispamérica* 15.45 (1986): 81-82.

————. "Pequeño manifiesto." *Hispamérica* 15.45 (1986): 82-83.

————. "My Deadly Doctorate." Trans. Evelyn Picón Garfield. *Review of Contemporary Fiction* 6.2 (1986): 7-8.

————. "The Other Face of the Pallus." *Reinventing the Americas: Comparative Studies of the Literature of the United States and Spanish America*. Eds. Bel Gale Chevigny and Gari Laguardia. Cambridge: Cambridge University Press, 1986. 242-48.

————. "A Legacy of Poets and Cannibals: Literature Revives in Argentina." *Lives on The Line: The Testimony of Contemporary Latin American Authors*. Ed. Doris Meyer. Berkeley: University of California Press, 1988. 290-97.

Criticism on the Works of Luisa Valenzuela

Alegría, Fernándo. *Nueva historia de la novela hispanoamericana*. Hanover, NH: Ediciones del Norte, 1986. 342-45.

Angulo, Elsa B. de and Dorothy S. Mull. "An afternoon with Luisa Valenzuela." *Hispania* 69.2 (1986): 350-52.

Araujo, Helen. "Valenzuela's *Other Weapons*." Trans. Rick McCallister. *The Review of Contemporary Fiction* 6.3 (1986): 78-81.

Callejo, Alfonso. "Literatura e irregularidad en *Cambio de armas*, de Luisa Valenzuela." *Revista Iberoamericana* 51.132-133 (1985): 575-80.

Case, Barbara. "On Writing, Magic, and Eva Perón: An Interview with Argentina's Luisa Valenzuela." *Ms*. 12.4 (1983): 12-20.

"*Cola de lagartija*." *Chasqui* 14.2-3 (1985): 77-79.

Cook, Carole. "*Strange Things Happen Here: Twenty-six Short Stories and a Novel*." *Saturday Review* 23 June 1979. 80.

Cortázar, Julio. "Luisa Valenzuela." *Review: Latin American Literature and Arts* 24 (1979): 44.

De Feo, Ronald. "Two from Argentina." *The Nation* 237.16 (1983): 239-42.

Forché, Carolyn. "Grasping the Gruesome." *Esquire* 100.3 (1983): 505-8.

Fores, Ana M. "Valenzuela's *Cat-O-Nine-Deaths*." *The Review of Contemporary Fiction* 6.3 (1986): 39-47.

García Pinto, Magdalena. *Historias íntimas: conversaciones con 10 escritoras latinoamericanas*. Hanover, NH: Ediciones del Norte, 1988. 215-49.

Garfield, Evelyn Picón. "Interview with Luisa Valenzuela." *The Review of Contemporary Fiction* 6.3 (1986): 25-30.

————. "Luisa Valenzuela." *Women's Voices in Latin America: Interviews with Six Contemporary Authors*. Ed. Evelyn Picón Garfield. Detroit: Wayne State University Press, 1985. 141-65.

————. "Muerte-Metamorfosis-Modernidad: *El gato eficaz* de Luisa Valenzuela." *Insula* 35.400-401 Mar-Apr. 1980: 17.

Gazarian Gautier, Marie-Lise. "Luisa Valenzuela." *Interviews with Latin American Writers*. Elmwood Park, Ill.: Dalkey Archive Press, 1989. 293-322.

————. "The Sorcerer and Luisa Valenzuela: Double Narrators of the Novel/Biography, Myth/History." *The Review of Contemporary Fiction* 6.3 (1986): 105-08.

Glantz, Margo. "Luisa Valenzuela's *He Who Searches*." Trans. Janet Perez. *The Review of Contemporary Fiction* 6.3 (1986): 62-66.

Gómez Engler, Raquel. "Borrón y cuenta nueva: Reflexión sobre el uso de las máscaras de belleza en un cuento de Luisa Valenzuela." *Alba de América* 3, 4-5 (1985): 123-28.

Grossman, Edith. "To Speak the Unspeakable." *Latin American Literature and Arts Review* 32 (1984): 33-34.

Hernández, Ana María. "Luisa Valenzuela's *The Lizard's Tail*." *World Literature Today* 58.2 (1984): 247.

Herron, Carol Olivia. "*The Lizard's Tail*." *Womanews* 8.1-2: 239-240.

Hicks, Emily. "That Which Resists: The Code of the Real in Luisa Valenzuela's *He Who Searches*." *The Review of Contemporary Fiction* 6.3 (1986): 55-61.

Josephs, Allen. "Sorcerers and Despots." *New York Times Book Review* 2 Oct. 1983: 15.

Kaminsky, Amy Katz. "Women Writing about Prostitutes: Amalia Jamilis and Luisa Valenzuela." *The Image of the Prostitute in Modern Literature*. Eds. Pierre L. Horn and Mary Beth Pringle. New York: Ungar, 1984. 119-31.

Katz, Jane. "I Was Always a Bit of a Rebel." *Artists in Exile*. New York: n.p., 1983. 59-70.

Lagos-Pope, María Inés. "Mujer y politica en *Cambio de armas* de Luisa Valenzuela." *Hispamérica* 16.46-47 (1987): 71-83.

Lauzen, Sarah E. "*Strange Things Happen Here*." *Review 28*. *Latin American Literature and Arts*. Center for Inter-American Relations 28 (1981): 81-2.

Lertora, Juan Carlos. "El estatuto de la ficción en *Cola de lagartija*." *Literatura Chilena: Creación y Crítica* 11.3-4.41-42 (1987): 12-13.

Maci, Guillermo. "The Symbolic, the Imagery and the Real in Luisa Valenzuela's *He Who Searches*." Trans. Janet Perez. *The Review of Contemporary Fiction* 6.3 (1986): 67-77.

Magnarelli, Sharon. "Censorship and the Female Writer—An Interview-Dialogue with Luisa Valenzuela." *Letras Femeninas* 10.1 (1984): 55-64.

————. "Gatos, lenguaje, y mujeres en *El gato eficaz* de Luisa Valenzuela." *Revista Iberoamericana* 45.108-9 (1979): 603-11.

————. "Humor and Games in *El gato eficaz* by Luisa Valenzuela: The Looking-Glass World Revisited." *Modern Language Studies* 13.3 (1983): 81-89.

————. "Juego/fuego de la esperanza: En torno a *El gato eficaz* de Luisa Valenzuela." *Cuadernos Americanos*. 247.2 (1983): 199-208.

———. "*The Lizard's Tail*: Discourse Denatured." *The Review of Contemporary Fiction* 6.3 (1986): 97-104.

———. "Luisa Valenzuela: From *Hay que sonreir* to *Cambio de armas.*" *World Literature Today: A Literary Quarterly of the University of Oklahoma* 58.1 (1984): 9-13.

———. *Reflection-Refractions: Reading Luisa Valenzuela.* New York: Peter Lang, 1988.

———. "Women, Language, and Cats in Luisa Valenzuela's *El gato eficaz*: Looking-Glass Games of Fire." *The Lost Rib.* Lewisburg: Bucknell University Press, 1985. 169-85.

Marcos, Juan Manuel. "Luisa Valenzuela: más allá de la araña de la esquina rosada." *Prismal/Cabral* 11 (1983): 57-65. Rpt. in *De García Márquez al postboom.* Madrid: Orígenes, 1986. 83-90.

Martínez, Nelly Z. "*El gato eficaz* de Luisa Valenzuela: La productividad del texto." *Revista Canadiense de Estudios Hispánicos* 4 (1979): 73-80.

———. "Luisa Valenzuela's *The Lizard's Tail*, Deconstruction of the Peronist Mythology." *El Cono Sur: Dinámica y dimensiones de su literatura: A Symposium.* Rose S. Minc. Ed. Montclair, N.J.: Montclair State College, 1985.

———. "Luisa Valenzuela's 'Where the Eagles Dwell': From Fragmentation to Holism." *The Review of Contemporary Fiction* 6.3 (1986): 109-15.

Marting, Diane. "Female Sexuality in Selected Short Stories by Luisa Valenzuela: Toward an Ontology of Her Work." *The Review of Contemporary Fiction* 6.3 (1986): 48-54.

Morello-Frosch, Marta. "*Other Weapons*: When Metaphors Become Real." *The Review of Contemporary Fiction* 6.3 (1986): 82-87.

Mull, Dorothy S. "Ritual Transformation in Luisa Valenzuela's 'Rituals of Rejection'." *The Review of Contemporary Fiction* 6.3 (1986): 88-96.

Mull, Dorothy S. and Elsa B. de Angulo. "An Afternoon with Luisa Valenzuela." *Hispania* 69.2 (1986): 350-52.

Ordóñez, Montserrat. "Enigmas y variaciones: Luisa Valenzuela y Cristina Peri Rossi: en el límite de la crítica." Instituto Internacional de Literatura Iberoamericana XXIV Congreso *La Crítica Literaria en Latinoamerica.* Stanford University 8-12 June, 1985. 97-106.

———. "Máscaras de espejos, un juego especular. Entrevista-asociaciones con la escritora argentina Luisa Valenzuela." *Revista Iberoamericana* 51.132-133 (1985): 511-19.

Paley Francescato, Martha. "*Cola de lagartija*: Látigo de la palabra y la triple P." *Revista Iberoamericana* 51.132-133 (1985): 875-82.

Resnick, Margery. "*Other Weapons.*" *New York Times Book Review* 6 Oct. 1985: 38.

Sabino, Osvaldo R. "Los nombres y los gatos: Luisa Valenzuela y sus siete libros." *Alba de América* 1, 1 (1983): 155-66.

Saltz, Joanne. "Luisa Valenzuela's *Cambio de Armas*: Rhetoric of Politics." *Confluencia: Revista Hispanica de Cultura y Literatura* 3.1 (1987): 61-66.

Saltz, Joanne Carol. "Stories of Power: The Short Narrative of Luisa Valenzuela." *DAI* 48.6 (1987): 1465A.

Sheppard, R. Z. "Where the Fiction is 'Fantástica'." *Time* Mar. 7, 1983: 78-82.

Tanner, Stephen L. "Reality by the Tail." *Chronicles of Culture* 8.12 (1984): 10-13.

Tobin, Patricia. "Voices in the Silence." *Review 76* Center for Inter-American Relations 18 (1976): 78-80.

Umpierre, Luz María. "Luisa Valenzuela: *Cola de lagartija*." *Revista Iberoamericana* 51, 130-31 (1985): 430-32.

Wilson, S. R. Review of *Aquí pasan cosas raras*. *Latin American Literary Review* 9.18 (1981): 67-69.

———. Review of *Cambio de armas*. *Latin American Literary Review* 12.24 (1984): 82-84.

RIMA VALLBONA
Costa Rica

R ima Vallbona was born in San José, Costa Rica, in 1931. She attended university in her native country and later in France, Spain, and the United States, where she completed her doctorate degree at Middlebury College. She has resided for many years in Houston, Texas, with her family and there she organized the Spanish Department of St. Thomas University, serving as its first chair. Since 1964 Vallbona has been a professor of Spanish literature in the United States, at the Universities of St. Thomas, Houston, and Rice.

Related to her academic interest, Vallbona has published two bodies of literary criticism: *Yolanda Oreamuno* (1971) and *La obra de Eunice Odio* (The Works in Prose of Eunice Odio, 1981). She has written two novels, as well as five collections of short stories and numerous children's stories. Her short-story volume entitled *Mujeres y agonías* (Women and Agonies, 1982) was awarded the SCOLAS Prize (Southwest Conference on Latin American Studies). She also has obtained such important prizes as the Jorge Luis Borges Short Story Award (Argentina, 1977), and the Ancora Prize for the best fiction book (Costa Rica, 1984).

Rima Vallbona's short stories reflect a deep feminist commitment and a continuous exploration into new levels of women's concerns. Some of her characters break new ground as they replace traditional patriarchal myths with vibrant, joyful women's experiences and unique achievements in self-fulfillment.

THE SECRET WORLD OF
GRANDMAMMA ANACLETA

Lying shipwrecked in the oceanic immensity of her baroque bed, framed by its twisted, leaf-covered columns, beneath the sheets and the fluffy feather comforter was the tiny, insignificant form to which nonagenarian Grandmamma Anacleta had shrunk. Seen from the vantage point of my ten years, and perhaps because of the lack of a better perspective, Grandmamma Anacleta was just a little heap of bones and corrugated skin. For many years she had spent her days lying still, moving her lips insistently, as if she were talking to herself. No matter how hard we tried, none of us could decipher the infinite mumbling that issued from her lips. At first, with the very patience of Job, we tried to communicate with her, straining to understand her incessant muttering. Little by little we began to give up until the day came when she mattered so little to us that we paid more attention to the TV, to the radio or even to the putt-putt of the lawnmower. To compensate for our indifference and to feel less guilty, we bought her a Walkman, a blessed modern apparatus that performed the amazing miracle of conclusively silencing Grandmamma Anacleta's jabbering and cleared away the lowering clouds of our guilt!

After that, we only reacted when she installed herself anew in our daily reality by filling the whole house with her booming rusty voice. Even today, in that distant memory, it seems incredible to me that that little heap of bones and skin was so powerful that it even caused the ever-present glass of water to vibrate on the bedside table. We all shook when that terrible rusted voice began to shout, "I want the bed pan right this minute! Water, a glass of ice water! Come straighten my sheets! Why doesn't anybody answer? Do you all think I'm just painted on the wall?" She spent her time making innumerable impertinent demands, like a captain at the head of his army, whenever she darned well felt like it, whenever it pleased her majesty to emerge from the silence of the sheets.

Her loud, rusty voice issued forth from the interminable baroque bed like a powerful projectile aimed unswervingly at each of us: it went straight through my body and was converted into remorse in the marrow of my conscience, asking if it were not my duty to ceaselessly weep over that tiny body lying like a useless rag on the bed, whose soul only joined it to become a great, despotic voice.

For Mamma, Grandmamma Anacleta's great, rusty voice was an indefinite sentence to remain by her side reading out loud to her: at first, only the Holy Scriptures, but to our surprise, she began to demand not only the usual classics, but also the more recent authors. However, they had better be substantial, because if they weren't, she would tear the books from Mamma's hands and furiously hurl them against the wall:

"Shitty writers who make fools of us by passing off a syrup of well-placed, dressed-up fancy words in order to cover up their emptiness! To hell with those imbeciles and their sleight-of-hand literature who fill our minds with nonsense! 'Straw, straw, straw,' as Unamuno said. They ought to learn from Goethe, Kafka, Hemingway, Borges, McCullers, Rulfo or Kundera . . ., now those are real writers! And what masterful writers!" Truly Grandmamma Anacleta gave us a hard time with the reading and my poor mother, although she enjoyed the books and the comments on them, stayed in a highly nervous state because when she least expected it the tyrannical voice would boom from the sheets, cursing the author, or some character, or Mamma, who from sheer fatigue would doze off as she read:

"I can't believe that at your age you're tired! Look at me, nearly a century old and I'm still alert! You people today are such delicate little touch-me-nots, with no spirit at all." It didn't even occur to Mamma to answer because Grandmamma Anacleta didn't listen to anyone and even less to her own daughter.

Grandmamma's big voice was a command that immediately made Norma, a good Samaritan-type grandchild, full of efficiency, race toward the heap of bones and corrugated skin and then the machine-gun orders burst from the bed: "Bring me the bed pan because I have to pee and take away the washbasin and towels because you've already bathed me enough, don't be messy, child, and fix this damned bed for me because it is my only refuge and my kingdom all day long, and today you're going to season the mashed potatoes the way I like them and add onions to the meat, oh, and I want caramel pudding for dessert, have Chela make it so I won't get diarrhea, and you fix me a watercress salad, yes, watercress and don't come to me saying it's not the season for watercress because that is what I want and that's that, but bring me the gown that I keep locked in the dressing table, here, unlock it and bring it on the double, because I'll catch cold lying here naked, hurry up, you little brat, just because I'm here shriveled up in this bed everybody thinks I'm a burden and no longer good for anything and they're wrong, re-member that tomorrow is my ninetieth birthday and in this house I represent the voice of knowledge and experience."

We all believed that too, even Dad, because she always, before some-thing happened, was psychic enough to foresee it and to forewarn us:

"Tell Anselma not to marry that fortune-hunter because she'll have a hard time of it, very hard," she declared, but no one paid attention and

Anselma, the eldest, married the fortune-hunter, who in fact only wanted the shelter of the family to squander everything that fell into his hands and to spend his time doing absolutely nothing.

"Don't be a fool, don't buy that lot because the real estate agent is a con man and he'll cheat you."

And she was right; at the end of a year we'd lost lock, stock and barrel since the lots that Dad bought were invented by the super-salesman in a part of the universe that never existed. That is what Grandmamma Anacleta was like, a little fistful of skin and bones, with a booming, rusty voice that shook the house and its inhabitants, and a clear and prescient mind when it suited her highness to take a hand in our affairs, because when it didn't suit her, even if we begged her, she stubbornly kept silent. Oh, I almost forgot that added to her foresight was her knowledge, up to the minute, of the news of the day. So well informed was she that when she deigned to speak, she referred to Gorbachev as if he were her neighbor, and even went so far as to affirm that she was becoming pro-Russian, if not downright Marxist, for she was always raving about the wastefulness of capitalism, while she rose up as the number one defender of the proletariat; she commented with exactness on the extermination of the rain forests of Brazil; on starvation in Africa; on the Panama Canal and its history. Moreover, she kept track of how many goals had been made by Maradona, Pele, and who knows what other famous soccer players. It was from my grandmother that I learned Virginia Woolf had said that for a woman to write novels and short stories she should have two things: money and a room to herself:

"A vain hope, because men always take away both rights from us so they can continue being our lords and masters," was her repeated and disconsolate litany. "Have you noticed that there are hardly any women composers in the music world? You could count them on your fingers. Have you ever heard of Ida Doukosky? Of course not! There's a reason, there's a reason . . . Music makes itself felt through its sound, while the pen glides silently across the paper when women secretly, as if they were committing a mortal sin, defy men with their books."

We knew the Walkman transistor, whose earphones were always plugged into her ears like a pair of leeches, was the source of her abundant knowledge, because she never wanted a newspaper nor condescended to look at television:

"Save me, Lord, from those two nuisances; they are the enemies of progress, truth and human aspirations." As she spoke, she crossed herself as if she were frightening away the devil.

Marcos was the one who had the idea of giving her two bowling balls for her birthday. They were jet black, as shiny as the entrance hall that Chela polished every day with the very persistence of Sisyphus. Dying laughing at our joke and imagining Grandmamma Anacleta's amazement when she saw them, we put them in a box which we wrapped with pretty baby pink paper and tied with a ribbon of the same color.

"Be careful, Sonia, don't get too close to Grandmamma Anacleta, because in one of her fits, her hands may get as strong as her voice. Wham! She'll throw the balls at you and knock you out flat with one blow. Watch out, I'm warning you, Sonia, don't forget!" Marcos advised me with the protective air of a big brother. I was touched and thanked him, because I was always climbing up on the mattress or on the edge of the bedframe.

"Can you imagine, Marcos, as weak and skinny as I am, how the bowling balls would flatten me? A cockroach would look big by comparison!"

We were so overcome by our irrepressible laughter that we couldn't even tie the bow on the gift. The next day, the birthday, was one long party for us as we anticipated the effect of our joke.

However, much to our surprise—of course, we waited to give her the bowling balls until the end of the festivities since we didn't want to take any risks before eating our share of the enormous cake with ninety candles that sparkled like little stars, and the strawberry ice cream that made our mouths water—well, I said to our surprise, those bony little arms with their parchment-like skin took the package as if it didn't weigh much. Marcos and I looked at each other in bewilderment, wondering if instead of the bowling balls, we had by mistake put some light object in the box; but there could be no doubt, we both knew perfectly well what was inside. We had an even greater surprise, for when we had moved well out of reach of any sudden destructive fit of fury, she opened the gift and her face lit up as if at that moment she were contemplating the Holy Grail and that present were the end of an interminable quest.

"Well! This is exactly what I wanted. How did you guess if I never told you?"

All of us who were present thought that her words were a pretense to hide her chagrin at our naughtiness. Nonetheless, it amazed us, because she *never, never*, as long as I could remember, had ever hidden anything. That's the way she was and we had suffered her and loved her just as she was up to then.

Following the bowling ball episode, my mother was freed from the enslavement of reading beside the big baroque bed. Foibles of the human race: Marcos as well as I joyfully believed we had done Mamma a favor, until we began to think that she missed the routine of reading, because so often she would come into Grandmamma Anacleta's room and would ask her if she didn't want her to read something.

"The Devil and all the demons in Hell! Didn't I tell you I'm not interested any more in all those wordy, inept writers who were clogging

my spirits? For me, the moment for action has arrived. *ACTION,* under-
lined and in capital letters, I'm telling you."

We all looked at each other wondering what she meant about the
"moment for action." To tell the truth we had utterly no idea, until one
sunny morning when the scent of orange blossoms perfumed the air,
and her voice, now clear, rang through the house like church bells on
Easter:

"Norma, bring me the black pants and jacket with the red blouse so
I can dress to go out."

To go out? How, when for twenty years she had been confined to the
big baroque bed and hadn't left it even for her most elemental needs?
We all feared that this was an evident sign that she was about to die
and wanted to go to the other world all dressed up in style.

"May I ask where you plan to go, Grandmamma Anacleta?" asked
Norma hesitantly, afraid the answer would be that she was dying. But
she just said:

"Stop asking questions, you silly child. Bathe me and be quick about
it because I want to go out right away."

We couldn't believe it! She jumped out of the big baroque bed with
agility and dressed herself with no help from anyone. Then we all
thought with one mind that that tiny old lady who seemed so fragile
had been torturing and enslaving us all that time for the purpose of
keeping us under her thumb; to be that agile and to work out her
long-term plan, she must have been exercising for years. At that instant
we understood the sound of footsteps and movement we had heard in
her bedroom late at night when the rest of the house was silent and
sleeping. We had even thought that there was a ghost in that room and
we called the priest to exorcise it. Now I understood why grandmother
was breaking up with laughter under her sheets while the priest sprinkled
the walls and furniture with holy water and Latin phrases.

"Where's the bowling alley? You, Marcos, drive me in your Volkswagen to the bowling alley."

"But Grandmamma Anacleta, what are you going to do at the bowling
alley?"

"Are you batty or do you just act that way? What does anybody do
at a bowling alley—why, bowl, of course, you impudent young pup!
Didn't you and your sister give me a pair of bowling balls for my
ninetieth birthday? Well, did you think that I, Anacleta Gutierrez del
Castillo, was going to let them gather dust when they were the best
present I've ever gotten in my life? That would be ridiculous! Come on,
brat, let's hurry to the bowling alley. You'll see that your grandmother
will set a world record and the news will be the sensation of the day.
Don't you believe it's necessary to fill the world with marvels to rid it
of all the brutality and porno that are everywhere? Besides, imagine the

double triumph, since I'm a woman, and all woman, and old, old, old. Can't you see the huge headlines in the newspapers that would broadcast to the four corners of the earth: 'NINETY-YEAR-OLD GRAND-MOTHER, WORLD BOWLING CHAMPION'?"

Translated by Bertie Acker

Bibliography: Rima Vallbona

Fiction

Vallbona, Rima. *Noche en vela*. San José: Editorial Costa Rica, 1968. Rpt. in San José: Editorial Costa Rica, 1984.

———. "Cementerio de camiones." *La Nación* 29 March 1969. 31-32.

———. "Una rosa al viento." *La Nación* 29 March 1969. 32-33

———. *Polvo del camino*. San José, Costa Rica: Lehmann, 1971.

———. "The Chumico Tree: A Modern Tale." *Nimrod--Latin American Voices* 18.1 (1973): 62-63.Rpt. in and Trans. Nuri Vallbona. *Five Women Writers of Costa Rica*. Ed. Victoria Urbano. Beaumont, TX: Lamar University Printing Dept., 1978. 113-14.

———. "El impostor." *El Urogallo* [Madrid] 34-35 (1975): 54-58.

———. "El árbol de chumico." *Letras Femeninas* 1 (1975): 20-21. Rpt. in *Posdata* [San José, C.R.] Jan. 1976. 6.

———. "Bajo pena de muerte." *Ancora* [San José, C.R.] 220 15 Aug. 1976. 4-5.

———. "Día de tinieblas." *La República* [San José, Costa Rica] Jan. 1976. 6.

———. "L'Imposteur." Trans. Juliette Decreus. *Fer de Lance* 99 (1977): 27-30.

———. "Parábola del amor imposible." *El Cuento--Revista de Imaginación* [Mexico] 75 (1977): 136-38.

———. "Más allá de la carne." *Foro Literario* [Uruguay] 3 (1978): 15-17. Rpt. in *Ancora* 22 Mar. 1987. 4D.

———. "Les Noces d'argent de Pénélope." Trans. Juliette Decreus. *Fer de Lance* 101-102 (1978): 13-18.

———. "Parable of the Impossible Eden." Trans. Nuri Vallbona. *Five Women Writers of Costa Rica*. Ed. Victoria Urbano. Beaumont, TX: Lamar University Printing Dept., 1978. 121-23.

———. "Penelope's Silver Wedding Anniversary." Trans. Nuri Vallbona. *Five Women Writers of Costa Rica*. Ed. Victoria Urbano. Beaumont, TX: Lamar University Printing Dept., 1978. 115-20. Rpt. in and Trans. Barbara Paschke. *Clamor of Innocence--Stories From Central America*. San Francisco: City Lights Books, 1988. 26-32.

———. "Bien au-déla de la chair." Trans. Juliette Decreus. *Fer de Lance* 103 (1979): 14-17.

————. "Penélope en sus bodas de plata." *Foro Literario* 5 (1979): 15-20. Rpt. in *Puerta abierta: la nueva escritora latinoamericana*. Ed. Caridad L. Silva-Velázquez and Nora Erro-Orthmann. Mexico City: Joaquín Mortiz, 1986. 259-65.

————. *La salamandra rosada*. Montevideo: Editorial Geminis, 1979.

————. "Beto y Betina." *Zona Franca* 18 (1980): 44-47.

————. "El hondón de las sorpresas." *Revista Chicano-Riqueña* 4 (1980): 35-37. Rpt. in *Ancora* 7 June 1987. 3D.

————. "Le Tréfonds de la surprise." Trans. Juliette Decreus. *Fer de Lance* 111-112 (1980): 12-14.

————. "Ame en Peine." Trans. Juliette Decreus. *Fer de Lance* 115-116 (1981): 33-37.

————. "Con los muertos al cinto." *Letras Femeninas* 7.2 (1981): 29-35.

————. "Desde aquí." *Garcín - Libro de Cultura* 3 (1981): 56-59.

————. "El juego de los grandes." *Letras femeninas en América* Montevideo: Asociación de Literatura Femenina Hispánica, 1981. 163-69.

————. "El monstruo de las cosas." *Maize* 5.1-2 (1981-1982): 62-64.

————. *Mujeres y agonías*. Houston, Texas: Arte Público Press, 1982.

————. "El muro." *La Costa de Oro* 21 (1982): 14-15. Rpt. in *Ancora* 22 Mar. 1987. 1D-2D.

————. *Barajas de soledades*. Barcelona: Ediciones Rondas, 1983.

————. "Los buenos." *Análisis* 84 (1983): 24-25.

————. "Iniciación." *Cuaderno Literario Azor* 37 (1983): 49-50. Rpt. in *Puro Cuento* 7 (Nov.-Dec. 1987): 46.

————. "El nagual de mi amiga Irene." La Palabra 1-2 (1983): 151-57.

————. *Las sombras que perseguimos*. San José: Editorial Costa Rica, 1983.

————. Tierra de secano." *Letras Femeninas* 1 (1983): 80-83.

————. "Los males venideros." *Alba de América* 2-3 (1984): 221-27.

————. "Mientras el niño Dios duerme en almohadonas de raso." *Foro literario* 8.13 (1985): 9-12.

————. "Cosecha de pecadores." *Ancora* Part 1: 20 Oct. 1985. 1D-4D; Part 2: 27 Oct. 1985. 3D-4D.

————. "Infame retorno." *Cultura* 73 (1984-1985): 49-57.

————. "Augusto discípulo de Pitágoras." *SUMMA-Revista de Cultura e Información* 3 (Dec. 1987): 93-100.

————. "Libelo de repudio." *El gato tuerto* [Miami] (Summer, 1987): 8.

————. *Cosecha de pecadores*. San José: Editorial Costa Rica, 1988.

————. "Una vez más Caín y Abel." *Ancora* 31 Jan. 1988. 1D.

Essays

Vallbona, Rima. "Divagaciones sobre *Nihil*." *La Nación* [San José] 2 July 1967. 8.

------. "Edward Albee: el arte y el público." *Indice* 248 (1968): 32-33.

------. "Ausentemente presente." *La Nación* [San José] 5 June 1969. 58.

------. "Por los pasillos de Jorge Luis Borges." *Insula* 274 (1969): 4.

------. *Yolanda Oreamuno*. Costa Rica: Ministerio de Cultura, 1972.

------. "Yolanda Oreamuno: el estigma del escritor." *Cuadernos Hispanoamericanos* 270 (1972): 1-27.

------. "La antipoesía de Virginia Grutter." *Troquel* [Costa Rica] I, II (June 1977): 16-17.

------. "El tiempo en siete relatos de Alejo Carpentier." *Troquel* [Costa Rica] II.13 (Aug. 1977): 5-11. Part 2 *Troquel* II.14 (Sept. 1977): 22-28.

------. "Hispanic Literature at the Secondary Level." *Bulletin* 4.2 (May 1975): 4-5.

------. "A Homeless Writer." *Five Women Writers of Costa Rica*. Beaumont, TX: Lamar University Printing Press, 1978. 44-50, 111-23.

------. "Trayectoria actual de la poesía femenina en Costa Rica." *Káñina* 2.3-4 (1978): 15-29.

------. "El escritor en Hispanoamérica." *Información* Part I (May 1981): 11. Part II (June 1981): 14.

------. "Eunice Odio: rescate de un poeta." *Revista interamericana de bibliografía/ Inter-American Review of Bibliography* 31.2 (1981): 199-214.

------. *La obra en prosa de Eunice Odio*. San José: Editorial Costa Rica, 1981.

------. "Trayectoria actual de la poesía femenina en Costa Rica." *Káñina* 5.2 (1981): 18-27.

------. "Las mujeres en los conventos del Nuevo Mundo." *Garcín--libro de cultura* (Uruguay) Part 1 5 (Mar.-Oct. 1982): 35-37. Part 2 6 (Nov.-Dec. 1982): 46-49. Rpt. in *Ancora* (Costa Rica) Part 1 12 Aug. 1984. 2. Part 2 19 Aug. 1984. 2-3.

------. "Alma en pena." *Woman of her Word--Hispanic Women Writers. Revista Chicano-Riqueña* [Special Issue] 3-4 (1983): 122-26.

------. "Búsqueda de Minerva en los ritos de las palabras." *Minerva: en el temor de las mudas paredes*. Ed. Cándido Gerón. Santo Domingo: Editorial Santo Domingo, 1983. 45-49.

------. "La mujer conquistadora: la Monja Alférez doña Catalina de Erauso." *Ancora* [Costa Rica] 28 Oct 1984. 1.

------. "La palabra ilimitada de Eunice Odio: *Los elementos terrestres*." *Los elementos terrestres*. Eunice Odio. Ed. Rima Vallbona. San José: Editorial Costa Rica, 1984. 11-36.

------. "Análisis ideológico de la poesía costarricense." *Ancora* [Costa Rica] 24 Nov. 1985. 1-D, 4-D. Rpt. in *Cuadernos de poética* [Dominican Republic] 9 (May-Aug. 1986): 45-53.

------. "Bibliografía de y sobre Yolanda Oreamuno." *Alba de América* 4-5 (1985): 415-29.

------. "Estudio valorativo de la obra de Eunice Odio." *Revista Atenea* [Puerto Rico] 1-2 (1985): 91-101.

------. "Jean Peytard et la Methode Semiotique dans l'Enseignement de la litterature." *Ca Parle . . . Hommage au Professeur Jean Peytard (articles/témiognages)*. Middlebury, Vermont: Ecole Francaise, Middlebury College, 1986. 97-100.

------. "*María la noche*--Erotismo, remembranzas tropicales y misterio." *Ancora* 9 Mar. 1986. 2-D.

------. "La mujer guerrera." *Ancora* 9 Feb. 1986. 2. Rpt. 20 April 1986. 2-D.

------. "La Musa de Guatemala." *Ancora* 8 June 1986. 2-D.

------. "La mujer pobladora." *Ancora* 1 Dec. 1986. 2.

------. "El populismo pictórico de Mario González." *Ancora* 2 Nov. 1986. 1D-3D.

------. "Amparo Dávila," "Catalina de Erauso," "Eunice Odio," and "Yolanda Oreamuno." *Women Writers of Spanish America--An Annotated Bio-Bibliographical Guide*. Ed. Diane E. Marting. New York: Greenwood Press, 1987. 109-11, 124-25, 281-83, 284-85.

------. "Costa Rica." *Handbook of Latin American Literature*. Comp. David William Foster. New York & London: Garland Publishing Inc., 1987. 191-202.

------. "Estructuras narrativas en los cuentos de Yolanda Oreamuno." *Evaluación de la literatura femenina de Latinoamérica*. San José, Costa Rica: Editorial Universitaria Centroamericana - EDUCA, 1987. 27-42.

------. "*La ruta de su evasión* de Yolanda Oreamuno: escritura proustina suplementada." *Revista Iberoamericana* 138-139 (1987): 193-217.

------. "Búsqueda de Minerva *En los ritos de las palabras*." *Hasta ahora*. Cándido Gerón. Santo Domingo: Editorial Santo Domingo, 1987. 129-34.

------. "Loreina Santos Silva en el umbral de la soledad." *Ancora* Part 1 6 Mar. 1988. 2d-3d. Part 2 13 Mar. 1988. 3D-4D.

Poetry

Vallbona, Rima. "Nanita triste." *La Urpila* 4-5 (Sept. 1981-Jan. 1982): 5-6.

------. *Poesía compartida--quince poetas latinoamericanos de hoy*. Montevideo: Ediciones Urpila, 1983. 48-50.

------. "Perpetua búsqueda." *La Urpila* 22 (1985): 11.

------. "En el mar de la nada." *La Urpila* 23-24 (1986): 11

------. "Tu voz de mar." *International Poetry*. Ed. Teresnika Pereira. Boulder, Colorado: International Writers Association, University of Colorado, 1987. 113.

Criticism on the Works of Rima Vallbona

Acker, Bertie. "*Mujeres y agonías* de Rima de Vallbona." *SCOLAS Bulletin* 6.2 (1982-83): 1-2.

------. "Revelación y hermetismo en *Mujeres y agonías*, Los nuevos cuentos de Rima de Vallbona." *Análisis* 80-81 (June-July 1983): 41-42.

Agosín, Marjorie. "*Mujeres y agonías*." *Third Woman* 2.1 (1984): 114-15.

Aldaya, Alicia J.R. "*La obra en prosa de Eunice Odio*." *The South Central Bulletin* 1-2 (1983): 30. Rpt. in *Letras Femeninas* 9.2 (1983): 60.

————. "Three Short Stories by Rima Vallbona." *Five Women Writers of Costa Rica*. Trans. Eduardo C. Bejar. Beaumont, Texas: Lamar University Printing Press, 1978. 124-127.

Amber, Angeles. *"Las sombras que perseguimos." La Religión* [Venezuela] 10 Nov. 1985. 5.

Armas, Wilson. *"Las sombras que perseguimos." Foro Literario* 14 (1985): 54-55.

Baeza Flores, Alberto. "Eunice, la mágica peregrina." *Revista Cultural 2001* Venezuela 4 Apr. 1982. 14.

Barahona Jiménez, Luis. "La estética en los novelistas del siglo XX (Período 1920-75)—Rima Rothe de Vallbona." *Apuntes para la historia de las ideas estéticas en Costa Rica*. San José: Editorial del Ministerio de Cultura, 1982. 88-90.

Bartolomé Pons, Esther. "Los cuentos de Rima Vallbona: dignificación de un Género." *Devenir* 7 (1982): 11-12.

Beltrán, Jorge. "El fatídico encuentro con la nada." *La Prensa* [Argentina] 10 May 1988. 3.

Burgos, Fernando. "La novela moderna hispanoamericana (Un ensayo sobre el concepto literario de modernidad)." *Inter-American Review of Bibliography/Revista Interamericana de Bibliografía* 4 (1986): 487-88.

Cerda, Flora et al. *La problemática de la mujer contemporánea en la narrativa de Rima de Vallbona*. Masters Thesis. University of Costa Rica, November, 1987. 146.

Cerezo Dardón, Hugo. *A la luz de los libros-Bibliografía Guatemalteca comentada (1980-1981)*. Guatemala: Editorial Universitaria, 1984.

————. *"La obra en prosa de Eunice Odio" La Prensa Libre* 13 Dec. 1981. 12. Rpt. in *Análisis* 69-70 (1982): 47-48.

Chase, Alfonso. "Eunice visita por Rima de Vallbona." *La República* [Costa Rica] 15 Aug. 1981. 9.

Chase. Cida S. "El mundo femenino en algunos cuentos de Rima de Vallbona." *Revista Iberoamericana* 53.138-139 (1987): 403-418.

Constanzó, Carlos M. "Sobre Rima de Vallbona." *Análisis* 90 (1984): 8.

"El cuidadoso estilo de Rima de Vallbona." [Editorial] *Ancora* 20 Jan. 1985. 6.

Decreus, Juliette. "Rima R. de Vallbona--Romancier du Costa Rica." *Fer de Lance* [France] 83 July, Aug. and Sept. 1973. 14-19.

Dowling, Lee. "Point of View in Rima de Vallbona's *Las sombras que perseguimos.*" *Revista Chicano-Riqueña* 13.1 (1985): 64-73.

————. "Rima de Vallbona: desafíos ideológicos y perspectivas de la narración en su obra literaria." *Letras* [Costa Rica] 11-12 (1986): 193-214.

————. "Rima Gretel Rothe de Vallbona." *Women Writers in Spanish America--An Annotated Bio-Bibliographical Guide*. Ed. Diane E. Marting. New York: Greenwood Press, 1987. 335-37.

Durán Cubillo, Ofelia. "Rasgos del relato moderno en el tiempo de *Noche en vela* de Rima Vallbona." Diss. Univ. de Costa Rica, 1976.

Fajardo, Miguel. "Eunice Odio." *La República* [Costa Rica] Jan. 17, 1982; *Análisis* [República Dominicana] 69-70 (1982): 20-22.

———. "Rima de Vallbona--una narrativa básica." *Análisis* 73 (1982): 41-42.

———. "Yolanda Oreamuno presentada por Rima de Vallbona." *Análisis* [República Dominicana] 73 (1982): 39-40.

Fernández de Ulibarri, Rocío. "Vallbona en el límite de lo real." *Ancora* 21 Aug. 1983. 2-3.

Gerón, Cándido. "Eunice Odio: poetisa costarricense." *La noticia* [República Dominicana] 31 Mar. 1982. 8.

Gruber, Vivan M. "*Mujeres y agonías.*" *The South Central Bulletin* (Winter 1983): 134.

———. "The Paradigmatic Story Mode of Carmen Naranjo, Eunice Odio, Yolanda Oreamuno, Victoria Urbano, and Rima Vallbona." *Letras Femeninas* 6.1 (1980): 14-24.

Jiménez, Esmeralda. "*Las astillas del viento.*" *Letras Femeninas* 3.2 (1977): 54-56.

Jurado Morales, José. "*Mujeres y agonías* de Rima de Vallbona." *Cuaderno Literario Azor* 36 (1982): 68.

Karsen, Sonja. "*Five Women Writers of Costa Rica.*" *Hispania* 63 (1980): 785.

Lázcaris, Constantino. "*Noche en vela.*" *Letras Femeninas* 4.1 (1978): 106-108.

Lindstrom, Naomi. "*Los elementos terrestres.*" *SCOLAS Bulletin* 10.1 (1985): 8.

Lojo, María Rosa. "*Mujeres y agonías.*" *Letras Femeninas* 1-2 (1987): 112-13.

Lojo de Beuter, María Rosa. "*Las sombras que perseguimos.*" *Alba de América* 3.4-5 (1985): 374-76.

López Oroz, María Luisa and Belén Lagos Oteíza. "Aproximaciones a la temática en *Las sombras que perseguimos.*" *Revista Estudios* 7 (1987): 227-34.

Luesma-Castán, Miguel. "Rima de Vallbona: *Baraja de soledades.*" *Heraldo de Aragón* 26 June 1983. 3.

———. "Sombra, dolor y realidad en Rima de Vallbona." *La República* [Costa Rica] 7 Mar. 1986. 11.

Monge, Carlos Francisco. *La imagen separada--modelos ideológicos de la poesía costarricense 1950-1980.* Rpt. in *Hispania* 69 (May 1986): 322.

Monté, Nydia. "*Mujeres y agonías,* un libro que Ud. debe leer." *Información* [Houston] 1 Apr. 1982. 7.

Moreira, Rubenstein. "*La obra en prosa de Eunice Odio.*" *El Diario Español* [Uruguay] 17 July 1982. 12.

Novo Pena, Silva. "*Mujeres y agonías.*" *La voz* [Houston] 1 July 1982. 10.

Oberhelman, Harley D. "*Las sombras que perseguimos. SCOLAS Bulletin* (1983-84): 5-6.

Páez de Ruiz, María de Jesús. "Mito y realidad en *Mujeres y agonías* de Rima de Vallbona." *Evaluación de la literatura femenina de Latinoamérica.* San José, Costa Rica: EDUCA, 1987. 81-90.

Parle, Dennis. "Vallbona, Rima. *La obra en prosa de Eunice Odio." SCOLAS Bulletin* 5.3 (1982): 6.

Porras, José A. *"La salamandra rosada* por Rima Vallbona." *La República* 7 Mar. 1981. 9.

Ramos, Lilia. "Rima Vallbona o *Noche en vela." Fulgores de mi ocaso.* San José: Editorial Costa Rica, 1979.

Ricci, Iris M. *"La obra en prosa de Eunice Odio. Foro Literario* 11 (1983): 48.

Rivera, Ana de. "Una escritora costarricense en los Estados Unidos." *La República* 18 April 1982. 16.

Salvo, Baccio. *"Baraja de soledades." Análisis* 84 (1983): 23.

Sandoval de Fonseca, Virginia. *"Las sombras que perseguimos* o práctica de relectura." *Evaluación de la literatura femenina de Latinoamérica.* San José, Costa Rica: EDUCA, 1987. 67-69.

Tatter, Federico. *"Barajas de soledades." La Ciudad* [Chile] 4 Oct. 1983. 5.

Vargas, Sonia. "Recuperación de valores femeninos." *La Nación Internacional* Aug. 1984. 23.

Velez, Joseph F. "Libro de agonías." *Ovaciones* [Mexico] 26 July 1984. 8.

———. "Una novela fascinante." *Ovaciones* [Mexico] 6 Apr. 1984. 8.

Zúñiga-Tristán, Virginia. *"Las sombras que perseguimos. Ancora* 21 August 1983. 2-3.

———. *"Mujeres y agonías." Káñína* 1-2 (Jan.-Dec. 1982): 126.

The Short Story, Feminism and Latin American Women Writers: A Bibliography

General Bibliography

Aguilera Garramuno, Marco Tulio. "La creación del cuento." *Plural: Revista Cultural de Excelsior* 15.8.176 (1986): 27-32.

Ainsa, Fernando. *Tiempo reconquistado: siete ensayos sobre literatura uruguaya.* Montevideo: Géminis, 1977.

Alarcón, Norma and Sylvia Kossnar. *Bibliography of Hispanic Women Writers.* Bloomington, IN: Chicano-Riqueño Studies Bibliography Series No.1, 1980.

Alcázar, Reinaldo M. *El cuento de carácter social en Bolivia entre 1935-1970.* La Paz: n.p., 1976.

Aldrich, Earl M. Jr. *The Modern Short Story in Peru.* Madison: University of Wisconsin Press, 1966.

———. "Recent Trends in the Peruvian Short Story." *Studies in Short Fiction.* 8.1 (1971): 20-31.

Anderson Imbert, Enrique. *El cuento español.* Buenos Aires: Columbia, 1959.

———. *Historia de la literatura hispanoamericana.* 2 vols., Mexico City: Fondo de Cultura, 1961. Rpt. in Mexico City: Fondo de Cultura Económica, 1964-1965.

———. *El realismo mágico y otros ensayos.* Caracas: Monte Avila, 1976.

———. *Teoría y técnica del cuento.* Buenos Aires: Marymar, 1977.

Andrés Gutierrez, Mariano de. "Ensayo de análisis estructural del cuento." *Bulletin Hispanique* 86.3-4 (1984): 403-34.

Arancibia, Juana Alcira, ed. *Evaluación de la literatura femenina de latinoamérica, siglo XX.* 2 vols. San José: Instituto Literario y Cultural Hispánico, 1985-1987.

Araújo, Helena. "Escritoras latinoamericanas: ¿Por fuera del boom?" *Quimera* 30 (1983): 8-11.

———. "Narrativa femenina latinoamericana." *Hispamérica* 11.32 (1982): 3-34.

———. *La Scherezada criolla: ensayos sobre escritura femenina.* Bogotá: Universidad Nacional de Colombia, 1989.

Araújo, Orlando. *Narrativa venezolana contemporánea.* Caracas: Ediciones Tiempo Nuevo, 1972.

Arias-Larreta, Abraham. *El cuento indoamericano.* Barcelona: Editorial Indoamérica, 1978.

Arrom, José Juan. *Esquema generacional de las letras hispanoamericanas: ensayo de un método.* Bogotá: Instituto Caro y Cuervo, 1963. Rpt. in Bogota: Instituto Caro y Cuervo, 1977.

Auerbach, Nina. *Woman and the Demon. The Life of a Victorian Myth.* Cambridge, MA: Harvard University Press, 1982.

Aycock, Wendell M, ed. *The Teller and The Tale: Aspects of the Short Story.* Lubbock, TX: Texas Tech. Press, 1982.

Baquero, Gastón. *Escritores hispanoamericanos de hoy.* Madrid: Instituto de Cultura Hispánica, 1961.

Baquero Goyanes, Mariano. *¿Qué es el cuento?* Buenos Aires: Columba, 1967.

Barbagelata, Hugo de. *La novela y el cuento en Hispanoamérica.* Montevideo: Talleres Gráficos de Enrique Míguez y Compañía, 1947.

Barceló, Victor Manuel. *Panorámica del cuento mexicano.* Bogotá: Instituto Colombiano de Cultura, 1973.

Barriga López, Franklin and Leonardo Barriga López. *Diccionario de la literatura ecuatoriana.* 2nd. ed. 5 Vols. Guayaquil: Casa de la Cultura Ecuatoriana, 1980.

Barthes, Roland. "Introducción al análisis estructural de los relatos." *Communicaciones/Análisis estructural del relato.* Trans. Beatriz Dorritos. Buenos Aires: Tiempo Contemporáneo, 1972. 9-43.

Barthes, Roland, et al. *Análisis estructural del relato.* Mexico City: Premiá Editora, 1984.

Bazán, Juan F. *La narrativa latinoamericana.* Asunción: Escuela Técnica Salesiana, 1970.

Beauvoir, Simone de. *The Second Sex.* Harmondsworth, England: Penguin, 1972.

Becco, Horacio Jorge and David William Foster. *La nueva narrativa hispanoamericana: bibliografía.* Buenos Aires: Casa Pardo, 1976.

Belevan, Harry. *Teoría de lo fantástico.* Barcelona: Editorial Anagrama, 1976.

Belsey, Catherine. *Critical Practice.* New York: Methuen, 1980.

Belensky, Mary et al. *Women's Ways of Knowing: The Development of Self, Voice and Mind.* New York: Basic Books, 1986.

Benedetti, Mario. *Letras del continente mestizo.* 2nd ed. Montevideo: Arca, 1970.

Blackwell, Alice Stone. *Lucy Stone, Pioneer Woman's Rights.* Boston: Little Brown, 1930. Rpt. in New York: Kraus Reprint Co., 1971.

Blackwell, Antoinette Brown. *The Sexes Throughout Nature.* New York: G.P. Putnam's Sons, 1895.

Block, Jeanne H. "Conceptions of Sex Roles, Some Cross-Cultural and Longitudinal Perspectives." *American Psychologist* (1973): 512-26.

Bolen, Jean Shinoda. *Goddesses in Every Woman: A New Psychology of Women.* New York: Harper & Row, 1984.

Bollo, Sarah. *Literatura uruguaya, 1807-1975.* Montevideo: Univ. de la República, 1976.

Bombal, María Luisa. *The House of Mist.* Trans. Richard and Lucía Cunningham. New York: Farrar and Strauss, 1947.

———. *New Islands and Other Stories.* Trans. Richard and Lucía Cunningham. New York: Farrar and Strauss, 1982.

———. *The Shrouded Woman.* Trans. Richard and Lucía Cunningham. New York: Farrar and Strauss, 1948.

Boulding, Elise. *The Underside of History: A View of Women Through Time*. Boulder, CO: Westview Press, 1976.

Bradú, Fabienne. *Señas particulares: escritora. Ensayos sobre escritoras mexicanas del siglo XX*. Mexico City: Fondo de Cultura Económica, 1987.

Brushwood, John. "Mexican Fiction in the Seventies: Author, Intellect and Public." *Ibero-American Letters in a Comparative Perspective*. Eds. Wolodymir T. Zyla and Wendell M. Aycock. Lubbock, TX: Texas Tech Press, 1978. 35-47.

———. *Mexico in its Novel: A Nation's Search for Identity*. Notre Dame, IN: University of Notre Dame Press, 1971.

———. *The Spanish American Novel. Twentieth-Century Survey*. Austin: Univ. of Texas Press, 1975.

Burns, E. Bradford. *Latin America: A Concise Interpretative History*. Englewood Cliffs, NJ: Prentice-Hall, 1982.

Burstyn, Joan N. *Victorian Education and the Ideal of Womanhood*. London: Croom Helm, 1980.

Butler, Josephine. *Women's Work and Women's Culture*. London: Macmillan, 1869.

Butler, Judith. *Gender Trouble: Feminism and the Subversion of Identity*. New York: Routledge, 1990.

Campos, Xorge del. "La narrativa joven de México." *Studies in Short Ficton* 8 (1971): 180-98.

Canby, Henry. *A Study of the Short Story*. New York: Henry Holt and Company, 1913.

Carballo, Emmanuel. *Narrativa mexicana de hoy*. Madrid: Alianza Editorial, 1969.

Carilla, Emilio. *El cuento fantástico*. Buenos Aires: Nova, 1968.

Carrera, Julieta. *La mujer en América escribe . . . Semblanzas*. Mexico City: Ediciones Alonso, 1956.

———. "La novela femenina mexicana." *Cuadernos* 3 (1953): 101-04. Rpt. in *Nuestra Década* 35.4 (1955): 32-41.

Carroll, Berenice A. "'To Crush Him in Our Own Country': The Political Thought of Virginia Woolf." *Feminist Studies* 4.1 (1978): 99-132.

Carvalho, Joaquim Montezuma de. "Alfonsina Storni: fundadora de la emancipación femenina hispanoamericana." *Norte-Revista Hispanoamericana. Frente de Afirmación Hispanista* 253 (1973): 44-52.

Castagnino, Raúl. *Cuento-Artefacto y Artificios del Cuento*. Buenos Aires: Nova, 1977.

Castellanos, Rosario. *Sobre cultura femenina*. Mexico City: Ed. de América, 1950.L
———. *The Nine Guardians*. Trans Irene Nicholson. London: Canguard, 1958. Rpt. in New York: Vanguard, 1960.

Castro Arenas, Mario. *El cuento de hispanoamérica*. Lima: Studium, 1974.

Chaney, Elsa. "Old and New Feminists in Latin America: The Case of Peru and Chile." *Journal of Marriage and the Family* 35.2 (1973): 331-43.

Chessler, Phyllis. *Women and Madness*. London: Allen Lane, 1972.

Chevigny, Bell Gale and Gari Laguardia, eds. *Reinventing the Americas: Comparative Studies of Literature of the United States and Spanish America*. Cambridge: Cambridge University Press, 1986.

Chodorow, Nancy. *The Reproduction of Mothering: Psychoanalysis and the Sociology of Gender*. CA: Univ. of California Press, 1978.

Coddou, Marcelo, ed. *Los libros tienen sus propios espíritus*. Xalapa: Universidad Veracruzana, 1986.

Coll, Edna. *Indice informativo de la novela hispanoamericana*. 2 vols. Puerto Rico: Edit. Universitaria, 1974.

——. *Injerto de temas en las novelistas mexicanas contemporáneas*. Puerto Rico: Juan Ponce de León, 1964.

Cornillon, Susan Koppelman. *Images of Women in Fiction: Feminist Perspectives*. Bowling Green: Popular Press, 1972.

Correas de Zapata, Celia. *Ensayos hispanoamericanos*. Buenos Aires: Ediciones Corregidor, 1978.

——. "Escritoras latinoamericanas: sus publicaciones en el contexto de las estructuras del poder." *Revista Iberoamericana* 51.132-133 (1985): 591-603.

——. "One Hundred Years of Women Writers in Latin America." *Latin American Literary Review* 3.6 (1975): 7-16.

Cortázar, Julio. "Algunos aspectos del cuento." *Casa de las Américas* 15-16 (1962-1963): 3-14. Rpt. in *Casa de las Americas* 31 (1968): 178-86.

Cortina, Lynn Ellen Rice. *Spanish-American Women Writers: A Bibliographical Research Checklist*. New York: Garland Publishing, 1983.

Corvalán, Graciela N. V. *Latin American Women Writers in English Translation: A Bibliography*. Los Angeles: California State Univ. Latin American Studies Center, 1980.

Cross Ethan, Allen. *The Short Story: A Technical and Literary Study*. Chicago: A.C. McClurg and Company, 1926.

Cruz Castelán, Charlotte A. *Vista general del cuento corto contemporáneo de México y de los Estados Unidos de Norteamérica*. Mexico City: Universidad Nacional Autónoma de México, 1956.

Cunningham, Lucía Guerra. "La mujer latinoamericana y la tradición literaria femenina." *Fem* 3, 10 (1979): 14-18.

——. *Mujer y sociedad en América Latina*. Santiago de Chile: Editorial del Pacífico, 1980.

——. "El personaje literario femenino y otras mutilaciones." *Hispamérica* 43 (1986): 3-19.

Daly, Mary. *Beyond God the Father: Toward a Philosophy of Women's Liberation*. Boston: Beacon Press, 1973.

——. *Gyn/Ecology: The Metaethics of Radical Feminism*. Boston: Beacon Press, 1978.

——. Foreword. *Women, Church and State: The Origional Exposé of Male Collaboration Against the Female Sex*. By Matilda Joslyn Gage. Watertown, MA: Persephone Press, 1980. vii-x.

Davies, Margaret Llewelyn. *Life as We Have Known It: By Co-Operative Working Women*. London: The Hogarth Press, 1931. Rpt. in London: Virago, 1977.

———. *Maternity: Letters from Working Women*. London: G. Bell & Sons, 1915. Rpt. in London: Virago, 1978.

Dijkstra, Sandra. "Simone de Beauvoir and Betty Friedan: The Politics of Omission." *Feminist Studies* 6.2 (1980): 290-303.

Dolz-Blackburn, Inés. "Recent Critical Bibliography on Women in Hispanic Literature." *Discurso literario* 3, 2 (1986): 331-34.

Donovan, Josephine. *Feminist Literary Criticism. Explorations in Theory*. Lexington: Univ. Press of Kentucky, 1975.

Dorn, Georgette M. "Four Twentieth-Century Latin American Authors." *SCOLAS Annals* 10 (1979): 125-33.

Durán-Cerdá, Julio. "Sobre el concepto del cuento moderno." *Explicación de Textos Literarios* 2 (1976): 119-32.

Dworkin, Andrea. *Woman Hating*. New York: E.P. Dutton, 1974.

Ehrenreich, Barbara and Deirdre English. *For Her Own Good: 150 Years of the Expert's Advice to Women*. New York: Anchor Press, Doubleday, 1978. Rpt. in London: Pluto Press, 1979.

Enloe, Cynthia. *Bananas, Beaches & Bases: Making Feminist Sense of International Politics*. Berkeley: University of California Press, 1989.

Fawcett, Millicent and E.M. Turner. *Josephine Butler: Her Work and Principles and Their Meaning for the Twentieth Century*. London: Association for Moral and Social Hygiene, 1927.

Fernández Olmos, Margarite. "El género testimonial: Aproximaciones feministas." *Revista/Review Interamericana* 1 (1981): 69-75.

———. "Sex, Color, and Class in Contemporary Puerto Rican Women Authors." *Heresies* 4.3 (1982): 46-47.

Figes, Eva. *Patriarchal Attitudes: My Case for Women to Revolt*. London: Faber & Faber, 1970.

Finot, Enrique. *Historia de la literatura boliviana*. 4th ed. La Paz: Gisbert, 1975.

Fleak, Kenneth. "Latin American Short Fiction." *Studies in Short Fiction* 20.4 (1983): 297-306.

Flexner, Eleanor. *Century of Struggle: The Woman's Rights Movement in the United States*. Rev. ed. 1959. Cambridge, MA: Belknap Press and Harvard University Press, 1979.

Flora, Cornelia Butler. "The Passive Female and Social Change: A Cross-Cultural Comparison of Women's Magazine Fiction." *Female and Male in Latin America: Essays*. Ed. A. Pescatello. Pittsburgh, PA: Univ. of Pittsburgh Press, 1973. 59-85.

Flores, Angel. *Bibliografía de escritores hispanoamericanos. A Bibliography of Spanish-American Writers 1609-1974*. New York: Gordian Press, 1975.

———. *Historia y antología del cuento y la novela en hispanoamérica*. New York: Las Americas Publishing House, 1957. Rpt. in New York: Las Americas, 1959.

Foster, David William and Virginia Ramos Foster. *Modern Latin American Literature*. 2 vols. New York: Frederic Ungar, 1975.

————. *Research Guide to Argentine Literature*. Metuchen, NJ: The Scarecrow Press, 1970.

Foster, David William. *Argentine Literary Research Guide*. 2nd ed. rev. New York: Garland Co., 1982.

————. *Chilean Literature. A Working Bibliography of Secondary Sources*. Boston, MA: G.K. Hall, 1978.

————. *A Dictionary of Contemporary Latin American Authors*. Tempe: Center for Latin American Studies, Arizona State Univ., 1975.

————. *Mexican Literature: A Bibliography of Secondary Sources*. Metuchen, NJ: The Scarecrow Press, 1981.

————. *Studies in the Contemporary Spanish American Short Story*. Columbia: University of Missouri Press, 1979.

————. *The 20th Century Spanish-American Novel: A Bibliographic Guide*. Metuchen, NJ: The Scarecrow Press, 1975.

Foucault, Michael. *Las palabras y las cosas*. Mexico City: Siglo XXI Editores, 1984.

Fox Lockert, Lucía. *Women Novelists in Spain and Spanish America*. Metuchen: The Scarecrow Press, 1979.

Franco, Jean. "Apuntes sobre la crítica feminista y la literatura hispanoamericana." *Hispamérica* 45 (1986): 31-43.

————. *An Introduction to Spanish American Literature*. Cambridge: Cambridge University Press, 1969.

————. *The Modern Culture of Latin America: Society and the Artist*. Harmondsworth, England: Penguin, 1970.

————. *Plotting Women. Gender and Representation in Mexico*. New York: Columbia University Press, 1989.

————. "Self-Destructing Heroines." *Minnesota Review*, ns 22 (1984): 105-15.

————. *Spanish American Literature Since Independence*. London: Breen Ltd., 1973.

————. "Teoría feminista en los ochenta." *FEM* 10.44 (1986): 52-55.

Freeman, Jo. *The Politics of Women's Liberation*. New York: David McKay, 1975.

Freudenthal, Juan R. and Patricia M. Freudenthal. *Index to Anthologies of Latin American Literature in English Translation*. Boston: G.K. Hall & Co., 1977.

Friedan, Betty. *The Feminine Mystique*. New York: W.W. Norton, 1963. Rpt. in Harmondsworth: Penguin, 1965.

Fuller, Margaret S. *Women in the Nineteenth Century*. New York: Greeley & McElrath, 1845. Rpt. in University of Southern Carolina Press, 1980.

Gage, Matilda Joslyn. *Woman, Church and State: The Original Exposé of Male Collaboration Against the Female Sex*. Chicago: Charles Kerr, 1873. Rpt. in Watertown, MA: Persephone Press, 1980.

Galerstein, Carolyn L., ed. *Women Writers of Spain. An Annotated Bio-Bibliographical Guide*. Westport, CT: Greenwood Press, 1986.

García Pinto, Magdalena. *Historias íntimas. Conversaciones con diez escritoras latinoamericanas*. Hanover, NH: Ediciones del Norte, 1988.

Garfield, Evelyn Picón. *Women's Voices From Latin America*. Detroit, MI: Wayne State University, 1985.

Garvon, Hannah. *The Captive Wife: Conflicts of Housebound Mothers*. London: Routledge & Kegan Paul, 1966. Rpt. in Harmonsworth: Penguin, 1968.

Gazarian Gautier, Marie-Lise. *Interviews with Latin American Writers* Elmwood Park, IL: The Dalkey Archive Press, 1989.

Giacoman, Helmy, Pedro Yañes and José Ramón de la Torre. *Perspectivas de nueva narrativa hispanoamericana: Países*. Puerto Rico: Ediciones Puerto, 1973.

Gil Polo, G., D.J.M. Pemán y Permatín. *La mujer a través de la literatura*. Barcelona: Universal, 1975.

Gilgen, Read G. "The Short Story of The Absurd: Spanish America's Contribution to Absurdist Literature." *Romance Notes* 18 (1977): 164-68.

Gilligan, Carol. *In a Different Voice*. Cambridge, MA: Harvard University Press, 1982.

Gilman, Charlotte Perkins. *His Religion and Hers: A Study of the Faith of Our Fathers and the Work of Our Mothers*. New York: Century Company, 1923.

———. *The Man Made World of Our Androcentric Culture*. New York: Charlton, 1911.

Gleaves, Robert M. "Fantasy in the Contemporary Mexican Short Story: A Critical Study." *DA* 26 (1969): 2261A.

Goldman, Emma. *Red Emma Speaks: Selected Writings and Speeches by Emma Goldman*. London: Wildwood House, 1979.

González, Patricia Elena and Eliana Ortega, eds. *La sartén por el mango: encuentro de escritoras latinoamericanas*. San Juan: Ediciones Huracán, 1984.

González Freire, Nati. "La mujer en la literatura de América Latina." *Cuadernos Hispanoamericanos* 414 (1984): 84-92.

Goreau, Angeline. *Reconstructing Aphra: A Social Biography of Aphra Behn*. New York: The Dial Press, 1980.

Goulianos, Jane. *By A Woman Writt: Literature From Six Centuries by and About Women*. London: New English Library, 1974.

Greer, Germaine. *The Female Eunuch*. London: McGibbon & Kee, 1970.

Guerra, Lucía. *La narrativa de María Luisa Bombal: una visión de la existencia femenina*. Madrid: Playor, 1980.

Guerra Cunningham, Lucía. *Splintering Darkness: Latin American Women Writers in Search of Themselves*. Pittsburgh: Latin American Review Press, 1990.

Gullason, Thomas H. "The Short Story: An Underrated Art." *Studies in Short Fiction* 2.1 (1964): 13-31.

Guttman, D. "Women and the Conception of Ego Strength." *Merrill-Palmer Quarterly* 11 (1965): 229-40.

Hahner, June E. *Women in Latin American History: Their Lives and Views*. Los Angeles: UCLA Latin American Center Publications, 1976.

Haneffstengel, Renate Von. *El México de hoy en la novela y el cuento*. Mexico City: De Andrea, 1966.

Harkess, Shirley and Cornelia B. Flora. "Women in the News: An Analysis of Media Images in Colombia." *Revista Iberoamericana* 4.2 (1974): 220-38.

Harris, Barbara J. *Beyond Her Sphere: Women and the Professions in American History.* Westport CT: Greenwood Press, 1978.

Harss, Luis and Barbara Dohmann. *Into the Mainstream.* New York: Harper and Row, 1967.

Hays, Mary. *Female Biography of Memoirs of Illustrious and Celebrated Women of All Ages and Countries, Alphabetically Arranged.* 6 vols. London: Richard Phillips, 1802.

Hernández, Julia. *Novelistas y cuentistas de la revolución.* Mexico City: Universidad Mexicana de Escritores, 1960.

Hill, Marnesba D. and Harold B. Schleifer. *Puerto Rican Authors: A Biographical Handbook. Autores Puertorriqueños: Una guía biobibliográfica.* Metuchen: The Scarecrow Press, 1974.

Hoberman, Louisa S. "Hispanic American Women as Portrayed in the Historical Literature: Types or Archetypes." *Revista/Review Interamericana* 4.2 (1974): 136-47.

Horner, Matina. "Fail: Bright Women." *Psychology Today* 3 Nov. 1969: 36.

Horno-Delgado, Asunción, et al. *Breaking Boundaries: Latina Writings and Critical Readings.* Amherst: University of Massachusetts, 1989.

Hunkins-Hallinan, Hazel. "A Revolution Unfinished." *In Her Own Right: A Discussion Conducted By The Six Point Group.* Hazel Hunkins-Hallinan. London: George G. Harrap, 1968. 9-17.

Hunter College Women's Studies Collective, ed. *Women's Realities, Women's Choices.* New York: Oxford University Press, 1983.

Jackson, Mary Garland. "The Roles and Portrayal of Women in Selected Prose Works by Six Female Writers of Peru." *DAI* 44.1 (1983): 181A.

Jaggar, Alison M. *Feminist Politics and Human Nature.* New Jersey: Rowman & Allanheld Publishers, 1983.

Jaquette, Jane. "Literary Archetypes and Female Role Alternatives: The Woman and the Novel in Latin America." *Female and Male in Latin America: Essays.* Ed. A. Pescatello. Pittsburgh: Univ. of Pittsburgh Press, 1973. 3-27.

Jaramillo Levi, Enrique. Prologue. *El cuento erótico en México.* Mexico City: Diana, 1975. 11-12.

Jiménez, Reynaldo L. "Cuban Women Writers and the Revolution: Toward An Assessment of Their Literary Contribution." *Folio* 11 (1978): 75-95.

Johnson, Harvey L. and Philip B. Taylor, Jr. *Contemporary Latin American Literature.* Houston: University of Houston, 1973.

Kaminsky, Amy. "The Real Circle of Iron: Mothers and Children in Four Argentine Novels." *Latin American Literary Review* 9 (1976): 77-86.

Keohane, Nannerl, Michelle A. Rosaldo and Barbara C. Gelpi, eds. *Feminist Theory: A Critique of Ideology.* Chicago: The University of Chicago Press, 1982.

Kerber, Linda K. *Women of the Republic: Intellect and Ideology in Revolutionary America.* North Carolina: University of North Carolina Press, 1980.

Kirby, M. T. *A Literary History of the Cuban Short Story.* Diss. University of North Carolina, 1971.

Kizner, Nora Scott. "Women Professionals in Buenos Aires." *Female and Male in Latin America.* Ed. Ann Pescatello. Pittsburgh: University of Pittsburgh Press, 1973. 159-90.

Klein, Viola. *The Feminine Character: History of an Ideology.* London: Routledge & Kegan Paul, 1946. Rpt. in Illinois: Univ. of Illinois Press, 1971, 1975.

Knaster, Meri. *Women in Spanish America. An Annotated Bibliography from Pre-Conquest to Contemporary Times.* Boston: G. K. Hall, 1977.

Kogan, Nathan. "Creativity and Sex Differences." *The Journal of Creative Behavior* 8.1 (1974): 1-4.

Kolodny, Annette. "Dancing Through the Minefield: Some Observations on Theory, Practice and Politics of Feminist Literary Criticism." *Men's Studies Modified.* Ed, Dale Spender. Oxford: Pergamon Press, 1981. 23-42.

Kostelanetz, Richard. "Notes on the American Short Story Today." *Short Story Theories.* Ed. Charles E. May. Columbus: Ohio University Press, 1976. 214-25.

Lagmanovich, David. "Images of Reality: Latin American Short Story of Today." *Dispositio: Revista Hispánica de Semiotica Literaria* 9.24-26 (1984): 53-63.

Lakoff, Robin. *Language and Woman's Place.* New York: Harper and Row, 1975.

Larguia, Isabel and John Dumoulin. "Toward a Science of Women's Liberation." *NACLA's Latin America & Empire Report* 6.10 3-20.

Larrazábal Henríquez, Oswaldo, Amaya Liebot and Gustavo Luis Carrera. *Bibliografía del cuento venezolano.* Caracas: Univ. Central de Venezuela, Facultad de Humanidades y Educación, 1975.

Larson, Ross. *Fantasy and Imagination in the Mexican Narrative.* Tempe, AZ: Arizona State University, Center for Latin American Studies, 1977.

———. "La literatura de ciencia-ficción en México." *Cuadernos Hispanoamericanos* 284 (1974): 425-31.

Lastra, Pedro. *El cuento hispanoamericano del siglo XIX, notas y documentos.* Ed. Helmy Giacoman. Santiago: Editorial Universitaria, 1972.

Lavrin, Ascension, ed. *Latin American Women: Historical Perspectives.* London: Greenwood Press, 1978.

Leal, Luis. *Breve historia del cuento mexicano.* Mexico City: De Andrea, 1956.

———. "Contemporary Mexican Novel and Short Story." *Contemporary Latin American Literature.* Houston: University of Houston, Office of International Affairs, 1973. 40-47.

———. *El cuento hispanoamericano.* Buenos Aires: Centro Editor América Latina, 1967.

———. "Female Archetypes in Mexican Literature." *Women in Hispanic Literature: Icon and Fallen Idols.* Ed. Beth Miller. Berkeley: University of California Press, 1983. 227-42.

———. *Historia del cuento hispanoamericano.* Mexico City: Studium, 1966. Rpt. in Mexico City: Ediciones De Andrea, 1966. Rpt. in Mexico City: De Andrea, 1971.

————. "Native and Foreign Elements in Contemporary Mexican Fiction: A Search For Identity." *Tradition and Renewal*. Ed. Merlin Forster. Urbana: University of Illinois Press, 1975. 102-28.

————. "El nuevo cuento mexicano." *El cuento hispanoamericano ante la crítica*. Ed. Enrique Pupo-Walker. Madrid: Castilla, 1973. 280-95.

Lemistre Pujol, Annie. "Los orígenes de la literatura femenina en Latinoamérica y Costa Rica." *Kañina* [Costa Rica] 9, 2 (1985): 85-90.

Leñero, Vicente. "Reflexiones en torno a la narrativa joven de México." *Mundo Nuevo* 38 (1969): 18-21.

León, Oliver Gilberto de. "Antología del cuento hispanoamericano: introducción." *Plural* 12.1 (1982): 124-26.

Letras femeninas en América. Uruguay: Asociación de Literatura Femenina Hispánica, 1981.

Lindstrom, Naomi. "Feminist Criticism of Latin American Literature: Bibliographic Notes." *Latin American Research Review* 15, 1 (1980): 151-59.

Liscano, Juan. *Panorama de la literatura venezolana actual*. Washington, OEA-Caracas: Publicaciones Españolas, 1973.

Lobo, Luiza. "Women Writers in Brazil Today." *World Literature Today* 61, 1 (1987): 49-54.

López, Ivette. "Puerto Rico: las nuevas narradoras y la identidad cultural." *Perspectives on Contemporary Literature* 8 (1972): 77-83.

Lozano, Stella. *Selected Bibliography of Contemporary Spanish American Writers*. Los Angeles: California State Univ. Press, 1979.

Magnarelli, Sharon. *The Lost Rib*. Lewisburg: Bucknell University Press, 1985.

————. *Reflection-Refractions: Reading Luisa Valenzuela*. New York: Peter Lang, 1988.

Maíz, Magdalena. "Una aproximación al paisaje cotidiano: narrativa femenina mexicana." *Cuadernos de Aldeeu* 1.2-3 (1983): 347-54.

Manrique Cabrera, Francisco. *Historia de la literatura puertorriqueña*. 4th ed. Puerto Rico: Edic. Culturales, 1971.

Martínez, Zulma Nelly. "La mujer, la creatividad y el eterno presente." *Revista Iberoamericana* 51.132-133 (1985): 799-806.

Martínez Bonati, Félix. *La estructura de la obra literaria*. Barcelona: Editorial Seix Barral, 1972.

Marting, Diane E., ed. *Spanish American Women Writers: A Bio-biographical Sourcebook*. New York: Greenwood Press, 1990.

————. *Women Writers of Spanish America. An Annotated Bio-Bibliographical Guide*. New York: Greenwood Press, 1987.

Masiello, Francine. "Texto, ley, transgresión: especulación sobre la novela (feminista) de vanguardia." *Revista Iberoamericana* 51.132-133 (1985): 807-22.

Mastrángelo, Carlos. *El cuento argentino: contribución al conocimiento de su historia, teoría y práctica*. Buenos Aires: Hachette, 1963. Rpt. in Buenos Aires: Nova, 1975.

Mathieu, Corina. *Latin American Women Writers, Yesterday and Today*. Pittsburgh: Carnegie Mellon, 1975.

McMurray, George R. "Recurring Themes and Technical Procedures in the Mexican Short Story of the Twentieth Century." *DA* 15 (1955): 1400.

———. "Thematic Incidence of the Revolution in the Mexican Short Story." *Bulletin of the Rocky Mountain Modern Language Association* 18 (1965): 5-8.

Meléndez, Concha. *El arte del cuento en Puerto Rico*. New York: Las Americas Publishing Company, 1961.

———. *Literatura de ficción en Puerto Rico: cuento y novela*. Puerto Rico: Editorial Cordillera, 1971.

Menton, Seymour. *El cuento hispanoamericano*. Mexico City: Fondo de Cultura Económica, 1980.

———. "'Sin embargo': La nueva cuentista femenina en México." *Tinta* 1.5 (1987): 35-37.

Mercier, Michel. *Le Roman Féminin*. Vendome: Presses Universitaires de France, 1976.

Meyer, Doris. *Victoria Ocampo: Against the Wind and Tide*. New York: Brazillere, 1979.

Meyer, Doris and Margarite Fernández Olmos. *Contemporary Women Authors of Latin America: Introductory Essays*. Brooklyn, NY: Brooklyn College Press, 1983.

Michael, Andrée. *Le féminisme*. Paris: Presses Universitaires de France, 1980.

Miguel, María Esther de. "La mujer en su literatura y su responsabilidad como escritora." *Universidad Nacional de Costa Rica* 10.1-2 (1969): 321-37.

Miller, Beth. *Mujeres en la literatura*. Mexico City: Fleischer Editora, S.A., 1978.

———. *Women in Hispanic Literature: Icons and Fallen Idols*. Berkeley: University of California Press, 1983.

Miller, Beth and Alfonso González. *26 Autoras del México actual*. Berkeley: B. Costa-Amic Editor, 1978.

Miller, Yvette E. and Charles M. Tatum. eds. *Latin American Women Writers: Yesterday and Today*. Pittsburgh: Latin American Literary Review, 1977.

Minc, Rose. *The Contemporary Latin American Short Story*. New York: Senda Nueva de Ediciones, 1979.

Miranda, Julio E. *Proceso a la narrativa venezolana*. Caracas: Universidad Central de Venezuela Ediciones de la Biblioteca, 1975.

Miró, Rodrigo. *La literatura panameña: origen y proceso*. 3rd ed. Panamá: Edit. Seviprensa, 1976.

Mitchell, Juliet. *Psychoanalysis and Feminism*. Harmondsworth: Penguin, 1974.

Moers, Elaine. *Literary Women: The Great Writers*. London: The Women's Press, 1978.

Moi, Toril. *Teoría literaria feminista*. Madrid: Ediciones Cátedra, 1988.

Mora, Gabriela. *En torno al cuento: De la teoría general y de su práctica en Hispanoamérica*. Madrid: José Porrúa Turanzas, S.A., 1985.

————. "Narradoras hispanoamericanas: vieja y nueva problemática en renovadas elaboraciones." *Theory and Practice of Feminist Literary Criticism*. Eds. Gabriela Mora and Karen S. Van Hooft. Ypsilanti, MI: Bilingual Press, 1982. 156-74.

Mora, Gabriela and Karen S. Van Hooft, eds. *Theory and Practice of Feminist Literary Criticism*. Ypsilanti, MI: Bilingual Press, 1982.

Morgan, Robin. *Going Too Far: The Personal Chronicle of a Feminist*. New York: Vintage Books, 1978.

La mujer en las letras venezolanas: homenaje a Teresa de la Parra en el año internacional de la mujer: Catálogo exposición hémero-bibliográfica. 5-26 octubre 1975. Caracas: Impr. del Congreso de la República, 1976.

Mujica, Tomas T. "Raíces del cuento popular en Colombia." *Boletín de la Academia Colombiana*. 34.146 (1984): 303-17.

Muriel, Josefina. *Cultura femenina novohispana*. Mexico City: UNAM, 1982.

Nares Santana, Alma Delia. "Secuencia temporal y narrativa en la novela mexicana contemporánea." *Estructura de la creación literaria hispanoamericana contemporánea*. Comp. Jesús Rodríguez Gurrola. Jalisco: Gobierno del Estado de Jalisco, 1986. 45-97.

Los narradores ante el público. 2 vols. Mexico City: Edit. Joaquín Mortiz, 1966.

Nas, June and Helen I. Safa, eds. *Sex and Class in Latin America*. New York: Praeger, 1976.

Navarro, Armando. *Narradores venezolanos de la nueva generación*. Caracas: Monte Avila, 1970.

Navarro, Tomas T. *La voz y la entonación en los personajes literarios*. Mexico City: Colección Málaga, 1976.

Oates, Joyce Carol. "Building Tension in the Short Story." *The Writer's Handbook*. Ed. A.C. Burack. Boston: The Writer, Inc., 1968.

Ocampo de Gómez, Aurora M. *Diccionario de escritores mexicanos*. Mexico City: Universidad Nacional Autónoma de México, Centro de Estudios Literarios, 1967.

————. *Novelistas iberoamericanos contemporáneos: obras y bibliografía crítica*. Mexico City: Universidad Nacional Autónoma de México, 1971.

Olivera, Otto. *Bibliografía de la literatura dominicana. 1960-1982*. Lincoln NE: Society of Spanish American Studies, 1984.

Omil, Alba and Raúl A. Piérola. *El cuento y sus claves*. Buenos Aires: Editorial Nova, 1967.

Orgambide, Pedro and Roberto Yahni, eds. *Enciclopedia de la literatura argentina*. Buenos Aires: Editorial Sudamericana, 1970.

Osborne, Martha Lee. *Woman in Western Thought*. New York: Random House, 1979.

Osen, Lynn M. *Women in Mathematics*. Cambridge, MA: MIT Press, 1974.

Paley de Francescato, Martha. "Onda y desonda: narradores jóvenes mexicanos." *Revista Canadiense de Estudios Hispánicos* 2 (1978): 296-302.

Parra, Teresa de la. *Mamá Blanca's Souvenirs*. Trans. Harriet de Onís. Washington D.C. and Mexico City: Pan American Union Washington D.C. General Secretariat, 1959.

Paz, Octavio. *Sor Juana Inés de la Cruz: o, las trampas de la fé*. Mexico City: Fondo de Cultura Económica, 1983.

Peden, Margaret Sayers, trans. *A Woman of Genius: The Intellectual Autobiography of Sor Juana Inés de la Cruz*. Salisbury, CT: Lime Rock, 1982.

———. ed. *The Latin American Short Story. A Critical History*. Boston: Twayne Publishers, 1983.

Peña, Margarita. *Entre líneas*. Mexico City: Universidad Nacional Autónoma de México, 1983.

Perez, Janet W, ed. *Novelistas femeninas de la postguerra española*. Madrid: José Porrúa Turanzas, 1983.

Perspectivas de nueva narrativa hispanoamericana. Piedras, PR: Ediciones Puerto, 1973.

Pescatello, Ann, ed. *Female and Male in Latin America*. Pittsburgh, PA: University of Pittsburgh Press, 1973.

Perspectivas de nueva narrativa hispanoamericana. Puerto Rico: Ediciones Puerto, 1973.

Pescatello, Ann, ed. *Female and Male in Latin America*. Pittsburgh, PA: University of Pittsburgh Press, 1973.

———. "The Female in Ibero-America." *Latin American Research Review* 7.2 (1972): 125-41.

———. Preface. "The Special Issue in Perspective: The Hispanic Caribbean Woman and the Literary Media." *Revista/Review Interamericana* 4.2 (1974): 131-35.

Plá, Josefina. *Literatura paraguaya del siglo XX*. 2nd ed. Asunción: Comuneros, 1972.

Pollmann, Leo. "Función del cuento latinoamericano." *Revista Iberoamericana* 48.118-119 (1982): 207-15.

Poniatowska, Elena. "La literatura de las mujeres es parte de la literatura de los oprimidos." *Fem* 6, 21 (1982): 23-27.

Pratt, Annis, *Archetypal Patterns in Women's Fiction*. Bloomington: Indiana University Press, 1981.

Propp, Vladimir. *Morfología del cuento*. Mexico City: Editorial Fundamentos, 1981.

———. *Las raíces históricas del cuento*. Madrid: Editorial Fundamentos, 1981.

Pupo-Walker. *El cuento hispanoamericano ante la crítica*. Madrid: Editorial Castilla, 1973.

Quesada, Ernesto. *El feminismo argentino. Tendencias y orientaciones*. Buenos Aires: n.p., 1920.

Rainwater, Catherine and William J. Schelk, eds. *Contemporary American Women Writers*. Lexington, KY: University Press of Kentucky, 1975.

Rama, Angel. *La generación crítica 1939-1969*. Montevideo: Arca, 1972. Rpt. in *Panoramas* Montevideo: Arca, 1972.

———. *Novísimos narradores hispanoamericanos en* Marcha *1964-1980*. Mexico City: Marcha Editores, 1981.

Ramos, Elías A. *El cuento venezolano contemporáneo (1950-1970): estudio temático y estilístico*. Madrid: Playor, 1979.

Ramos Foster, Virginia. "La crítica literaria de las profesoras norteamericanas ante las letras femeninas hispánicas." *Revista Interamericana de Bibliografía/Interamerican Review of Bibliography*. 30.4 (1980): 406-12.

Raviolo, Heber. *Panorama del cuento chileno*. Montevideo: Ediciones de la Banda Oriental, 1981.

Rea Boorman, Joan. *La estructura del narrador en la novela hispanoamericana contemporánea*. Madrid: Hispanova, 1976.

Rela, Walter. *Guía bibliográfica de la literatura hispano-americana desde el siglo XIX hasta 1970*. Buenos Aires: Casa Pardo, 1971.

——. *Spanish American Literature: A Selected Bibliography 1970-1980*. East Lansing, MI: Michigan State University, 1981.

Resnick, Margery and Isabel de Cortivron, eds. *Women Writers in Translation: An Annotated Bibliography*. New York: Garland Press, 1984.

Rigney, Barbara Hill. *Madness and Sexual Politics in the Feminist Novel: Studies in Bronte, Woolf, Lessing and Atwood*. Madison, WI: The University of Wisconsin System, 1978.

Rivera de Alvarez, Josefina. *Diccionario de literatura puertorriqueña*. Puerto Rico: Instituto de Cultura Puertorriqueña, 1970.

Robles, Martha. *La sombra fugitiva: Escritoras en la cultura nacional*. Mexico City: Editorial Diana, 1989. Vol. I - II.

Rodríguez Gurrola, Jesús, coord. *Estructura de la creación literaria hispanoamericana contemporánea*. Jalisco: Gobierno del Estado de Jalisco, 1986.

Rodríguez Monegal, Emir. *El arte de narrar*. Caracas: Monte Avila, 1977.

——. *Literatura uruguaya del medio siglo*. Montevideo: Alfa, 1966.

Rodríguez Rea, Miguel Angel. "El cuento peruano contemporáneo: índice bibliográfico, I: 1900-1930." *Lexis: Revista de Lingüística y Literatura* 7.2 (1983): 287-309.

Rodríguez-Alcalá, Hugo. *Historia de la literatura paraguaya*. Mexico City: De Andrea, 1970.

Roffé, Reina. "Omnipresencia de la censura en la escritora argentina." *Revista Iberoamericana* 51.132-133 (1985): 909-15.

Rose, Phyllis. *Woman of Letters: A Life of Virginia Woolf*. London: Routlege & Kegan Paul, 1978.

Roy, Joaquín, ed. *Narrativa y crítica de nuestra América*. Madrid: Edit. Castilla, 1978.

Russ, Joanna. "What Can a Heroine Do? Or, Why Women Can't Write." *Images of Women in Fiction: Feminist Perspectives*. Ed. Susan Koppelman Cornillon. Bowling Green: Bowling Green University Popular Press, 1972. 3-20.

Ruth, Sheila. *Issues in Feminism: A First Course in Women Studies*. Boston: Mifflin, 1980.

Sabrosky, Judith A. *From Rationality to Liberation: The Evolution of Feminist Ideology*. Westport, CT: Greenwood Press, 1979.

Sarfati-Arnaud, Monique, and Lillo Gaston. "El cuento mexicano a traves del título: Apuntes sobre la ideología de los años 1940 hasta 1958." *Imprevue* 2 (1983): 7-46.

Scott, Rivers. "Rebecca West: *Women's Lib and Why I'm For It.*" *Sunday Telegraph* 24 Dec. 1972. 6.

Sefchovich, Sara. *Mexico: país de ideas, país de novelas.* Mexico City: Editorial Grijalbo, 1989.

Serra, Edelweis. *Tipología del cuento literario.* Madrid: Cupsa Editorial, 1978.

Shea, Maureen. "A Growing Awareness of Sexual Oppression among Contemporary Latin American Women Writers." *Confluencia: Revista Hispánica de Cultura y Literatura* 4, 1 (1988): 53-59.

Shimrose, Pedro. *Diccionario de autores iberoamericanos.* Madrid: Ministerio de Relaciones Exteriores, 1982.

Shons, Dorothy. "Nuevos datos para la biografía de Sor Juana." *Contemporáneos* 9 (1929): 161-76.

———. "Some Obscure Points in the Life of Sor Juana Inés de la Cruz." *Modern Philology* 24 (1926): 141-62.

Showalter, Elaine. *Women's Liberation and Literature.* New York: Harcourt Brace Jovanovich, 1971.

Silén, Juan Angel. *La generación de escritores de 1970 en Puerto Rico (1950-1976).* Puerto Rico: Editorial Cultural, 1977.

Silva Castro, Raúl. "Mujeres en las letras chilenas." *Cuadernos* 94 (1965): 75-80.

Simpson, Hilary. "A Literary Trespasser: D.H. Lawrence's Use of Women's Writings." *Women's Studies International Quarterly* 2.2 (1979): 155-70.

Smith, Dorothy. "A Peculiar Eclipsing: Women's Exclusions From Man's Culture." *Women's Studies International Quarterly* 1.4 (1978): 281-96.

Solé, Carlos A. and María Isabel Abreu, eds. *Latin American Writers.* 3 vols. New York: Charles Scribner's Sons, 1989.

Sosa de Newton, Lily. *Diccionario biográfico de mujeres argentinas.* Buenos Aires: Editorial Plus Ultra, 1980.

Spender, Dale. *Feminist Theorists: Three Centuries of Women's Intellectual Traditions.* London: The Women's Press, 1982.

———. *Man Made Language.* London: Routledge & Kegan Paul, 1980.

———. *Men's Studies Modified: The Impact of Feminism on the Academic Disciplines.* London: Virago, 1978. Rpt. in Oxford: Pergamon Press, 1981.

———. *These Modern Women: Autobiographical Essays from the Twenties.* New York: The Feminist Press, Old Westbury, 1978.

———. *Women of Ideas and What Men Have Done to Them: from Aphra Behn to Adrienne Rich.* London: Ark Paperbacks, 1983.

———. *The Writing or the Sex?: or Why You Don't Have to Read Women's Writing to Know It's No Good.* New York: Pergamon Press, 1989.

Stacey, Margaret and Marion Price. *Women, Power and Politics.* London: Tavistock, 1981.

Steele, Cynthia. "Toward a Socialist Feminist Criticism of Latin American Literature." *Ideologies and Literature* 4, 16 (1983): 323-29.

Stewart, Grace. *A New Mythos, the Novel of the Artist as Heroine, 1877-1977*. Montreal: Eden Press, 1981.

Stineman, Esther F. "Simone de Beauvoir: An Autobiographical Blueprint for Female Liberty." *University of Michigan Papers in Women's Studies* 2.3 (1977): 88-122.

Summers, Hollis. *Discussions of the Short Story*. Boston: D.C. Heath and Company, 1963.

Teutli Teyssier, Margarita. *Los cuentistas de la revolución mexicana: aportación*. Mexico City: Universidad Nacional Autónoma de México, 1956.

Todorov, Tzvetan. *Introducción a la literatura fantástica*. Mexico City: Premiá Editora, 1981.

Traba, Marta. *Mothers and Shadows*. Trans. Jo Labanyi. Mexico City: Siglo XXI Editores, 1981.

Ugalde, Sharon Keefe. "Process, Identity, and Learning to Read: Female Writing and Feminist Criticism in Latin America Today." *Latin American Research Review* 24, 1 (1989): 222-32.

Urbano, Victoria. *Una escritora costarricense: Yolanda Oreamuno: ensayo crítico*. Madrid: Eds. Castilla de Oro, 1968.

Urrutia, Elena. "¿Qué escribe la mujer en México ?" *Fem* 3, 10 (1979): 9-12.

Uslar Pietri, Arturo. *Breve historia de la novela hispanoamericana*. Madrid: Mediterráneo, 1974.

Valadés, Edmundo. "El cuento mexicano." *Armas y Letras*. 3.4 (1960): 19-39.

Valadés, Edmundo y Luis Leal. *La revolución y las letras. Dos estudios sobre la novela y el cuento de la revolución mexicana*. Mexico City: Instituto Nacional de Bellas Artes, Departamento de Literatura, 1960.

Valdés, Bernardo. *Panorama del cuento chileno*. Miami: Ediciones Universal, 1976.

Valdivieso, Mercedes. "Literatura femenina: momentáneas permanencias críticas." *La Critica Literaria en Latinoamérica* Stanford University 8-12 July 1985. 245-49.

Valenzuela Rodarte, Alberto. *Contemporary Latin American Writers*. New York: Las Americas, 1971.

Valenzuela, Victor M. *Grandes escritores hispanoamericanos, poetisas y novelistas*. Bethlehem, PA: Lehigh Univ., 1974.

Valis, Noel and Carol Maier. Eds. *In the Feminine Mode: Essays on Hispanic Women Writers*. Lewisburg, Pa.: Bucknell University Press, 1988.

Anthologies

Aguilera Malta, Demetrio and Manuel Mejía Valera, eds. *El cuento actual latinoamericano*. Mexico City: De Andrea, 1973.

Ahern, Maureen. *A Rosario Castellanos Reader*. Austin: University of Texas Press, 1988.

Anderson Imbert, Enrique and Eugenio Florit, eds.. *Literatura hispanoamericana: antología e introducción histórica*. New York: Holt, Rinehart and Winston, 1960. Rpt. in New York: Holt, Rinehart and Winston, 1970.

Antología del joven relato latinoamericano. Buenos Aires: Compañía General Fabril Editora, S.A., 1972.

Arkin, Marian and Barbara Shollar, eds. *Longman Anthology of World Literature by Women 1875-1975*. New York: Longman Inc., 1989.

Barradas, Efraín, ed. *Apalabramiento: cuentos puertorriqueños de hoy*. Hanover, NH: Ediciones Del Norte, 1983.

Barroetavena, E. Esquiu, ed. *Parnaso femenino*. Buenos Aires: Argentinidad, 1936.

Benitez Rojo, Antonio, ed. *Un siglo del relato latinoamericano*. La Habana: Casa de Las Américas, 1976.

Borges, Jorge Luis, Bioy Casares and Silvina Ocampo. *Antología de la literatura fantástica*. Buenos Aires: Ed. Sudamericana, 1940. Rpt. in Barcelona: HEDHASA, 1981.

————. *El cuento argentino contemporáneo*. Buenos Aires: Centro Editor de América Latina, 1977.

Bosco, María Angélica and Haydée M. Jofré Barroso, eds. *Antología consultada del cuento argentino*. Buenos Aires: Compañía General Fabril Editora, 1971.

————. *Antología del joven relato latinoamericano*. Buenos Aires: Fabril, 1972.

Cahill, Susan, ed. *Women and Fiction: Short Stories by and About Women*. 2 vols. New York: New American Library, 1975-1978.

Campodónico, Luis,ed. *Diez relatos y un epílogo*. Montevideo: Fundación de Cultura Universitaria, 1979.

Carballo, Emmanuel, ed. *Narrativa mexicana de hoy*. Madrid: Alianza Editorial, 1969.

————. Prologue. *El cuento mexicano del siglo XX*. Mexico City: Empresas Editoriales, 1964. 9-18.

Cardoso, Heber, ed. *El cuento uruguayo contemporáneo*. Buenos Aires: Centro Editor de América Latina, 1978.

Cartagena, Aída, ed. *Narradores dominicanos*. Caracas: Monte Avila Ediciones, C.A., 1969.

Castro Arenas, Mario, ed. *El cuento en Hispanoamérica*. Lima: Studium, 1974.

Catorce cuentistas. La Habana: Casa de las Américas, 1969.

Cerda, Martín, ed. *Nuevos cuentistas chilenos*. Santiago: Editorial Universitaria, 1985.

Chang-Rodríguez, Raquel and Malva Filer, eds. *Voces de hispanoamérica. Antología literaria*. Boston: Heinle and Heinle, 1988.

Chase, Alfonso, ed. *Narrativa contemporánea de Costa Rica*. San Juan, Costa Rica: Ministerio de Cultura, 1975.

Chicanas Speak Out. New York: Pathfinder Press, 1971.

Correas de Zapata, Celia C. *Short Stories by Latin Women: The Magic and the Real*. Houston, TX: Arte Público Press, 1990.

Correas de Zapata, Celia C. de and Lygia Johnson, eds. *Detrás de la reja: antología crítica de narradoras latinoamericanas del siglo XX*. Caracas: Monte Avila, 1980.

Cortina, Lynn Ellen Rice, ed. *Spanish American Women Writers*. New York: Garland, 1983.

Cotelo, Rubén, ed. *Narradores uruguayos*. Caracas: Monte Avila, 1969.

Crow, John A. and Edward J. Dudley, eds. *El cuento*. New York: Holt, Rinehart and Winston, 1966.

Dale, Carter E., ed. *Antología del realismo mágico*. New York: Odissey Press, 1970.

Díez Rodríguez, M., ed. *Antología del cuento literario*. Madrid: Editorial Alhambra, 1985.

Doce mujeres cuentan. Buenos Aires: La Campana, 1983.

Domínguez, Mignon, ed. *Cuentos fantásticos hispanoamericanos*. Buenos Aires: Editorial Crea, 1980.

Donoso Pareja, Miguel, ed. *Prosa joven de América Hispana*. Mexico City: Sepsetentas, 1972.

Fernández, José B. and Nasario García, eds. *Nuevos horizontes. Cuentos chicanos, puertorriqueños y cubanos*. Lexington: D.C. Heath and Company, 1982.

Fernández-Marcané, Leonardo, ed. *Cuentos del Caribe*. Madrid: Playor, 1978.

Flores, Angel, ed. *Narrativa hispanoamericana 1968-1981 historia y antología: la generación de 1939 en adelante*. (Centroamérica/Colombia/Cuba/Ecuador/Puerto Rico/República Dominicana/Venezuela). Vol. 5 Mexico City: Siglo XX Editores, 1983.

———. *Spanish Short Stories*. New York: Bantam Books, 1981.

Fornet, Ambrosio, ed. *Antología del cuento cubano contemporáneo*. Mexico City: Era, 1967.

Fremantle, Anne, ed. *Latin-American Literature Today*. New York: New American Library, 1975.

Gandolfo, Elvio E, ed. *Cuentos fantásticos y de ciencia ficción en América Latina*. Buenos Aires: Centro Editor de América Latina, 1981.

Garfield, Evelyn Picón, ed. *Women's Fiction From Latin America*. Detroit: Wayne State University Press, 1988.

Garicini, María del Carmen and Eugenio Matus, eds. *Antología del cuento hispanoamericano*. La Habana: Editora del Ministerio de Educación, 1963.

Gómez, Alma, Cherríe Moraga and Mariana Romo-Carmona, eds. *Cuentos: Stories by Latinas*. New York: Kitchen Table, Women of Color Press, 1983.

Gómez-Gil, Orlando, ed. *Literatura hispanoamericana. Antología crítica*. 2 vols. New York: Holt, Rinehart and Winston, 1972.

González Curquejo, A, ed. *Florilegio de escritoras cubanas*. 3 vols. Habana: El Siglo XX, 1910-1919.

Gregorich, Luis, ed. *Doce mujeres cuentan*. Buenos Aires: La Campana, 1983.

Gregorich, Luis, ed. *La guirnalda literaria, Colección de producciones de las principales poetisas y escritoras contemporáneas de España y América*. Guayaquil: Calvo, 1870.

Handelsman, Michael H, ed. *Diez escritoras ecuatorianas y sus cuentos*. Guayaquil: Casa de la Cultura Ecuatoriana, Núcleo del Guayas, 1982.

Howes, Barbara, ed. *The Eye of the Heart: Short Stories From Latin America*. New York: Avon, 1974.

Jofré Barroso, Haydée M, ed. *Nuevos cuentos del Brasil*. Buenos Aires: Ediciones de La Flor, 1972.

Katz, Esther and Anita Kapone, eds. *Women's Experience in America: An Historical Anthology*. Brunswick and London: Transaction Books, 1980.

Latcham, Ricardo, ed. *Antología del cuento hispanoamericano*. Santiago de Chile: Zig Zag, 1962.

Lawaetz, Gudie, ed. *Spanish Short Stories, Cuentos Hispánicos*. 2 vols. Maryland: Penguin Books, 1972.

Leal, Luis, ed. *Cuentistas hispanoamericanos del siglo veinte*. New York: Random House, 1972.

Leal, Luis and Frank Dauster, eds. *Literatura de hispanoamérica*. New York: Harcourt, Brace and World, Inc., 1970.

Lewald, Herald Ernest, ed. *Diez cuentistas argentinas*. Buenos Aires: Ediciones Riomar, 1968.

————. ed. and trans. *The Web: Stories of Argentine Women*. Washington D.C.: Three Continents Press, 1983.

Lijeron Alberdi, Hugo and Ricardo Pastor Poppe, eds. *Cuentos bolivianos contemporáneos. Antología*. La Paz: Ediciones Camarlinghi, 1975.

Llarena, Elsa de, ed. *14 mujeres escriben cuentos*. Mexico City: Federación Editorial Mexicana, 1975.

Llarena, Elsa de and Josephina Torres López, eds. *Así escriben los mexicanos*. Buenos Aires: Orión, 1975.

Luby, Barry J. and Wayne H. Finke, eds. *Anthology of Contemporary Latin American Literature 1960-1984*. London-Toronto: Associated University Press, 1986.

Mancini, Pat McNees, ed. *Contemporary Latin American Short Stories*. Greenwich, CT: Fawcet Publications, 1974.

Manguel, Alberto, ed. *Other Fires, Short Fiction by Latin American Women*. Toronto: Lester & Orpen Dennys, 1986.

Marañon, Gregorio, ed. *Cuentos y narraciones de hispanoamérica*. Valencia, España: Ediciones Prometeo, 1969.

Menton, Seymour, ed. *El cuento hispanoamericano*. 2 vols. Mexico City: Fondo de Cultura Económica, 1972.

————. *The Spanish American Short Story: A Critical Anthology*. Berkeley: University of California Press, 1980.

Meyer, Doris, ed. *Lives on the Line: The Testimony of Contemporary Latin American Authors*. Berkeley: University of California Press, 1980.

Meyer, Doris and Marguerite Fernández Olmos, eds. *Contemporary Women Authors of Latin America: New Translations*. Brooklyn, NY: Brooklyn College, 1983.

Millán, Maria del Carmen, ed. *Antología de cuentos mexicanos*. 2 vols. Mexico City: Nueva Imagen, 1977.

Mínovez Sender, José Miguel, ed. *Antología del cuento chileno*. Barcelona: Editorial Bruguera, S.A., 1970.

Montero, Jenny, ed. *La cuentista dominicana*. Santo Domingo, República Dominicana: Biblioteca Nacional, 1986.

Morgan, Robin, ed. *Sisterhood is Global. The International Women's Movement Anthology*. Garden City, NJ: Anchor Press, Doubleday, 1984.

Mujeres chilenas cuentan. Santiago del Chile: Zig Zag, 1978.

Mullen, Edward J. and John F. Garganigo, eds. *El cuento hispánico*. New York: Random House, 1984.

Navajo, Ymelda., ed. *Doce relatos de mujeres*. Madrid: Editorial Alianza, 1983.

Ocampo, Aurora M, ed. *Cuentistas mexicanas siglo XX. Antología*. Mexico City: Universidad Nacional Autónoma de México, 1976.

Ortega, Julio. *El muro y la intemperie: el nuevo cuento latinoamericano*. Hanover, NH: Ediciones del Norte, 1989.

Panorama del cuento mexicano. 2 vols. Montevideo: Banda Oriental, 1980.

Partnoy, Alicia, ed. *You Can't Drown the Fire: Latin American Women Writing in Exile*. Pittsburgh: Cleis Press, 1988.

Poletti, Syria, ed. *Cuentos desde el taller, Taller "Leonar Alonso" dirigido por Syria Poletti*. Buenos Aires: Plus Ultra, 1983.

Quince cuentistas. La Habana: Casa de Las Américas, 1974.

Rela, Walter, ed. *20 cuentos uruguayos magistrales*. Buenos Aires: Plus Ultra, 1980.

Reyes, Chela, ed. *Mujeres chilenas cuentan*. Santiago: Zig Zag, 1978.

Rodríguez Monegal, Emir, ed. *The Borzoi Anthology of Latin American Literature*. 2 vols. New York: Alfred Knopf, 1977.

Rojo, Grinor, and Cynthia Steele, eds. *Ritos de iniciación*. Boston: Houghton Mifflin Co., 1986.

Rovere, Susana, ed, *Cuentos hispanoamericanos del siglo XX*. Buenos Aires: Huemul, 1979. Rpt. in Buenos Aires: Editorial Crea, 1980.

Ruiz, Elisa, ed. *Antología de las escritoras argentinas: 1840-1940*. Buenos Aires: Centro Editor de América Latina, 1980.

Sáinz, Gustavo, ed. *Los mejores cuentos mexicanos*. Barcelona: Ediciones Océano, 1984.

Sefchovich, Sara, ed. *Mujeres en espejo I. Narradoras latinoamericanas siglo XX*. Mexico City: Folios Ediciones, S.A., 1983.

———. *Mujeres en espejo II. Narradoras latinoamericanas siglo XX*. Mexico City: Folios Ediciones, S.A., 1985.

Shapard, Robert and James Thomas, eds. *Sudden Fiction International*. New York: W.W. Norton, 1989.

Silva-Velázquez, Caridad, and Nora Erro-Orthmann, eds. *Puerta abierta: la nueva escritora latinoamericana*. Mexico City: Joaquín Mortiz, 1986.

Sorrentino, Fernando, ed. *35 cuentos breves argentinos. Siglo XX*. Vol.1. Buenos Aires: Plus Ultra, 1976.

————. *36 cuentos argentinos con humor. Siglo XX*. Buenos Aires: Plus Ultra, 1979.

Sosa de Newton, Lily, ed. *Las argentinas, de ayer a hoy*. Buenos Aires: L.V. Zanetti, 1967.

Sullivan, Rosemary, ed. *Stories by Canadian Women*. Toronto: Oxford University Press, 1984.

Tanak, Yukiko and Elizabeth Hanson, eds. *This Kind of Woman. Ten Stories by Japanese Women Writers 1960-1976*. New York: The Putman Publishing Group, 1984.

Togno, María Elena, ed. *Así escriben las mujeres*. Buenos Aires: Orión, 1975.

Trece cuentos colombianos. Montevideo: Arca, 1970.

Un siglo del relato latinoamericano. La Habana: Casa de las Américas, 1976.

Urbano, Victoria, ed. *Five Women Writers of Costa Rica: Short Stories by Carmen Naranjo, Eunice Odio, Yolanda Oreamuno, Victoria Urbano, and Rima Vallbona*. Beaumont, TX: Asociación de Literatura Femenina Hispánica, 1978.

Valera, Benito, ed. *El cuento hispanoamericano contemporáneo. Antología*. Tarragona: Ediciones Tarraco, 1976.

Vélez, Diana. ed. *Reclaiming Medusa: Short Stories by Contemporary Puerto Rican Women*. San Francisco: Spinsters/Aunt Lute Book Company, 1988.

Verdevoye, Paul, ed. *Antología de la narrativa hispanoamericana, 1940-1970*. 2 vols. Madrid: Gredos, 1979.

Visca, Arturo, ed. *Antología del cuento uruguayo: los nuevos*. Vol. 5 Montevideo: Ediciones de la Banda Oriental, 1986.

————. *Nueva antología del cuento uruguayo*. Montevideo: Banda Oriental, 1976.

Yáñez, Aval de Agustín, ed. *Pasos en la escalera. La extraña visita. Girándula*. Mexico City: Porrúa, 1973.

Yates, Donald A, ed. *El cuento policial latinoamericano: introducción, antología y biografías*. Mexico City: Ediciones De Andrea, 1961.

Yates, Donald A. and John B. Dalbor, eds. *Imaginación y fantasía*. New York: Holt, Rinehart and Winston, 1983.

Selected Books from Cleis Press

Latin American Studies

Beyond the Border: A New Age in Latin American Women's Fiction edited by Nora Erro-Peralta and Caridad Silva-Núñez. ISBN: 0-939416-42-5 24.95 cloth; ISBN: 0-939416-43-3 12.95 paper.

The Little School: Tales of Disappearance and Survival in Argentina by Alicia Partnoy. ISBN: 0-939416-08-5 21.95 cloth; ISBN: 0-939416-07-7 9.95 paper.

You Can't Drown the Fire: Latin American Women Writing in Exile edited by Alicia Partnoy. ISBN: 0-939416-16-6 24.95 cloth; ISBN: 0-939416-17-4 9.95 paper.

Fiction

Cosmopolis: Urban Stories by Women edited by Ines Rieder. ISBN: 0-939416-36-0 24.95 cloth; ISBN: 0-939416-37-9 9.95 paper.

Night Train To Mother by Ronit Lentin. ISBN: 0-939416-29-8 24.95 cloth; ISBN: 0-939416-28-X 9.95 paper.

The One You Call Sister: New Women's Fiction edited by Paula Martinac. ISBN: 0-939416-30-1 24.95 cloth; ISBN: 0-939416031-X 9.95 paper.

Unholy Alliances: New Women's Fiction edited by Louise Rafkin. ISBN: 0-939416-14-X 21.95 cloth; ISBN: 0-939416-15-8 9.95 paper.

Literature/Animal Rights

And a Deer's Ear, Eagle's Song and Bear's Grace: Relationships Between Animals and Women edited by Theresa Corrigan and Stephanie T. Hoppe. ISBN: 0-939416-38-7 24.95 cloth; ISBN: 0-939416-39-5 9.95 paper.

With a Fly's Eye, Whale's Wit and Woman's Heart: Relationships Between Animals and Women edited by Theresa Corrigan and Stephanie T. Hoppe. ISBN: 0-939416-24-7 24.95 cloth; ISBN: 0-939416-25-5 9.95 paper.

Women's Studies

Don't: A Woman's Word by Elly Danica. ISBN: 0-939416-23-9 21.95 cloth; ISBN: 0-939416-22-0 8.95 paper.

Fight Back! Feminist Resistance to Male Violence edited by Frédérique Delacoste and Felice Newman. ISBN: 0-939416-01-8 13.95 paper.

Peggy Deery: An Irish Family at War by Nell McCafferty. ISBN: 0-939416-38-7 24.95 cloth; ISBN: 0-939416-39-5 9.95 paper.

The Absence of the Dead Is Their Way of Appearing by Mary Winfrey Trautmann. ISBN: 0-939416-04-2 8.95 paper.

Voices in the Night: Women Speaking About Incest edited by Toni A.H. McNaron and Yarrow Morgan. ISBN: 0-939416-02-6 9.95 paper.

With the Power of Each Breath: A Disabled Women's Anthology edited by Susan Browne, Debra Connors and Nanci Stern. ISBN: 0-939416-09-3 24.95 cloth; ISBN: 0-939416-06-9 10.95 paper.

Women & Honor: Some Notes on Lying by Adrienne Rich. ISBN: 0-939416-44-1 3.95 paper.

Sexual Politics/Lesbian Studies

AIDS: The Women edited by Ines Rieder and Patricia Ruppelt. ISBN: 0-939416-20-4 24.95 cloth; ISBN: 0-939416-21-2 9.95 paper.

A Lesbian Love Advisor by Celeste West. ISBN: 0-939416-27-1 24.95 cloth; ISBN: 0-939416-26-3 9.95 paper.

Different Daughters: A Book by Mothers of Lesbians edited by Louise Rafkin. ISBN: 0-939416-12-3 21.95 cloth; ISBN: 0-939416-13-1 8.95 paper.

Different Mothers: Sons & Daughters of Lesbians Talk About Their Lives edited by Louise Rafkin. ISBN: 0-939416-40-9 24.95 cloth; ISBN: 0-939416-41-7 9.95 paper.

Sex Work: Writings by Women in the Sex Industry edited by Frédérique Delacoste and Priscilla Alexander. ISBN: 0-939416-10-7 24.95 cloth; ISBN: 0-939416-11-5 12.95 paper.

Susie Sexpert's Lesbian Sex World by Susie Bright. ISBN: 0-939416-34-4 24.95 cloth; ISBN: 0-939416-35-2 9.95 paper.

Since 1980, Cleis Press has published progressive books by women. We welcome your order and will ship your books as quickly as possible. Please write for a complete catalog. Order from: Cleis Press, PO Box 8933, Pittsburgh PA 15221. (412) 937-1555. Individual orders must be prepaid. Please add 15% shipping. PA residents add sales tax. MasterCard and Visa orders welcome; $25 minimum—include account number, exp. date, and signature. Payment in US dollars only.